T0032137

SAVING SCOUT

MICHELLE CHRISTINA

HIGHERLIFE
PUBLISHING & MARKETING

HigherLife Publishing & Marketing
 PO Box 623307
 Oviedo, FL 32762
 AHigherLife.com

ISBN 978-1-958211-18-2 Paperback
ISBN 978-1-958211-19-9 Ebook
LOC # 1-12768214245

Printed in the United States of America

10 9 8 7 6 5 4 3 2 1

Dedicated to

Nathaniel Henry Edward Brunhoff III

"You don't get to choose how you're going to die, or when. You can only decide how you're going to live. Now."

-Joan Baez

Prologue

Beep ... beep ... beep ...

Awakened by the sound of my alarm, I get ready every morning to go to work, then to three hours of school, and later to a night of waitressing as my mother walks out the door to start her work day. Although this may sound like a stressful daily routine (for a high school student), it actually makes me feel good about myself. We don't always get to choose the type of life we are given in our early years, but it is our choice (and opportunity) to set it right for our future. I realize having an education is very important to society today. Anyone can live a productive life if they choose to, although, it is not something we can obtain without effort; it takes work. For the past twelve years of my education, I have worked hard to get where I am today and my achievements will speak for themselves. From the early days of my elementary education, when I was always a top finalist in the spelling bees, to my high school years being nominated Princess, I have always been an achiever. I believe I am a good investment.

As a senior of Newaygo High School, and soon to be student at Grand Valley State University in Grand Rapids, Michigan, USA, unlike many students, extracurricular activities have always been a luxury. I have only been able to squeeze in time for two years on the high school dance team and one year on the volleyball team. I have been raised by a hard-working single mother, and if I ever want anything, I have to work to pay for my own living. I began working at the age of fifteen as a "salad bar girl" at a local, hometown restaurant. When I turned sixteen, I received my first raise and began waitressing to save enough money to buy my first car. Four months before my seventeenth birthday, I began my second job at Great Lakes Energy as a Customer Service Representative. Working two jobs has never allowed much time for extracurricular activities, but nothing has ever got in the way of the importance of my schoolwork.

Education is important to me. I have a grade point average of 3.8 and have been on the honor roll since sixth grade. My favorite class has always been English and I'm currently enrolled in the accelerated Senior Literature class. This is an extremely challenging class, but I have learned to improve my writing skills and styles through much hard work, a necessary talent for the profession I want to pursue; I am going to become a journalist. I am choosing a career in journalism. First, because I love to manipulate the English language into short stories or writings that interest people. Secondly, I admire writings with strong, powerful words, full of emotions, which persuade me to understand an author's opinion or purpose of their piece (regardless of time). Third, this skill may offer the opportunity to travel and see the world for a while and then allow me to settle down in one area to begin a family.

Community service is also an important part of my life. Roadside pickup and food drives have been the main focus of my involvement. I have also spent many hours tutoring fellow students in science and have helped a migrant summer school program as a teacher's aide. While all of my community service involvement has been highly motivating, when I was a teacher's aide at the migrant summer school program, I was most inspired. The children were so grateful and eager to learn. It was amazing to learn that they had such hard, difficult lives, but yet were so happy, friendly and accepting of others.

Acquiring a higher education is very essential and important to becoming successful, but (I believe) we often misjudge the importance. We all have a choice of which path we choose to take in life. I (personally) am choosing the path of higher education and to go to college. I have worked very hard to get to where I am already and will not give up. I will accomplish my dream and aspirations in life. It is not life who makes us who we are; on the contrary, we make life what it is. I am living for tomorrow.

. ◆ .

That was my high school graduation paper, titled "Living for Tomorrow" (1999). I was prepared for college, filled with hopes and big dreams. I never did become a journalist. And, actually, my path turned out to be nothing like what I either planned nor expected.

What I have learned is that there's really not much that can prepare you for the trials and challenges you'll experience through life. And, just as soon as you think you have it all figured out, something crazy will happen to make sure you remember that you don't.

Chapter 1

I can't help but mindlessly stare into the office across the hall. I hear whispers between our company VP and her assistant. When the office door starts to shut, I turn my attention to a beautiful photo hanging on my office wall. It's a reflection of auburn and yellow leaved trees over the Potomac River. The calendar page hanging below says October 2014. The U.S. is fighting ISIS and politicians are campaigning for the November elections, but none of this matters right now. Not the whispers behind the closed door or the stack of work on my desk, and definitely not any of the news reports on war and campaigning.

"I can understand your hesitation, but be assured that you will never lose Nate again," I re-read the closing of the email again. It comes from a recently discovered stranger whom I was told I should call my great aunt. And yet, even though I know nothing of her, I can't help but feel immediately drawn to her loving spirit. Her small profile pic, which lives in a bubble at the top of the screen, shows an elderly woman, striking with silver-white hair and ice blue eyes. Her words are comforting and kind, and she seems genuine and true. She truly cares and is excited to be connecting with me.

"I just want to do everything right, and I don't want to lose him again," I type and hit send back, before closing out the email.

As badly as I want to overcome my fears and jump on a plane from Washington, D.C., to his home in Escondido, California, I am scared. No, I'm not scared. I am terrified. Not only did I just find him and have a million questions about who he is and what are his intentions, but can the hard news also be true? Is he really sick? How sick?

I open a new message and address it to the mysterious man who's newly entered my life and claims I can call him father. After thirty-three years of curiosity and wondering, can I now know and accept this man as my dad? The words on the screen appear just as quickly as I type them, "I'm worried about you," and then my fingers fall silent. I lift a hand to reach and hit delete, but instead raise them both up to let my face fall in my hands, using my forefingers to plug the pooling water in the corner of my eyes. I quickly wipe them clean and return to the screen, reading aloud the words I had typed, "I'm worried about you," and shake my head. Seriously? Should I also tell him to take his vitamins? It's only been eighteen days since his first email arrived in my inbox and here I am sounding like I'm trying to assume the parental role (one which, I'm not going to lie, has always come naturally in taking care of myself and my mother). I go for it again, and this time with success. I hit delete and all the words disappear. Focus, I tell myself. Focus on work. I close out the email and get back to work.

It's nearing 8:30 p.m., and I finally realize how late it is as I start wrapping up. I had managed to squeeze in a few extra hours of work, but not another attempt to write that email. I quickly shut down and start packing up to leave the office, hitting again the "remind me tomorrow" for computer updates. I turn off the lights and close the office door behind me to walk the dark and empty halls of the old building in McLean, Northern Virginia, located not far from the outskirts of Washington, D.C. It's always a relief to exit the revolving doors in the downstairs lobby and get within eyesight of my car in the dimly lit parking lot. I hit the button on my key fob to unlock the car with an audible "beep" and quickly throw open the door and toss my purse and bag to the passenger side. Sigh. It's been another long day of work. I let my head fall back to the headrest, while an audible exhale escapes my lips. Then so do the tears from my eyes, but I wasn't expecting this. Like a heavy rainfall, they start spotting my light khaki dress pants. Here I am, feeling pathetic, sitting in an empty dark parking lot and in the silent confines of my own car ready to shout at the top of my lungs, "But I just found him…. You can't take him from me already!" But no words escape; it's only the soft patter of tears on my pants that I hear as I sit with myself and God in the silence.

Following the unexpected wave of anger and frustration, a moment of peace finally finds me like a cool breeze. I regain composure, start the car and turn down the radio, hoping to find clarity in the silence. I pop the car in reverse and lift my head to look in the rearview mirror, catching a glimpse of myself and the mess of mascara that has given me raccoon eyes. I jump on the brakes and grab a wipe from the glove box to clear the black from my face. Looking in the mirror again, I whisper aloud, "Alright." I remind myself, "You don't know this man beyond the name on your birth certificate and here you are crying like a mother who lost a child, a boy who lost his dog, or a wife who just learned her husband is being shipped off to war. Calm your horses."

When I realize I just gave myself a pep talk, I laugh. Feeling oddly relieved to get all that out of my system, I reach my hand not to the volume on the radio, but instead to the sky and shout, "You!" Smirking, wondering if it could be possible to all be part of His cleverly schemed plan, or some kind of trickery or teaching that has awaited me all these years. "Of course it is," I continue saying aloud, "there just has to be some kind of dramatic twist now, doesn't there."

I arrive home, give Bernie (my husband's and my now graying labradoodle) a quick snuggle and make my way quickly to the closet to pull off these wretched heels. I grab my "dad" file off a dresser nearby and lay it open, taking a seat on the bed. Picking up my phone, I text Alice. I don't know much about her yet, but I figure she is surely my best bet to figure out what's going on. I've been told that Alice, my father's lady, is a doctor. They are not married but have been together for over twenty years. I also know, or feel fairly confident, that if he's not going to tell "Great Aunt Maura" about being sick, then he sure isn't going to tell me. I type the message and hit send.

> Hi Alice! I was emailing with Maura today and she mentioned health concerns ... for Nathan. It took me a few hours to work up the courage to text you. I'm so nervous to hear ... is he going to be OK?

· ◆ ·

JOURNAL ENTRY

October 20, 2014

The words are still ringing in my head, playing over and over again. Is it true, you think? Why they said they started the same search to find me? And just ten days before I find them. Does he know he's dying? Is this a last-minute attempt for redemption or is he finally able to surrender whatever indifference it was that prevented him from reaching out to me for thirty-three years?

I'm really not upset. Not in general. And especially not at God above, who knows my life's journey and fate.

On my drive home from work tonight, I convinced myself to think more intuitively and rationally. I wondered. Maybe it's true that the love is or can be just inherently there? But even if that's true, would my fear of such a loss be comparable to those who have known and enjoyed many years together? And what about a miscarriage? The parents do not know their child any more than that child knows what it's like to see light, but yet they seem to mourn the loss just the same. Whilst they have carried the child for a number of months, is it the thought of them or the actual inherit connection to them that they mourn?

I just need to be thankful.

Thankful of whatever time I have, because I have it. And I have dreamed, prayed, and waited all my life for this very moment to happen.

· ♦ ·

Lying in bed now with pajamas on and a bowl of warmed chili in one-hand, "dad" file in the other, and old puppy Bernie at my side, I begin sifting through the papers and reading our first emails.

The first was from him.

It all started earlier this month on what was just another, late summer night. My husband, Charlie, retired to bed early, so I was left to my own devices. Searching Facebook, I found a Brunhoff Family group page. Feeling adventurous, as well as oddly and exceptionally confident, I sent a request to join the group page. I included a brief explanation of who I was, proud of my life and marriage as well as company and career in D.C., followed by what I know is my father's name on my birth certificate, as well as my interest to learn more about the family medical history, especially in case we should want to have children. I was chatting on the phone with Cara, a good friend, when she brought up a familiar suggestion—let's Google your dad. That's when she found him living in Escondido, California, with an Alice, D.O. I, too, looked her up on Facebook and sent a request to connect.

It was that night, September 30, 2014, that I received a notification from Facebook that would change my life forever. I was accepted to join the Brunhoff Family group page.

With sheer excitement, and a swift swarm of butterflies that instantly inhabited my belly, I scanned every post on the group page to see when it started, ended, and everything in between. What was unpromising was that the last post was made in June 2011, three years ago. With my worrying thoughts fluttering away like escaping butterflies, I had to remind myself that someone was active in the group because they just accepted my request. I quickly typed a message and posted it to the group page:

"Hi everyone! Does anyone still use this group? I'm so excited to connect with all of you. Per my birth certificate, my father is Nathan Henry Brunhoff. I am married and live in Washington, D.C."

The first ding to my phone was nearly immediate and was another notification that sent my spirit flailing, spiraling into a tireless night of posting, commenting, and liking back and forth with multiple members in the group. Others had quickly joined in the conversation and that's when I met and became keen to Great Aunt Maura. We exchanged our personal email addresses and continued messaging privately into the next morning. It was then, after getting into the office late the next morning, that a new message came, not from her but him … my father.

* ◆ *

From: Nate Brunhoff

Date: Thursday, October 2, 2014 at 11:24 AM

To: 'Michelle'

Subject: Good morning from the west coast

Michelle:

Several of your correspondences have ricocheted to my attention.

I think it takes substantial courage and confidence to reach into the unknown as you have. I could be a jerk. A gun-toting right wing tobacco chewing skin head or a raging vegan who secretly attends pit bull terrier fights on the weekend. I could have a cantilevered beer gut and attitude, drag one foot and drool profusely. In those respects I hope that I don't disappoint.

Since we are clearly at the cross roads, I suggest we continue.

Nathan B.

· ◆ ·

Attached was a photo of him and Alice. He was tall and handsome, thin in stature with very light blonde hair peeking out under a cowboy hat. His glasses, a classic style with thin gold circle rims and his smile, ever so coy, giving way to what seems to be a warm and interesting soul. He was dressed nicely in a white, button-down dress shirt and fitted leather vest. I noticed the Movado watch on his right wrist. Alice was equally as captivating, wearing a loosely crocheted black sweater over a silky black tank and a slender red pencil skirt. If anyone would've walked by my office at that moment, they'd have seen me childishly grinning from ear to ear. I couldn't help but to be so elated by how much I loved his email, seeing this picture of him, and how excited I was to write him back.

· ◆ ·

On October 2, 2014, at 12:07 AM, Michelle wrote:

(smiling)

Hello there, Nathan.

I must admit that I was forewarned to be prepared for the worst, and raging vegan who secretly attends pit bull terrier fights was one of my top fears. Nonetheless, I have thought about this day for many years and felt confident that I am ready to be "shot" down or drooled on. ;)

You could never disappoint. We are who we are and the past is behind us. Now at this crossroad, we have nothing but the future ahead of us. I'm in. Let's dance!

Smiles,

Michelle

PS—Cute pic! Saving that one on my phone. What were you dressed up for? You and Alice are very cute together. How long have you been together? She seems wonderful.

· ◆ ·

My anticipation of his next message, I remember, had me insanely checking my email all day and then later again at night at home, and then again the next day, and the next! Thankfully, Charlie and I drove to the family cottage that weekend, which helped take my mind off things. The cottage is a beautiful home on Lake Anna, nearly two hours outside of the city and south of D.C. into Virginia. The area is country at its very finest. You can barely get a signal of service on your phone, one can find the best Amish food and antique markets, and at night you can see the stars and hear the crickets. It's beautiful there, which makes it easy to take your mind off anything you want to leave behind in the city. Plus, there's so much fun to be had in the simplicity of it all; cruising on the pontoon boat and floating in the water all day, sipping tequila and listening to music while fishing, jumping in the truck to go antiquing, visiting nearby wineries for good food and wine, bundling up to bonfires and feeling the warmth of sun-kissed skin, or waking early to see the sun rise over the lake and watching the fog break as the cows "moo" in the pasture near-by—it's unmatchable. These are the simple joys in life you can't possibly experience and appreciate in the hustle and bustle of the city. For me, it's a little slice of heaven.

It's always on the Sunday drive back to the city from the cottage that my phone starts to ding again with service. All the messages and emails from the weekend flood in. And there it was, buried deep in work email, a new message from this man whom I wondered if I may one day openly call Dad.

* ◆ *

On October 5, 2014, at 2:23 PM, Nate wrote:

Michelle:

A hearty yes !->

In reverse order of your query and in artless transition, Alice and I have been together for 28 years. But more than that. Here is the page worn story. In 1972, I picked her up hitch-hiking in my black VW bug outside of Hanover, New Hampshire. It was safe to do that back then. She was hiking with her two roommates and left her notebook in the back. I ransomed it for dinner and we became an item for a year and half. For reasons that are not entirely clear, we went our separate ways but always kept in touch with snail mail. Then, in 1986, I came to California to help a friend with his construction project and I looked her up. We settled on dinner but spent the weekend together, and the next, and the next, and we hooked up as though no time had ever passed. That was 28 years ago.

She's a little hard to describe. Very smart is very true. Funny also. She is French Canadian and so every once in a while she will mangle the language like wearing "a chip on your sleeve" or "your heart on your shoulder." She loves animals. I was raised with dogs, but she likes cats so we have six and -0-. I think I lost in that equation.

The pic of us two was from a 50th wedding anniversary of a couple we know. Theme was of course western. There was a band that played Texas Swing and Blue Grass, and two dance instructors for line dancing. Some guests dressed as robbers and took money from the 200 attendees which in turn went to a charity. They even found an old-timely photo booth which worked. The food was marginal but the company and music excellent.

Alice noted that you had 100+ likes from your Facebook inquiry so I don't need to be concerned about acceptance or silence. Nice splash!

I did notice a giraffe in one of your pics and so conclude it most likely came from the Wild Animal Park in Escondido. If true that would have put the two of you about 4 miles from the house. You landed a smart good looking dude by the way. I grew up in East Grand Rapids, where he is from, back in the 50's and 60's. Then we moved to Ada in the mid 60's. Back then, there was only East Grand Rapids and Forest Hills—considered sister schools. Each high school had a boat load of friends in the other school, as well as dates, and the parties were huge.

Electrostatic painting ? ? ?

Is that your company ?

Nathan B.

PS—Nice work on the website by the way ...

· ◆ ·

I'll never forget when we returned to the house that evening; I shared his message with everyone. I felt like an insane child on a sugar rush after eating a handful of pixie sticks, bouncing off the walls with pure, inno-cent joy. Charlie and the rest of the family seemed just as entertained to read it, too.

I eventually leveled out, unpacked, and got dressed for bed, before warming up a cup of tea to write him back.

" ◆ "

At 9:57 PM, Michelle wrote:

Hello Nathan,

How I do love getting your messages. It brings a smile to my face every time.

And so, it is true. You indeed are a lucky man. Imagine back to that day when you picked up Alice on the side of the road ... who would have thought that you would be together today, 28 years later. What an incredibly romantic story. We'll title that one "The Notebook."

Charlie and I met through a mutual friend shortly after I moved home from California (moved out to LA after college to start my career). Sitting in a tapas restaurant on our first date, we ordered a glass of sangria and I was served the fact that he had just turned 21. I was 23, turning 24 later that year. I couldn't believe it. He was just a baby I thought. However, his persistence and maturity quickly won me over and we have been together for eight years now. We tied the knot in Puerto Vallarta, Mexico, the day after Thanksgiving in 2010. It was a beautiful and intimate wedding in a private rented villa filled only with close friends and family ... with a jubilant donkey across the river who kept belting "hee haw" throughout the ceremony, making everyone laugh.

I love cats and all of their personality (easily categorized as sassy), but I am most definitely a dog girl. Yeah, you clearly lost that battle. ;) We rescued Bernie, a yellow haired labradoodle, shortly after we moved into our first apartment together. The story was heartbreaking. Another puppy mill story and a rescuer who saved him from being shot in the head.

The giraffe, that was in Africa. And it was amazing! I'll never forget that drive. It was a two-track dirt road and we were hanging off the back of the jeep while Charlie's mom was screaming for us all to keep our limbs inside. The side of the road was only 2 feet from an edge that led to a cliff into the great depths of the Ngorongoro Crater. When we reached the break in the peak of the climb out, we hit a bend in the road that opened to a sudden and surprising landscape filled with bigger-than-life, grazing giraffes. They are dinosaur-like in real life, yet somehow elegant; breathtaking and unreal. I swear, I took over 3,000 pictures on that trip and a good percentage was just of them. That night ended at a tented camp in the Serengeti. I could fill up a whole email on this adventure. We have lots of time, so I'll leave those "tails" for another.

Ada ... 1960's ... our world may be getting that much smaller.

Charlie's grandfather, known as Dick, founded Green Tree Farms and had a big hand in building Ada township. If you don't mind me asking, how old are you and what is your birth date, school and year of graduation? I am wondering if you may know any of my aunts or uncles on their side.

Charlie is a prodigy of his father's work in electrostatic painting. His father owns an electrostatic painting company in Grand Rapids and instilled in him the drive and passion for entrepreneurship. When Charlie told me he was ready to part ways and start his own business, I hesitated at first but then quickly warmed to the idea of a challenge and excited to apply the skills I have used to help other companies succeed.

Clever and witty you are. And smart.

What do you do, Mr. Nathan B.?

To end this, I just want to say thank you. Thank you for your willingness to fill in the missing pages of my book; all chapters that could never be written without you, and quickly becoming a "can't-put-it-down" story I have always wanted to read.

Turning the page ...

Enjoy your night,

Michelle

· ♦ ·

From: Nate Brunhoff

Date: Tuesday, October 7, 2014 at 11:40 AM

To: 'Michelle'

Subject: In defense of

My adolescence.

Back in the day, 1964-67, we weren't hooligans. The graduating class before ours was always in trouble for having a "club" which was looked upon as a gang back then. "Unsponsored" clubs were literally against state law. But they, The Riatta, met in a barn on the river and did painting and poetry and, of course, got fall down drunk. But they were harmless. They graduated, got drafted, and never came back from Vietnam.

Our group met in fields to sing Joan Baez and Judy Collins with those who brought guitars and got fall down drunk—but we didn't burn cars.

The exception to the good part was more good parts. Back in the day, driver's licenses were unguarded pieces of paper with a background which resembled that of bank checks. Thus, we were able, with the help of a serious Xerox machine and a razor, to make fake licenses to equal 21. Then we rented an apartment on the west side of GR—just across the river, and everyone brought one piece of furniture from their basement or kitchen and, Viola! furnished. It was our alternate place for parties or dates. If someone got too drunk, we took the keys to their car (if they drove) and it was up to them to deal with the parental fallout. The smart ones made excuses ahead of time to their parents. One final addition was canoeing. Once a month, in the better weather, we would pick a river that had some white water. We would fill the canoes with beer and sandwiches and shove off into a mix of hilarity and stupidity. A lot of beer was lost to poor steerage.

NB

* ♦ *

Thumbing through more printed pages and email exchanges stuffed in the manila folder titled "dad," I continue giggling and smiling with every read. We continued to share and connect on our semi-rebellious, but still good, adolescent memories. Similar to him, my friends and I were just an average group of considerably smart girls who wanted to achieve things in life but also wanted to have fun. We were good, never in trouble, thankfully, but always pushing the limits and finding ways to entertain ourselves in the vast fields of corn, acres of woods, and many dirt roads that surrounded us.

I told him about my school-age parties in the woods (because there was nothing more to do in our sleepy town in the 1990s) and the fibs we told each other's parents, including one clever lie that we were old enough to drive (when we clearly were not). One night, we got the keys to a large and long white commercial van; we had no idea it was going to be the vehicle of a parent's friend whom we talked into the deal. We appropriately named it "The Marshmallow" on our adventures driving it on the dirt roads.

I still remember us all sitting at the very front, one girl in the driver's seat, one in the passenger's seat, and the rest on a handful on buckets and boxes pulled from the back. We were all hysterical, wondering how in the world to drive the huge thing. Whenever we pulled this stunt, we never knew what kind of vehicle we'd end up getting. We would just claim to be old enough and ask to borrow their keys.

That night in the Marshmallow, we accidently almost tipped it on its side going around a corner. We had no idea, never having driven anything of that size, and were going way too fast. We had taken the van to a clearing in the woods the high schoolers called Consumer's Beach. It was set atop a nearly mile-high hill of pure, white beach sand that rolled down to the water of Croton Hardy Dam. We enjoyed a few dips, and a few sips of beer, before returning home with one of our fondest memories that has lasted a lifetime.

Chapter 2

Nearly twenty-four hours after inquiring about my dad's health, my nerves are a little calmer, but my heart is still twisted in knots. I must have woken at least five times throughout the night and into the early morning, constantly checking to see if Alice texted back about my father's sickness. Each time I was met with silent disappointment, I'd grab another chocolate chip cookie and suppress my anxiety with its sweetness. Finally at work, full still from cookies and ready to skip lunch like breakfast, around 11:30 a.m. a "ding" and notification lights my phone home screen—it's Alice!

ALICE

> Yes. Nathan does have medical issues and I am optimistic. Please write him and ask him about his health.

I try to take a deep breath but choke on the exhale. I hadn't realized I was holding my breath. I turn up my palms and catch my face again. After some time with my face hidden in my hands, I collect myself and return my focus to the computer screen. I save my open projects, minimize the design programs, and open a blank email. I type in his email address. After a few sentences, I pause to read over what I've typed. I start hitting backspace and delete. I know what I want to say. I need to start over and speedily begin typing again. Now a few paragraphs in, I pause again to re-read and check for formalities and errors. Nope, I don't like it. I delete it all over again.

I can't quite figure it out. How the heck do I express my sincere, deep concerns to a man who's basically still a stranger? What a juxtaposition. What if I come across too strong, do I try again, and then, what if it comes across too distant and insincere? And how do I keep my thoughts composed about something I have no understanding of? I'm also sitting on two open invitations to visit him for the first time, one from Alice and another from Great Aunt Maura, but yet I haven't heard a peep from him about it. He hasn't even responded yet to the last message I wrote, nearly four days ago. This is incredibly awkward. This man … my father, he is such a mystery. What is he thinking? And how will he react to such a note? I wonder.

· ◆ ·

From: 'Michelle'

Date: Tuesday, October 21, 2014 at 9:13 AM

To: Nate Brunhoff

Subject: Good morning :)

Hi Nathan,

I hope the sun is shining for you this morning. How was your time spent with your brothers? I received a special birthday book in the mail last weekend that was filled with pictures of you, Alice, and the family. I am sure she shared my appreciation with you, but I also wanted to say thank you to you as well. It is a treasure and I hope that in the next few months I will be able to point out everyone in the book by name, including the furry ones.

In my writings back and forth with Great Aunt Maura, I have been learning a lot about the family history and health. She recently mentioned that you may be dealing with a few health concerns yourself. I cannot trust that it is not something I should not know about. Could you possibly divulge?

I thought of something that may be fun, too. Have you ever talked via Skype where you can see each other and talk at the same time? There is also FaceTime, if you or Alice have an iPhone. What do you think, phone date?

Also, Aunt Maura suggested a visit, and then Alice so kindly shared an invite as well. I must admit that in a surreal bubble of excitement came a sudden burst of hesitation and nerves. I thought, maybe more time would be best to continue to get to know you and the family before the first visit. I am curious to know your thoughts …

Thinking of you,

Michelle

＊◆＊

On October 22, 2014, at 10:40 AM, Nate wrote:

Yes. I am too short of time so I will mention in passing that I am far too ugly for Skype (on my mac or iphone). People have been known to light their hair on fire and go shrieking off into the distance. Others just want to take long showers. A very disappointing result.

More later today.

nb

＊◆＊

So quickly he responds … and yet, so disappointing is his response. Incredible, he so confidently and auspiciously dodges the question. And am I surprised? Ugh, no I am not. This quiet, hidden, and very mysterious man.… Why on earth would he reveal himself to me now? I have to ask. It has taken him all these years to come forward, and ironically the same age that I am today, thirty-three, matches to exactly how old he was when I was born, thirty-three. So, why now, and to pull open the curtain only to reveal whatever angle of light he so desires to display? With much disdain and frustration, but yet a heart full of love, curiosity, and a yearning for acceptance, I continue and press on—responding quickly and considerably foolishly. But what do I have to lose, him?

＊◆＊

On October 22, 2014, at 10:52 AM, Michelle wrote:

We could always wear Halloween masks. Cool shades and a hat?

I think you are handsome.

Can't wait till you pop in my inbox again. :)

-M

＊◆＊

JOURNAL ENTRY

October 22, 2014

His short-lined response to my questions bring back old memories. A single sentence that so cleverly avoids any seriousness.... "Yes. I am short of time so I will mention in passing that I am far too ugly for Skype.... " This may be my biggest fear.

Could this man be any more elusive? How does one manage to cleverly dodge any serious question I ask? And then I go to the beginning ... "Yes." And that's his response to: a) Will you please tell me about your health problems? or b) Have you ever talked via Skype where you can see each other while you talk? The answer is unknown.

He's short of time. It's like reading the last sentence of a novel. You know it's impactful and has deep meaning (and purpose), but for one who has not read the book in its entirety, it is simply just a sentence with no true meaning or understanding.

But the following sentences.... "People have been known to light their hair on fire and go shrieking off into the distance. Others just want to take long showers. A very disappointing result." What is this, some kind of code I'm supposed to decipher? Are these instances from a movie or maybe Shakespeare that I have heard he so much enjoys?

\- ♦ -

Riddle me this.
    Riddle me that.
    My hand slaps the journal shut.
    I find myself reflecting on my childhood. It was 1998 and I was sixteen years old, working at an energy company that serviced our county, headquartered in our small town. I worked there with Lo and Missy, two of my bestest girlfriends since grade school. It was an employment opportunity we had unexpectedly won after scoring exceptionally high on fake interviews arranged by our business school teacher.
    Many years earlier, when we first moved to the town (Mom, myself, and my brother), I was snooping through one of many, many boxes.

Hidden away and filling all corners of the basement, stacked in closets, or set out in the open on bookshelves, boxes were always a part of our home growing up, no matter where we lived. And every one of them always held my curiosity because you never knew what you would find inside. Pay stubs, books, papers, toys, yearbooks, baby clothing, MSU college memorabilia…. Mom never got rid of *anything*. One day, I found a box filled with paper bills (utility, loan, car, etc.) and for some reason I spent nearly an hour rummaging through it as though I knew I would find something cool. And then, sandwiched in between two pieces of paper was victory. I found an old two-dollar bill! I shoved it in my pocket, put the box away, threw on a pair of dirty, worn-out tennis shoes, ran outside to jump on my bike and pedaled to the party store down the road. What did I buy? Candy, of course. We never had sweets in the house (only at Grandma's).

This curiosity with Mom's boxes and the possibility of uncovering hidden treasures never ceased. In my eyes, everything undiscovered was a potential treasure. And then, one day, I found it. It was my birth certificate and for first time, I learned my father's name. It read:

FATHER – NAME

Nathan	Henry	Brunhoff
(first)	(middle)	(last)

The rest of my days following the discovery, my girlfriends and I would fill his story with all kinds of mystery and drama. The "what if" was so exciting and the unknown…. Well, it was practically dehydrating. I wanted, I needed, and I had to know more, especially as I got older. If I couldn't uncover his truth, I felt like I would wilt away. Teenagers are, indeed, dramatic, and I was one of them.

Now, back to my sixteen-year-old self working at the energy company. It was our junior year of high school, and we got access to the internet for the first time, the "world wide web" (www). It was so new, and we were so curious about its possibilities. Even as teenaged novices, we understood its search capabilities. On a warm day in early September, the sun was shining and Lo and I opted out of our regular cruise to the park to smoke cigarettes and listen to music. Instead, for break, we parked ourselves in a quiet conference room at work. We logged onto a computer with questionably more excitement than sneaking out on a warm, summer night to see cute boys (and maybe taking a few swigs of their forbidden beer). On a Yahoo search page, we typed the letters "B-r-u-n-h-o-f-f" and hit enter.

The results that populated were so few that there wasn't even an option to hit next to see another page. No detective work needed here. Holy smokes! You can only imagine the feeling we had at that exact moment. Could this be? Are these all the answers right here!? We stared at the results in silence. There were only two names listed. It was both interesting and unexpected to learn the name is so rare. And then all of a sudden, nearly in unison, we both broke from our mesmerized trance and screamed with (teenage girl) excitement!

After all the time spent daydreaming, and in just a matter of seconds and a few clicks of the mouse and fingertips on the keyboard, there before us was the glimpse of a part of life that had always been a mystery. The part of me that was unknown. Did I have relatives? Maybe I had a grandma and grandpa, and possibly a stepmom? Brothers and sisters? We hit print and spent a few minutes being giddy school girls babbling about what to say, most of it serious and some joking. Admittedly, we have called strangers before, but that was for prank calling (wink).

"Hi! I'm looking for my dad and I just found my birth … " I said aloud, practicing. We both agreed it didn't sound right. "Hi, Dad, it's me!" we both laughed. The more I practiced, the more it seemed absurd and ridiculous. Screw it. "I'm just going to go for it!" I remember telling Lo. I grabbed the conference room phone and dialed the first number.

The area code and address were for Fort Pierce, Florida, and the name was Betty. It was an elderly woman who answered the phone. She had a tempestuous voice that was sweet but unconvincing. As I quickly explained my story, I finished by asking if the name was familiar or if there was any family information she could provide.

"Well, honey," she said almost apprehensively. Then the words that followed left me looking at Lo in absolute disbelief and amazement as her story revealed exactly nothing I had expected and everything I was hoping to hear. The tears started flowing down my cheeks.

"I am sorry that I have not heard anything about you," she apologized. "But I also have not spoken to Nathan in many years. If what you say is true, then I would be your step-grandmother, darling. Your grandfather has passed. His name was Henry Edward Brunhoff. Nathan has two brothers and, last I knew, he was living in California near San Diego. He would be around fifty years old now. He was going to school to get a degree in law. Let me give you the number to his brother Ed. He is a computer scientist. I think this number should still work. It has been a while since I have spoken to any of the boys."

My heart was fluttering and I was choking to get any words out. And while her words were filled with some sort of mystery, they provided more answers than I could have ever hoped. I jotted down the number and notes. Before we hung up, I paused to let her know how great it was to meet her.

As I hung up the phone, in a hurried voice I shared every detail with Lo. She pointed out that Ed was the only other person listed in the search results. The number Betty had provided was different. We gave it a whirl....

The other end of the line was answered again by a woman, but with a younger and more welcoming voice. She, too, had not heard anything of me, and while surprised by my call, promised she would give Ed my message when he returned home from work. She took down my name and number.

This time, when I hung up, we realized the time was five minutes past three o'clock, and five minutes past our break! We scurried out of the conference room giggling, full of excitement. The rest of the afternoon was spent in a dream of what my next days and what the rest of my life would be like.

Later that evening, around 8:00 p.m., the phone rang and Mom said it was for me.

"Hello?"

"Hello, is this Michelle?" said the voice on the other end.

"Yes, it is."

"Hi. My name is Ed. Ed Brunhoff."

"Oh, yes! Hi! Thank you so much for.... "

"I received your message and wanted to return your call. So, you say that Nathan is your father?" he interrupts.

"Yes, I know it sounds crazy," I look at my mom and then quietly sneak out of the room with the cordless phone. "I am just looking for answers. I found my birth certificate a few years ago and underneath the entry for father it says, Nathan Henry Brunhoff. I wasn't sure if I would even find anything. My friends and I were at work today and thought we would search for the last name on the internet. Only two names came up, you and a Betty living in Florida. I called her first and she suggested I call you and gave me your phone number."

Silence.

In a nervous sounding laugh, he finally filled the awkward silence with more words.

"And have you asked your mom?"

"No, she doesn't know anything about this yet," I quickly and quietly responded. "She doesn't even know I found my birth certificate or that I have access to the internet to try and find him."

"Alright. Well, I haven't spoken with him yet, but I will give you his phone number."

"Okay," I gasped. My entire throat filled with a boulder-size rock.

"Do you have a pen handy?" he asked.

"Ohhh … (ack) … ummm, yeah, yes, I'm ready!" I squeezed out in a mumbled voice as quick as a buzzing bee. I was so disconnected from reality and just trying to find ANYTHING to write on. Any writing surface will do. I hung up and stared at the numbers written on the face of my desk. I remember thinking, "THIS is my father's phone number."

I paced. I prayed. I cried. I swore up and down to heaven and earth that I would never be more thankful for anything. I wondered, "What is he like? Am I like him? Do we like the same things? What does he look like? Do I look like him? Has he thought of me?"

But I left no time for courage-building. There was no coaxing myself into it. I just went for it. After all the time spent filled with dreams and mirages, I was ready to see the sand fall from the hourglass. I wanted to see inside the time capsule of everything I did not know.

"Hello?" a woman's voice answered my call, cheerful and charismatic.

"Hello. Hi. My name is.… "

"Yes, you must be Michelle," she interrupts.

"Yes!" I responded quickly and full of bewilderment.

"I have been waiting for you to call for a long time."

There are no other words that could have ever had such great impact on me. I've searched for my dad for a thousand years in my mind. At that moment on the phone, I wanted to rejoice. I found him! This was real!

The woman on the phone kept it short and sweet, not privy to the frantic screaming I had happening on the inside. She told me my father was looking forward to speaking with me and wanted to set up a date. We scheduled it for the next Tuesday, September 15, at 6:00 p.m. I jotted the time and date on the same printed piece of paper from our internet search results earlier in the top right corner and highlighted it with blue marker:

TUESDAY EVENING 6 P.M.
(NATE IS CALLING)

Thinking back on that first, real phone conversation I had with my father, I wish now I would have seized every minute. But how was I to know what would happen next? I thought it was all just the beginning, and the start of the rest of our years together. Oh, to be young and (to put it frankly) dumb. So oblivious to reality but full of dreams and hopes.

The phone call was nothing like what I made up and played over again in my head. I recall him asking if I liked the movies and which one I had seen lately. He also asked me what I liked to eat. I remember thinking his questions were kind of strange and boring. He wanted to know if I ate healthy. In turn, both of my responses were equally as poor, but it was all nothing I wanted to talk about. Eating healthy and watching movies? What about my school, my job, or my friends? What about my goals and aspirations? Didn't he want to know of my accomplishments or dreams?

It was a bit of an awkward conversation, but I tried my best to reflect the maturity on the other end. We exchanged email addresses and promised to stay in touch. Unfortunately, my level of maturity ended with the conversation. Later that week, instead of hanging out with friends on a Friday, I went to Grandma's and started a chain of very embarrassing and one-way conversation emails ... you know, those of a sixteen-year-old girl expressing her innermost feelings, just talking to herself and thinking anyone else on the other end is going to be invested, care, and listen.

‹ ♦ ›

From: 'Michelle'

Date: Friday, September 18, 1998

To: Director of the Western Hemisphere

Subject: It's Me!

(You might want to print this off before you start to read it. It is quite long and I think you would find it much easier to read than on screen. ☺)

Dear Dad,

Hi!

How are you? I tried to e-mail you this morning from Voc. School, but I ended up spending all my time trying to re-install the scan program on the computer. I wanted to scan pictures of me to send you. Well the program was mainly for just scanning text so the pictures didn't turn out too well. When I have time, I am going to scan a few pictures of me and my friends in the computer lab at high school and email you them from my grandma's house.

I am at my grandma's right now. It's about 7:00 p.m. After I write you, I am going to go home to get ready to see my boyfriend. His name is Wade and we have dated for a while now but have also broken up a few times. I really like him though and we have been friends now for about four years. He always makes me laugh and takes me out places. We have a good time together. He is taking classes at Grand Valley State University right now, where I am going to school next year to study journalism.

O.K., are you ready? I am going to tell you about my life. I was born at Butterworth on October 15, 1981. I have one brother and his name is Jay. He is older than I and we have different dads, obviously. My favorite color is blue (I love blue) and I like a lot of things. I am a very wishful person. I also have a lot of faith. I believe in fate, miracles, and that prayers can be answered.

As a child, I grew up in Rockford, Michigan. After I finished my third grade year, we moved to Newaygo on Brooks Lake. I really liked that house but not the memories. Just to inform you, I have had a few bad things happen to me, which I don't mind talking about.

At that house, my mom had brought home a new boyfriend who eventually moved in with us. His name was Chip and I didn't like him from the beginning. Well, he started sexually molesting me and I was very young then, only nine years old and I was afraid to tell my mom. It's true what they say, when you are that young you don't have enough self-esteem or courage to tell your parents or anyone else what is going on when something like that is happening. I remember (crazy me) that I had thought that my mom would get mad at me and boy was I wrong! After about a month of it happening, I had written on a piece of paper "I hate Chip, I love my mom" over and over and over. It covered the entire piece of paper front and back. I had crumpled it up and thrown it in the trash and somehow my mom found it. When she questioned me, I couldn't help but let it all out. And when it came out, he was out of there and in jail. I remember the day in court so good. I cried so hard. Chip's lawyer was such an ********! They finally let me get off the witness stand when I couldn't talk anymore because I was crying so hard. My mom thought that I would need counseling, but I didn't. When I first went to counseling, I couldn't stand the lady. I thought she was so nosey. Then she just let me play games, color, and draw pictures ... I got out of school for it so I didn't mind. I guess eventually my mom said the lady told her that counseling wasn't needed and I agreed, so then I never had to go again.

Anyways, after that house we moved to one on Hess Lake. After living there for about a year, my friend Blossom and I had stopped at my house after babysitting some kids in the trailer park down the road. I was always home alone then because my mom was always working. Ever since I can remember, I have babysat myself. I was very responsible as a child and have always been independent. Anyways, I unlocked the door and we went right to my bedroom so I could get some money to go to a movie with her family. We had been in the room for only a few minutes when a guy about 6′2″ with blue jean cutoffs, a turquoise t-shirt, and a black ski-mask came into my room behind Blossom and grabbed the both of us. I will never forget her screaming. It was so loud and it was only pissing him off more, so I had to keep telling her to be quiet. He had tied up her arms and hit the back of her head with a thick, old fashioned glass Coca Cola bottle I had in my room and it knocked her out. Then he started hitting me over the head. The third time I blocked it with my hand and was being kind of cocky reminding him that he had promised he wouldn't hurt us. Then he started to strangle me and I got scared. I started praying. It's hard to explain what it is like to not be able to breathe or even catch a breath because someone else won't let you. All I could do was pray for strength over and over again. Then, all of the sudden, I got a spurt of energy that seemed unexplainable. I started kicking my legs and trying to find balance and found a wall. I used it as leverage and started pushing against him with everything I had. I was only about 90 lbs. but I think adrenaline can do wonders. I ended up breaking free from him and crawling to the other side of my room. Soon after that he left.

Blossom still tells me to this day that she can't believe how brave I was to be so cocky to him. She had come back to and said she heard me still giving him crap right before he left saying that he said he wouldn't hurt us. He ended up being a convicted rapist from Grand Rapids. He was my neighbor. He got caught trying to rape two girls from Grand Rapids and bring them to his house. How can a person be so mentally ill in the head? A few years later he was proven to be the guy who had assaulted us. My detective was a really nice guy. I see him every now and then. He always tells me that I am such a brave girl and that I only keep getting more beautiful. I realize these things have happened to me in my lifetime, that's it ... they did and I can't change it. It doesn't bring me down at all, and I don't feel that they should either. I use these experiences to warn others that it can happen to them, too. I never, not in my wildest dreams, thought it would happen to me. I have given many speeches and written papers about these experiences and still do to this day.

My life has been very wonderful though. Although it has been hard, I don't ponder on the bad times. What's the point in doing that? I see it as I need to cherish the good times and let the bad times only be of the past. I have so many wonderful friends and family. I have had a lot of great times in my life too and I have a great time at school. I guess you could say I am kind of popular in school but I am friends with everyone, even those that some people call "nerds." Seriously, I don't see them as that at all. I can't imagine having to put up with other people thinking that I was lower than them and have them pick on me for it. In my eyes, no one is better than anybody. One of the greatest things that has happened to me in my life though, even though there are many, this one beats them all—finding you!

I have always wanted to know who you are, talk to you, meet you, start a relationship with you, but I guess I thought that would actually never happen. I know you think that you could never be a good father (your brother told me), but you can. It doesn't matter to me though whether you are good or bad, that isn't important. What is important is that we have a relationship now. I would really love to have a relationship with you of great friendship and to meet you and your family. I like you for who you are, you are my father. I just want you to know that you are my prayers answered.

Well, I have now written you a novel about me, it is your turn. I really wish I could write some more (I will have to send you some of my poems next time I email you), but I need to start typing my paper for my senior literature class, look up some information for my speech in speech class and then leave to go see my boyfriend.

I hope you had a wonderful day and have a great night. Tell your family I said "Hi ☺". Sleep tight and don't let the bed bugs bite.

Love always and forever,

Michelle

P.S. When you look outside your window tonight and see a bright star in the night sky, just remember that even though we are miles away we are looking at the same star.

▪ ◆ ▪

Yikes. Talk about telling your life story in ONE email. Is it fair to say, if you give a young girl a keyboard and let her know on the receiving end is a father she's never met, you'd expect nothing less? But yet, it indeed was not received well and my continuous and ever-long messages were to my own detriment. I scared him away, 100 percent. I didn't realize it at the time, but that novel email and those that followed terrified this man who was not ready to be a father or have any kind of relationship with his daughter.

Blah, blah, blah … I wanted to tell him *everything*. How embarrassing for me, and how terrifying for my father who I imagine clenched his teeth and massaged an inflamed vein on his temple after reading every word, after word, after word. I only ever received a few short responses back. It crushed me.

▪ ◆ ▪

From: Director of the Western Hemisphere

Date: Wednesday, September 30, 1998 at 11:03 PM

To: 'Michelle'

Subject: [Fwd: It's Me!]

Dear Michelle:

I am sorry I haven't replied earlier. I have been busy packing to move to Seattle Washington.

I have a new e-mail address until I get settled which is just below.

. ◆ .

His new email never worked and then neither did his current one. I always wondered, even back then, if I had scared him off. It's quite the conundrum. Funny, because you would think a father-daughter relationship would be different than a relationship of a boy and girl—turns out, in this case, it feels far too much the same. If a young girl were ever to fall in love too fast and make a complete ass of herself, only to lose the boy … well, that was me and the boy was my father. I lost him within just a week of finding him. This could possibly be a record of some sort.

Chapter 3

Jumping again to 2014, emailing again with my dad. This time it's his writing that has stymied me. Do I need to decode a riddle? Maybe pass some kind of test? Although it's late and my body is tired, my mind is not. His response yesterday riddled me, but I'm convinced I'll solve it. When in doubt, you can always count on trusty Google.

Enter Google Search: "Shakespeare Long Showers"

Results populate with *Richard II*, ACT II, Scene I.

CLICK!

My face is lit only by the blue-hued glow of the screen in front of me and the rest of the room is blanketed with the dark of night. I can feel the answer is here, hidden somewhere in this strange script. I read line 715:

"His rash fierce blaze of riot cannot last,

For violent fires soon burn out themselves;

Small showers last long,

But sudden storms are short."

The story is about John of Gaunt. In this Shakespeare play, chock-full of situations forcing characters to choose between political and family ties, John of Gaunt finally gets it—he realizes that being a good dad is more important than being loyal to the king. Unfortunately, Gaunt's big "ah ha" moment comes a little too late. Deprived of his banished son, sick and dying, he decides to offer the king some real guidance … and that's what comes (again) in line 715.

I am convinced I was meant to find this. I'm also known to overthink things. So, there's that. But regardless, I swipe off my phone and join it in sleep mode with a contented smile on my face.

With a bit of time to kill before work in the morning, I leave early and find an empty spot in the parking lot to sit and park. I roll down the window, take a sip of hot coffee and light a cigarette, pulling open our last email again on my phone. I hit reply and re-title the subject, adding a dash and "response v II" to parody Act II. Then I type in the exact words of those lines from the play. I write nothing more and nothing less and hit send with the same contented smile that I went to bed with last night.

· ♦ ·

From: 'Michelle'

Date: Thursday, October 23, 2014 at 6:16 AM

To: Nate Brunhoff

Subject: Good morning - response v II

His rash fierce blaze of riot cannot last,

For violent fires soon burn out themselves;

Small showers last long, but sudden storms are short.

· ♦ ·

At 10:27 AM, Nate wrote:

Richard the II !

· ♦ ·

Yesssss! That's it, Richard the II.
    BOOM. High five to self? #winning
    That may also be the quickest response I've received yet, and it won't be the last time Shakespeare enters our relationship. That contented smile is now confidently glowing on my face. It's a feeling like when you gamble another quarter in the claw machine and finally grab a hold of a stuffed animal *and* hold it all the way to the victory drop!
    Little do I know though, my winnings are yet to come.

· ♦ ·

From: Nate Brunhoff

Date: Thursday, October 23, 2014 at 11:16 AM

To: 'Michelle'

Subject: Re: Good morning - response v II

Here's the deal, Oldsmobile ...

As you know—Aunt Maura is coming down from the bay area on the 7th–10th November. Because of time and circumstance this could be a one-time event for her. We have some extra miles on our American Airlines account. I would like to offer to you and your husband to fly you to San Diego round trip. We have a furnished apartment close by (12 minutes) that is used for patients and family (you). That will give you lots of privacy and a retreat. We have an extra car for you to zip around in. There is wi-fi at the apartment for your laptop. We have some food in the fridge at the house—so foraging is not necessary.

Would this be of interest?? I know it is rather short notice.

Nathan III

· ◆ ·

Of all the wonderful words in our English language, this email does not include a single one that could allude to the description, feeling of or resemblance of glory, yet I am feeling all of it and am floating in the clouds. Nor does a single word say what I believe to be true and am hearing from reading it, but seems to be in the unwritten; he wants to meet me.

His message comes just as swiftly and unexpectedly as a storm on the beach sands of Lake Michigan. With very little warning and a surprising gust of cool wind, you're left chasing a beach towel as it flies down the shoreline and the skies begin to roll. The once brilliant sun becomes matched with a foray of clouds and a rainbow prism wall of misted rain drops. Magnificent colors spray across the sky and reflect on the endless brilliant blue waters below. You are left standing alone now with the sand stuck between your toes. Awe-struck by the beauty and grace of life's natural turmoil, you naturally let the towel blow away; because you know it is special and not something everyone gets to see.

The invitation is now real, because it is from him. My joy is insurmountable. I want to elatedly scream and jump and, at the same time, fall down with great gratitude and disbelief.

Pinch me.

Is this real? Is this *really* happening? I have thought of this day for so many years. I have longed to meet him since as far back as I can remember, far before I ever found that birth certificate and read his name for the first time.

Without hesitation, I forward the email to Charlie and send him a text at the same time to make sure he reads it immediately. The thought of bugging him is of no concern. Any hesitations about leaving our business unattended for the first time or being out of office at work are suddenly trivial and inconsequential. Thankfully, his response comes right away. I'm not sure I could've waited a second longer.

"Yes, let's do it. This is important and everything else can wait. It's a once in a lifetime opportunity. We'll figure out how to make it work. Let's talk about it tonight, but respond Yes!"

These are not butterflies. It is my actual stomach rising to the back of my throat. It's matched with an insanely fast and loud palpitating heart that feels as though it could vibrate nearby objects like the sound of bass from a souped-up low rider on the strip of Las Vegas. Thankfully, I'm at home for lunch. I make my way to the bathroom to splash water on my face.

- ◆ -

At 2:44 PM, Michelle wrote:

Alright Cadillac,

I'm not sure how I could ever say no ... and therefore, I will not. YES. 100% yes. You made the invitation pretty hard to refuse. Thank you—so incredibly generous. Charlie said he will make it work and not to worry about the business and I also just cleared the dates with my office.

This truly is beyond generous. Please let me know how we can help and assist with the travel arrangements, and I sincerely mean that. I don't want to use up all your miles and we can most definitely cover any costs.

Wow. Is this really happening?

Michelle I

﹡ ◆ ﹡

Michelle "the first" is how I sign off with my acceptance response (ha!). Sometimes I entertain myself, but also am feeling wildly confident.

﹡ ◆ ﹡

At 7:35 PM, Nate wrote:

Thank you for accepting the invite! It will be fun.

We will begin to assemble the flights tonight as close as possible to non-stop and no red-eye flights. I'll keep you posted as soon as possible as well—and my thanks to Charlie with apologies for dragging him rather unceremoniously away from his business.

Nathan B.

﹡ ◆ ﹡

I'm lying in bed restless tonight, feeling like a child again, but this time one who cannot sleep because of the pure joy and excitement for what tomorrow brings. It feels like Christmas. It's not, but it sure does feel like it. I rewind the day and reflect back on how it started, sitting in the parking lot smoking a cigarette and brilliantly guessing the answer to his riddle, much less confidently than any contestant in the history of Jeopardy. Did I solve it or was it just coincidence? Oh, John of Gaunt. Oh, life.

﹡ ◆ ﹡

At 7:11 AM on October 24, 2014, Michelle wrote:

It will be so much fun! I am finding it difficult to even explain my excitement and happiness.

Charlie mentioned without a doubt, it was never a question after reading your email. It's good for everyone. He asked me to also express his thanks for including him. He is a good man and my best friend. I'm so thrilled for us all to meet!

I must also tell you that I made a decision at the beginning of this venture that I would not tell my mother until I was ready. Not thinking that I would actually find you, but once I did, I decided to remain true to that original plan. I feel strongly that I must take this journey myself with a clear mind and only positive thoughts. The last time I spoke of you with her was many years ago and it was not in fair judgment on her part. Since, it has remained a quiet and clouded conversation without any interests on my part to reignite. When I'm confident in my feelings, I know the time will be right to share.

So, as far as the social media story goes, I have had to refrain from shouting my excitement to the rooftops. It is not my intention to keep you secret, but just to be cautious in my steps. For the time being, I am sharing my joy only with close friends and family, and an old friend—my trusty journal.

Pinch me. I am so excited to meet you.

-M

• ◆ •

And just like you would've never predicted, the curiously connected world of Facebook sends me a notification again from the twisted hands of fate. Posted on my wall at 10:19 a.m. is a message from Frank, my father's younger brother, my uncle.

Good morning, Michelle.

I thought about saying welcome to the family but—you have always been a part of the Brunhoff family. I can only imagine how curious you must be about all of us, so I will try to put together a little info about myself this weekend. I guess one could say I am the wanderer and the explorer of the brothers.

Nate has always been a really cool older brother. If there were an Oscar for the role, he would have a shelf full of the statues.

If I may ask, I would like to communicate by email. I am not very big on Facebook messaging.

I send him a private message and give him my work email. And like a coastal city flooded by the waves of a once silent earth rattled by an earthquake, I feel like my new world is now threatening to overtake me.

• ◆ •

At 10:38 AM, Nate wrote:

A tiny favor I must ask ...

When Charlie goes to the refrigerator—or pantry for a snack—what does he grab?

When you go to the pantry or fridge for a snack—what catches your attention?

In exchange therefore I promise to bathe.

NB

• ✦ •

At 10:52 AM, Michelle wrote:

We are truly not picky eaters. No allergies and we enjoy pretty much all ethnicities. We are not vegan or vegetarian, and we love our gluten and carbohydrates. And anything that says diet is usually gross and doesn't taste anything like its normal counterpart.

Honestly, please not to worry. We will enjoy anything and everything. Anything that we feel is necessary or wanted, we can simply go grab at the closest convenience store.

Please still shower.

;)

• ✦ •

And now, a surprise!

• ✦ •

From: 'Frank'

Date: Friday, October 24, 11:55 AM

To: 'Michelle'

Subject: Re: And the Oscar goes to ...

Hi Michelle,

Thanks for the open door.

The stories are many! But I will try to put together an outline for you this weekend and as time goes along fill it in. Questions are welcomed by family. I tend to be quiet and reserved about my life but something inside me says you are OK!

I have been involved in construction since 1971, starting as a carpenter helper/apprentice/house farmer. My career and work focus quickly shifted to commercial—industrial projects.

As a young man, I wanted to work on projects that were too remote, too difficult, too dangerous and so I did for many years, accumulating with 8 years in Iraq & Afghanistan in what we on the inside would call combat construction. Because of this wild goal, I lived & worked on the edge for nearly 40 years. I do not consider myself particularly special in any sort of way, just a dreamer and a hard worker. The projects I was fortunate enough to get on have taken me many—many places.

This has been off set for a love of Tibetan Buddhism which I have studied for longer than I have worked in construction—not a likely mix.

My home is now in Thailand where we have a beautiful garden and in a few years a home to retire in. All this is possible because of a fantastic lady (Yenja!) that I met in late 2004 in Thailand and married in August of 2006. I currently reside in Little Rock, AR where I hope to be joined by Yen in a few months. I am putting Yen's daughter Nyafon through college in Bangkok so—more work is needed. :)

Photo from 2011

More this weekend.

Frank

· ♦ ·

Attached to his email is a photo of a modern-day rendition of the 1930 iconic American Gothic painting by Grant Wood, more commonly referred to as the farmer and his wife. Surrounded by the greenery of a bountiful garden and "wooded" Thailand backdrop, sits a new Ford F-150 truck, Frank with a balding head and circle glasses seated on a small wooden chair holding a shovel, and next to him stands a small and quaint Taiwanese girl who looks about twenty years younger and rises only a head taller on her feet than him sitting on his chair. She is also holding a rake and smiling cheerfully from ear to ear.

Feeling inquisitive and completely perplexed by all the information shared in his message, I stare intensely at the photo until an alert slides across the screen distracting my focus. It's a new message from my father.

· ◆ ·

At 11:57 AM, Nate wrote:

Hummmmm. Do you like

Berries

English Muffins

Small toasty trolls

Corn chips

A particular dip

Coffee

Lattes, etc.

A favorite tea

Red Bull Rocket Fuel

Peanut butter

Sparkling water

Cold water

Room temp water

Milk, 2%, whole, raw

Cottage cheese small curd, large curd ...

Help me out here ...

· ◆ ·

His message makes me laugh-out-loud, and little thought is needed to quickly respond. Berries? Yes. English muffins are okay. Small toasty trolls are delightful. Corn chips are delicious with salsa or homemade guacamole. Coffee is a morning must and a vanilla latte is a luxury. I should drink tea, but instead I drink wine. We drink red bull with vodka to get our wings. Peanut butter is a staple. Sparkling water sounds fancy. Cold water is preferred and room temp water is for the toilet. Milk 2% will do, so you can give Betsy a night off from milking the night before we arrive. Cottage cheese large *or* small curd!

A few hours later, Alice sends over flight options and I forward them to Charlie. When I get home, we quickly make a decision and respond back with our preference. By 7 o'clock, we have itineraries in hand.

• ♦ •

JOURNAL ENTRY

October 24, 2014

In two weeks, I will be spending my first day ever with a man who bears the exact name printed on my birth certificate; a man who has spent thirty-three years knowing nothing of me and I knowing nothing of him; a man I had accepted as someone whom I may live all my years and never know; a man who has lived as a scar on my heart and that I learned to accept, even intentionally making it a tattoo to forever be a part of me.

Not a single other ink mark exists on my body, only the one small marking I chose in my twenties. It's approximately one inch in width and one inch in height, discretely hidden under my small left breast, and directly on top of my heart. It's a Chinese symbol that reflects in one character a lifetime journey that I have always, but now more proudly, borne; the symbol 父 for "Father."

Chapter 4

"**1**70!" Charlie says, flailing his hands and acting as air traffic control. "Back up and park right there."

I slide the car in reverse and back up to a spot just in front of our storage unit.

Charlie gets out first and unlocks the storage unit door to let it fly up. BANG! The bright orange, metal door rolls up and smacks the top of the unit. Charlie and I pause, standing there looking in, almost perfectly poised side by side and centered before the storage unit in front of us. It's a 10' by 20' box space built of compressed wood walls and stacked full of wilting, dusty cardboard boxes, plastic totes, tables, chairs, furniture, tools, lawn equipment, and everything else that once comprised our life and filled our home in Michigan, before our move to D.C. The cement slab floor is barely visible underneath, and after only a few steps in, your only options are to either move or climb over boxes.

"There's our life," I say turning to look at him.

"Yep, or just stuff from it," he quickly adds and gives me a kiss.

I turn my gaze back to look again, and realize he's right. It is just stuff from it.

Up until now, living in D.C., I have moved a total of twenty-three times. I am very comfortable living simply, or so I thought. I really thought I had purged and downsized at every move, but am realizing now (looking at this unit stacked full to the brim) that maybe I still have too many belongings. When we arrived to D.C., we put everything in storage and only allowed one box of special belongings that we felt "necessary" along with our totes of clothes and shoes. That's it. Everything else went into this storage, and we've never pulled anything out since. Now it's been two years and we've never opened this door or thought about any of it. Ironically, our lives feel richer today than the day we moved.

It's true. That is not our lives in there. Our lives are right here. We both take a step in and begin pulling things out. Charlie helps make me a path, but quickly I hop up and start climbing to get all the way to the back. Balancing one foot on a table and another on a stack of boxes, I open a large and dingy white tote.

"Man, everything is so dusty in here!" I say as I swipe off a layer of dust caked so thick you wouldn't feel mistaken to call it dirt. My black yoga pants are striped from every edge I've touched.

"What's in there?" Charlie asks anxiously and tries to make his way towards me, continuing to move boxes.

It's full of outdoor cushions, kitchen towels, and a large wooden Santa. I pull out the Santa knowing it'd give Charlie a good chuckle. "It's going to be like Christmas when we finally move and open all of this," I say and we both laugh again.

This is not the right box, so I start repacking it and reach to grab the lid. Then I remember, "I think it's either in a box labeled 'books' or one from the living room." I snap shut the lid and make my way to another familiar box stacked high in the opposite corner.

"This one says 'Worldly Treasures,'" I cheer as I pull it down.

"I know what one that is," Charlie says. "That might be it!"

Our living room back home in Michigan was filled with trinkets and memories collected throughout our travels around the world … Africa, Mexico, Abu Dhabi, Canada, and more. The small box of worldly treasures was from the same room, so I thought.

Nope.

"Ugh!" I sigh and stuff everything back in the box and restack it on the others. I continue the hunt, now for a box labeled "Books." I climb, balance, and pull away boxes, stacking and moving and restacking.

"I think I found it!" I shout to Charlie, who was now back towards the front of the unit tinkering with his John Deere. I rip apart the silver duct tape that holds the box shut and reassure myself that is it before opening it. I remove all the contents before getting to the very bottom where a shiny, graphite-colored box sits—inside is our engagement album. I open the magnetic flap and find our marriage license in an envelope on top. "Yes, this has got to be where it is!" I yell over to Charlie again.

Flip, flip, flip….

"Oh, man … " I say in disbelief, turning to the last page of the book and then flipping back through all the pages again. "It's not here."

I feel deflated. How am I ever going to find it? I swore it would be with our marriage license. I have no idea where or what to even look for now.

"Why exactly do you want it?" Charlie asks.

I think about it, and even have to ask myself before I respond.

"I don't know," I admit. "I just really wanted to see it."

Maybe I just want to assure myself that it is all true? Or if anybody questions, I can prove that it is true? As I continue to look around and rack my brain, Charlie loses interest and lets me know all the heavy boxes are out of the way, so he's going to head back to the shop. I let him know I understand and that I'll ride back with him to grab my car. While I'm fairly convinced myself that I won't find it in this massive mess, I do want to look for just a bit longer.

Driving back, I try to envision packing everything up and dig deep in my memory. I remember a pink tote. It was the only pink tote I bought for the move and I used it to pack up my office. Now on a mission for the pink tote, peering through the stacks up, down, and sideways, I find it in the center of the unit and closer to the back under a large stack of blue-colored totes (blue was from the kitchen). I make my way towards it, balancing and moving boxes out of the way. It's about five totes down from the top. Determined, I super-woman out the fifty-pound totes, all while standing on stacks myself. When I open the lid, I feel a new wave of memories rush over me. I pull out a shoebox of cards from friends and family, a stack of all my old high school yearbooks, a bunch of childhood journals, and then an old poem book—it's a spiraled Five Star legal notepad with a dark blue vinyl cover. On it is a smiley face sticker and a cut-out from a Ramona Quimby journal. Scallop-cut edges border the bolded words "Your Wish" with the image of a star and questions, "Have you made a Star Wish? What was it?" Written in childlike penmanship is my answer, "That I can always love my family."

This, I was not looking to find, nor have I looked at it in years. Shaking off the goose bumps, I open the cover and there sit the printed Yahoo search results from high school with scribbled notes …

Betty S. Brunhoff – Step Grandma

Ed & Bettie Brunhoff – Uncle & Aunt

Nathan Henry Brunhoff – 50 years old, degree in law

"Alice" was written to the side of Nathan's name and I had also jotted down that Uncle Ed was a computer scientist. Underneath the paper is a stack of printed emails from when I connected with mister-mystery-man (a.k.a. my father) as a teenager.

Cool, at least I found these memories. I set aside the notebook on a nearby flower planter stacked on top of a chair and turned upside down. I continue to sift through the rest of the tote's contents. A brightly colored hot pink, lime green, orange, and yellow kaleidoscope-designed shoe box quickly reveals itself. It's a memory box from our wedding in

Puerto Vallarta, Mexico. I open the lid and pull out my white veil with tiny little flowers, a handful of congratulations cards, a printed menu from our dinner that night, some dried roses, a homemade travel book and itinerary I made for our guests, pictures, a CD.... So fun. I keep pulling out and admiring every piece. Lost in a delirium of memory land, I see it! Nearly everything is pulled out of the box. At the bottom is a white envelope titled U.S. Government Official Mail. My heart jumps.

I open the envelope and pull out my birth certificate. I read it as intently again as the first time I found it. I'm all alone in the dark of night in this storage unit that's lit up like a Christmas tree, and I proudly hold this baby up and flap the envelope like a winning lottery ticket, clamoring alone in a victorious cry after seeing his name printed exactly how I remembered it!

Okay, it's 1000 percent true. Validated and confirmed, just as I knew it to be. I just needed to see it again. It's been years since I looked at this birth certificate and I found myself starting to question my own memory, even when no one else was. I wonder, can you just write anyone's name on a birth certificate? What if my mom slept around and just guessed who my father was? What if this, what if that.... I just needed to see it again to feel reassured. It is hard to believe this all to be true. I close up and restack the box, climb down from the Mountain of Life, lock up the storage unit, and head home to get some much-needed sleep.

It's the next morning and Charlie wakes up late, and only because I start cooking bacon. He comes down the stairs "coughing" and I know him well enough to know it's fake. I pretend like I believe his parade and ask how he feels. Like a mother who knows her child or a pet owner who knows their dog, so does a wife know her husband. All the while, as he's explaining his aches and pains and oncoming headache, I am totally okay with it. I'm not dealing with you, is what I think to myself. Today is too important. I grab my purse, keys, and coffee mug and jog out the door without hesitation, leaving his bacon on the stove for him to serve up himself.

He was supposed to come with me. We've had this planned for weeks. Now I'm stewing, making myself more frustrated than when I left, madly weaving in and out of traffic on the miserable 495. I roll down a window for some fresh air and turn up the tunes. The four-lane highway loops around the entire city of D.C. and has nearly every species of terrible drivers in every lane. I pick up my phone and type a quick text. According to Siri, the world's beloved phone assistant powered by artificial intelligence, I'm going to arrive ten minutes late, and that's only if I have no trouble finding parking. The woman I'm to meet responds quickly and lets me know she's already there. I do wish Charlie was with me. I'm nervous!

Walking the streets of Alexandria is like walking through an upscale heritage community in New York or Chicago. The townhomes are all narrow and tall, full of character and color. It feels quaint here with a bit of individual personality from home to home. You can also find a mix of delightful boutiques and bistros in between, like La Fontaine, where I'm meeting Jenny, who is Great Aunt Maura's daughter. Technically, she's a second cousin on my father's side, and is the first Brunhoff I am meeting.

She's outside, standing near the door entrance between the sidewalk and curb, dressed in a white turtle neck and long slimming black skirt that goes all the way down to her ankles. Her black leather purse hangs by a long strap over her shoulder. She's thin, sweet-faced with a quirky cute smile, big blue eyes, and a head full of wild, blonde curly ringlets. She is simple but classy. She reminds me of a Hollywood actress, Meg Ryan.

"Jenny?" I ask.

"Michelle," she says back confidently with a big smile.

"Oh, it's so wonderful to meet you!" I reach out and we hug. "Thank you again for taking the time to do this. I honestly have so many questions and it's so nice to finally meet someone in person."

"I knew it was you as I soon as I saw you," she says, turning to open the door to the restaurant. She asks the hostess for a table for two before turning back to talk with me again. "I could tell you were a Brunhoff right away, tall with the blonde hair and blue eyes."

As we sit, she pulls out a pair of bright red, circle-rimmed glasses from her purse to read the menu. I am fully charmed. When we order, we order the same exact thing for both food and drink, which makes us laugh—the Norwegian (cold salmon dressed in caramelized onions and cream fraiche) with a diet coke.

When our food arrives, I am completely entranced in our conversation. We continue to talk and I barely eat. Jenny has no TV. She's not married and defends the fact that she has no television because she has no time. "There's nothing worthwhile on anyways," she explains. She likes to make pottery at a place down the road.

She tells me stories about the Brunhoff family. Everyone's names and how we're related quickly become blurred. Every time I grab my notebook and start taking notes, I just as quickly set my pen down to listen intently. But when she starts talking about our family lineage that links to Mary Todd, I stop short on taking a drink of diet coke and set it back down on the table to catch a breath to swallow. "Mary Todd … " I ask, "As in Mary Todd Lincoln?"

"Yes," she assures me.

Mary Todd, first lady of one of our country's greatest presidents. To be here in Washington, D.C., and hear this news is humbling, exciting, and motivating.

Yet, as exciting as it is to learn about the family lineage, I really want to learn more about my father. So, I redirect the conversation back to him and she continues. Jenny hasn't seen him since she was eleven, and it's a bit difficult for her to recall memories of him. "Hank," she says and then pauses. "That was his name back then. That's how I always remembered him. There were Hank, Ed, and Frank, his two brothers. I was in New York for my mom's second wedding when I saw him last. He was a hippie. I remember him lighting some cool cigarette and I asked to take a hit." She pauses to laugh and we both stand up harmoniously grabbing our jackets off the back of our chairs. As we exit, she pulls out an American Spirit box from her purse and pulls out a cigarette.

"You smoke?" I say, stating the obvious, gently resting my hand on her back in a mixed state of relief and disbelief.

"Do you want one?" she asks.

"That would be great," I say. "I smoke too, but I left mine in the car so I wouldn't be tempted to smoke in front of you."

She hands me a cigarette and lighter.

I put it to my mouth and ask, "Please don't tell my father."

She laughs a big chuckle and reminds me I'm thirty-three years old. We walk the next few blocks, smoking and laughing, enjoying an easy and natural conversation.

"Hank the hippie!" I yell out in proud laughter, thinking of how she remembered my dad the last time she saw him.

"Just be sure not to ever call him that," she quickly responds, and with surprising concern. The mood quickly turns as she recalls and starts to share something deeper and unexpected.

The family business, Brunhoff Manufacturing, was very successful. Jenny tells it as a true story of riches to rags, and its downfall was all thanks to the unhelpful hands of Henry Brunhoff, my father's dad, my grandfather. Henry, or Hank, was a generational name and she explains that there was a huge falling out between Hank and his father. It was at that point that she remembers my father asking that the family start to call him by his first name, Nathan. This was just before he gave a substantial amount of effort to separate and distance himself from the family name, which at that time still carried a lot of weight and expectations.

"Was his dad stern?" I ask.

"No," she continues. "He just lived a life of self-entitlement."

. ♦ .

From: Nate Brunhoff

Date: Sunday, October 26, 9:12 AM

To: 'Michelle'

Subject: Forgive the presage of 20 questions

... but I don't have 6 months to get to know the beautiful and curious quirks of you and Charlie so I ask tangential nearly silly questions like

Does he like beer? Dark or light?

Ha! Do YOU like beer?

Do either of you prefer your wines dry. red or white

What was the last tune(s) you and he downloaded from iTunes or its equivalent?

What is your and his preferred Ice Cream (even though it may change next week)

Do you have an espresso machine?

Any food either of you are allergic too, such as fish, peanuts, bok choy, cats?

I personally have a mild inexplicable aversion to coconut, but I do not have a phobia regarding frogs.

nb

. ♦ .

I love his curiosity and am even more thankful for his character and wit to open the floor and give us an opportunity to get to know one another more. It shows me he really does care this time and is interested to get to know me, too. Finally, I'm not the only one who wants to know all the things! Equally so, I also find enjoyment in the fact that he has an aversion to coconut. Not that he's allergic; there's just something about it. I have an aversion, too. The only way I will touch it is with chocolate, dark chocolate preferred.

I respond to his comical questions with equal parts of seriousness and wit. I hope to also get some ideas for a small gift for Alice.

* ◆ *

At 11:24 AM, Michelle wrote:

Neither of us are avid beer drinkers unless we're working on a summertime project outside.

I definitely love our wine and seem to always consume what's his as mine.

Red or white, and I prefer dry.

Charlie doesn't drink much, and when he does it's usually vodka and red bull.

He's chocolate. I'm vanilla.

He's techno and rap. I'm country and hip hop.

I should have an espresso machine. Where did we go wrong?

No allergies to anything.

Charlie has a strange phobia to tomatoes and mayonnaise, but he loves ketchup and aioli.

Can you tell me what Alice likes—a few of her favorite things?

P.S. A few members on my family side are on Facebook, and they now all know. They are completely supportive and understanding, so I am feeling more comfortable about sharing our story in the public light. It is getting harder and harder to keep my excitement under wraps, so consider yourself warned. You're lucky I can't tag you. ;)

-M

« ♦ »

At 12:15 PM, Nate wrote:

Whales, snails, and puppy dog tails.

Really ? No.! Please. Don't tag me! OMG. All my friends (2) will know **EVERYTHING** ! ARRRrrrggg.

Chapter 5

"**D**o you know where I can find Shakespeare?"

The store clerk looks up at me and places his feet on the ground to stand from a wooden stool beneath him. For the first time since I walked in, he looks up from his book and acknowledges me. "Hmmm ... " he audibly groans before waving me to follow.

We weave through the tight aisles, each one lined with bookcases stretching from the floor to the ceiling. The shelves are lined with colorful card labels. There are stacks of books on the ground everywhere, an overflow of those that cannot fit on the shelves.

He stops and points me to a shelf in front of us with a bright yellow card that says "Shakespeare" and then walks back to his reading stool in the front.

The bookshelves are intimidating. I really don't have much of an idea what I am looking for, except for anything besides the obvious *Romeo and Juliet* or *Julius Caesar*. It needs to be something special, to gift to my father for when we first meet. I know he likes used books. It's one of the few things I remember from our first call so long ago. He told me about his favorite job, and it was when he was a librarian at a used bookstore. He not only loved the books but oddly, their distinct smell, he told me.

The first book I pull off the shelf opens to a page filled with notes and writings and two theatre stubs stuck in the center. How cool! I wonder whose book it was and about these moments locked inside. It's a book which holds a story within its story.

I close its cover and set it to the side, as I do with many of the others that follow. Nearly a full hour passes rather quickly. I'm pulling and thumbing through every book on the shelf, Googling titles and reading reviews to learn more about the stories, until I finally find the perfect pair to finish my quest. One is a tale of King John and the other a biography of William Shakespeare by S. Schoenbaum. I proudly carry them to the counter to check out and inconveniently disrupt the store clerk from his story again.

When I get home, I head straight upstairs to our bedroom and open the bag of books. I quietly admire each book with its unique old cover and dingy colored pages. Out of curiosity, I pull each one up to my nose; he's right, they do have a special smell.

King John is a smaller sized book. A thicker paperback with a bright red cover and stamped on the inside with "U.S. Army." It's filled with thin and fragile browning pages that soften the air with a warm musk at the turn of every page. The Shakespeare biography is a larger hardcover, lined with beautiful blue linen and imprinted with red foil. When you open the book, its inside cover is decorated with maroon and tan-colored illustrations of villages and angels. I decide it's here that I will write him a poem:

A single blade of grass moves
to the slightest breath of wind;
A pebble on the road less traveled
finds flight to those daring around the bend.
Beauty exists in the darkest of gray;
close your eyes to see what they cannot purvey.
Pull your hand to your heart
and feel the rhythm of life;
Wiggle your toes and awaken a new day
where confidence prevails and joy is rife.
The gift of life,
by Michelle Christina

The words came quickly and completely unplanned. As I wrote each line, I never paused, I didn't hesitate, nor did I question. I had seized the moment confidently without a single word second-guessed and let it flow from my heart, even feeling inspired myself with every line.

I proudly close the cover and stack the books on our nightstand. For the rest of the evening, I keep catching myself glancing over at them, admiring my finds and excited to gift them to my father.

* ◆ *

From: 'Frank'

Date: Sunday, October 26, 3:42 PM

To: 'Michelle'

Subject: The start of a story,

An outline of my life started on October 25th, 2014

Michelle,

As I have met and talked with people over the past 10 to 15 years, many have encouraged me to write my life's story. I often think they are being polite because I certainly don't consider it anything unique or exceptional. Possibly it's because I've done things that most people don't have the opportunity to do. So for the past three years I have made short notes about events in my life, including the wars in Afghanistan and Iraq and their impact on me.

As I start this outline, I quickly realized it will have a dual purpose; a bit of my life story for you and a document of my life's story for me ... 3rd grade foot race at East Grand Rapids Elementary School—I won & had a red plaid tie on. The first time I realized I could succeed at anything I put my mind to.

6th grade I bought a Red Rhone [sic] horse named Fou Rouge which is French for crazy red. I spelled it "Fouru" for short.

I recall my mother reading the story of Black Beauty to me as a very young child. The brilliant pictures of the beautiful black horse, the train, and the fields that the horse ran. From that moment on I wanted a horse and often talked to my mother and father about it. They told me that if I really wanted a horse I would have to save my money and buy it myself. Between first and sixth grade, I saved almost $750 doing odd chores, mowing lawns, anything that neighbors would pay me to help them with.

I rode English and showed in dressage and jumping. I was often encouraged by instructors to pursue my natural abilities to ride and set a goal to join the Olympic team. The way that story ends broke my heart. Trust me it will surprise you....

In the early summer of my eighth grade year, I was to join my family to go to Estes Park Colorado on summer vacation, a trip that we made almost annually for a number of years. In Estes Park there is a cabin that still belongs to the family that my mother's father and older brother built in the 1930's. It sits at about 10,000 feet above elevation and oversees the North entrance of the Rocky Mountain National Forest. This is set by a backdrop of Longs Peak at its north face....

9th grade proved to be quite difficult in a number of ways. School was becoming a very hard challenge for me because of my slow reading and inability to learn how to spell correctly. It wouldn't be until the mid-1990's that I learned that I have dyslexia. Of course in ninth grade, 1965, I wanted to be in a rock n' roll band and starred in one with some friends, learning to play the rhythm and lead guitar. Unfortunately, this ended quite abruptly when mowing the lawn, a weekend chore required by my father. I accidently cut off three fingertips on my left hand. Fortunately, there was a doctor at Butterworth Hospital in East Grand Rapids that would later become famous for his ability to reconstruct hands and fingers which he did for me that summer, restoring up to three fingers completely. Unfortunately, four weeks later at a school dance I put my hand through a window in the door. The breaking glass severed several arteries and a number of my tendons to my fingers in my right hand. Cut my fingertips and four weeks later my wrist ... my music career ended abruptly. In retrospect, probably a good thing.

My 10th grade year in high school was even more difficult. Math had been one of my best subjects and easiest, but suddenly it changed to word problems and the frustration was way too much as I watched other kids come to school with their homework all done never thinking a thing about it while I would still be struggling to finish that next morning at school. By the spring of the 11th grade year, I dropped out of high school and never finished.

At this same time, it had become crystal clear that my parents were going to be divorced. I was 17 years old sitting alone on a spring night on the front yard that overlooked a valley with a pond and our land that expanded beyond for possibly a mile. That very night I realized if I was not to have the same flaw in me that my parents had (for they had been my gods and heroes) I must relearn everything. I had no idea how long it would take, nor where it may lead me.

I did take a GED and scored very high in Denver, Colorado in 1970. I have continued to learn and read over all these years, always interested in so many things and reading at libraries was the way to find new things. Despite my reading challenges, to this day I read every day. This was probably instilled in me by my mother, your grandmother, Martha Ruth Palmer Brunhoff. After high school, mom and I became quite close and I doubt there was a subject that we didn't discuss, sometimes welding into it over tea or coffee in great depth at her dining room table. I think you'll find that Nate and Ed share a profound respect and love, as do I, for our mother.

Well at any rate. Do let me know if this makes sense and feel free to ask questions.

Frank

  · ◆ ·

From: Nate Brunhoff

Date: Monday, October 27, 10:48 AM

To: 'Michelle'

Subject: Re: A few of her favorite things :)

Michelle:

Curious to note your dislike of coconut as well.

Alice's favorite things, in rotating random order, are: her cats, Lifetime movies, Pilates, her work, her car (like a 17-year-old) ... and her iPad. I gave her one two+ years ago for xmas and I haven't seen her since. Most recently she is very UN-humble about her iPhone 6+ and that nifty big screen. Yes. I confess jealousy.

She likes dry white wine, but not red and not mixed drinks. She is SUCH a delicate creature. Mostly salmon for fish, and eggs in the dairy dept. (albeit eggs are not cowish). There isn't a vegetable on the planet she doesn't like. Personally I think most vegetables should be left in the bowl because they look good there. She's a good cook but seldom displays any interest and this is especially true of dishes. A small amount of debris tends to gather in spots where she comes to rest.

For music, anything that has harmony and a beat. Clarity of presentation. That rather excludes Metallica. Lately she is very captivated by chess and in short time has become very formidable.

NB on the run.

· ◆ ·

From: 'Michelle'

Date: Monday, October 27, 1:28 PM

To: 'Frank'

Subject: Re: The start of a story,

Hi Frank,

I read your email, and then again, and at least two more times before closing my eyes last night. I love learning about you and the family. I must also share that it warmed my heart to hear you were excited to learn about me. I am so humbled and elated to be accepted as a Brunhoff.

While I have many questions, I will limit them to only a few, as I feel that some of your story may answer other questions and I do want to read on.

Question 1—What happened to Fouru when you moved to Denver?

Question 2—When you left at 17, did your mother stay with your brothers at the house or did everyone move? Is she still alive?

Question 3—Do you ever go back to Estes Park? Is it a cabin?

Now for a little bit about me … I'll start off with 1st grade and give a quick rendition through junior high. Here we go.

1st Grade: I have no idea how you remember that far back! Instead, I will focus on 1st–3rd grade and share my most exciting highlight being on The Bozo Show, which may also sound ridiculous in retrospect.

My mom surprised me in the middle of a school day when she got me out of class. In the car, she handed me a bright pink t-shirt with a big black smiley face on the front and told me I'd want to wear it. When I asked her why and where we were going, I could NOT believe her response … "The

Bozo Show!" she exclaimed. It was the most popular show at the time for a kid. It's popularity was similar to the Price Is Right for adults, but the Bozo Show games were for kids and you could win candy and toys instead of TVs and cars.

We met up with one of my mom's friends who had a daughter I knew pretty well. Her name was Carlena and she was close to my age. Carlena's younger brother was standing in front of me in line to get into the show, and there were two mean boys standing in front of him that kept picking on him. I remember getting so mad because they were calling him names, and when I couldn't take it anymore I broke outside of my comfort (naturally, a very super shy girl) and yelled at them. Then I put myself in his place and moved him behind me. And it worked! The stupid boys never said a peep again.

Throughout the show, every kid had a number and they would call the numbers to go down on stage and participate in an activity. The largest groups called would be up to twenty or so for a crowd of kids to dance on stage between commercial breaks. As we were closing in on the end of the show, I remember getting so upset at the last commercial break. My number was NEVER called the entire time! I remember thinking ... I can't even get called down to dance?

So, you can imagine my surprise when it's literally the last activity before the show ends (and also the biggest) and my number was called! I was the Bucket Bonanza girl. It's my claim to fame lol. It is the last segment of the show and the grand finale where you toss a ping pong ball into a row of buckets to try and win all of the show's largest prizes. I did not win every bucket, but I remember realizing, even at that young of age, that I would've never had the opportunity if I hadn't switched spots with Carlena's younger brother to protect him. I had been rewarded for doing a good deed.

4th Grade: This is when we moved from the city to a small country town up north in Michigan, yet I still wore a dress to school nearly every day. This was the first time I met Lo, who is still my bestest friend today. Our teacher was Mr. Manciu, an old school friend of my mom's growing up in the same small town. He would talk about her often with me, about their days in school together, and he always would make it a point to tell me he liked my dresses, like a true gentleman and in a courteous way. Mr. Manciu also owned the best drive-in burger joint in town, ironically the same place where my mom spent her high school evenings on skates serving customers. Mr. Manciu kept our class for two years in a row, which he said he never did before, and that made us feel really special. People just don't realize how much of an impact they have on a child's life. I will never forget him and his kind heart. He was a true gentle giant.

6th – 8th Grade: By this time, Lo and I had officially become besties. We sat on the school bus one day and started singing. From that point forward, we were inseparable. We even added a few more girls to the crew, Missy and Elsa, and we all remained best friends through junior high and high school, even had our senior pictures taken together. (All of us, except for Elsa, are still best friends today.) I ran the two mile in track during Junior High and was beat by only one girl. The first time I raced her, she had that look; she knew she was going to beat me. She had that confidence. In 8th grade, my last year in Junior High and my final race, I beat her—and I nearly beat the school record at the same time!

Can't wait to read on and share more of our life stories!

Smiles,

Michelle

Chapter 6

Shutting the car door, I quickly walk around to open the back, grab my work bag and start sprinting to the front door of the townhouse as soon as I hear his cry. He's terrible, and it's so embarrassing. Every day, when I arrive home, our dog Bernie recognizes the sound of my car and decides to pierce the ears of every townhome resident in our corridor. He literally sounds like someone is dying, and I am not exaggerating. I snap open the code box, enter the code, and can hear all three animals running down the stairs like a stampede. I greet the furry welcome committee and shepherd them to the backyard for poops and pees. Charlie's parents' dogs are a ridiculously adorable mix. One is a big, brown, and very floppy lab mix named Roger. In his mind, he is and will always be a puppy. And the other is a white, feisty little guy named Georgie, a Shitzu whom we call the "little terrorist."

It's a decent time that I'm getting home tonight from work. I slip off my heels and trade them for a pair of ballet flats out of the downstairs closet. I check the food and water for the dogs and then head right back out and walk up to the Town Center. Today, I need to look for a gift for Alice.

It's a fun walk, and I love the Town Center. It's in a fairly new suburb of Washington, D.C., on the Northern Virginia side, just stretching past the outskirts of town as they plan for a new railway system. It's quaint, classy, and clean. I know a few boutiques where I can find something special for her but also maybe add to the books for Dad. The past few days, I've started pulling together a random (and what I think is maybe "cool") stack of personal items to share. If I can find a simple kraft box, I may make a memory box and fill it with some things from my childhood to adulthood. Not too much, though. I'll keep it simple, but thoughtful and meaningful. My friend Cara is flying in on Thursday, so I can ping ideas off her, too. It's crazy how much has happened since her Google search during one of our phone calls. She will be flying in to visit just before I fly out a few days later to meet him.

It's always a little surprising when you exit our townhome community to discover a four-lane street that separates us from the entrance of the Town Center. It feels a little overwhelming and dramatic, especially with its well-landscaped median, but one has to assume it's the plan for continued growth. Only two blocks after the crossing, I arrive at one of my favorite gift boutiques, Paper Source. Regardless of the occasion, I can always find something perfect here, whether cute, funny, clever, or sentimental with heart. Roaming inquisitively through the store, there are so many treasures. You could walk around twice and find new things you missed before.

Score! I grab a large cream-colored kraft box. Then I find a set of black calligraphy pens, two adorable kitty print kitchen towels (for Alice), a package of 4x4 kitty cocktail napkins (also for Alice), a small plastic prescription bottle with a clown nose inside, and an off-white linen scarf with gold printed elephants (that's for me, definitely, so cute).

Back at home, I head straight upstairs again and all the way to our bedroom to pull out the craft box, calligraphy pens, and the bottle with a clown nose. I just can't wait to put everything together for him. And then, on some trip of newly-found-father high, I pull out my birth certificate and start cutting hearts out of a note pad.

◦ ◆ ◦

JOURNAL ENTRY

October 27, 2014

You're about to be famous. That's what I said when I sent a text to him today! I did it! All fears aside. If I make an *** of myself, I don't care. And I'm confident that I won't lose him again. Should anyone even try to tell me that I will lose him, it will be because of an illness, and I will remind them again, that I will never lose him.

I am connected to him now and in ways I cannot explain. I just feel it, I know it. It feels as though we have always been together, just separated and lost along the way, but it was only a matter of time before the forces of life would bring us together.

I posted to Facebook: **FOUND! A name that once was just a name written on the line under Father ... for all these years I've dreamed and I wondered. A journey in discovering more of my story. I'm excited to share that I have found my father (and he's pretty awesome)!**

The support and happiness from family and friends is overwhelming, but what Alice writes steals my heart, "And when your name comes into conversation ... he just beams. I have known him since I was 18 and have never seen that look on his face."

At that moment, my world really did stop for a second....

■ ◆ ■

I close the journal and crawl in bed, looking over again to the dresser where the box and gifts sit. I pause, reaching over to turn off the light. I feel such peace in my heart. Somehow, magically, this box is what makes sense and is going to "show and tell" my life story: tokens of special moments, hints of past memories, a few thoughtful gifts, and a bit of laughter. I pull my hand back from the lamp and switch to grab my heart, as if to keep it from leaving my chest, and then remember ... what an awkward conversation this is going to be if he ever finds out about the tattoo.

■ ◆ ■

From: 'Frank'

Date: Tuesday, October 27, 11:19 PM

To: 'Michelle'

Subject: Re: The start of a story,

I can tell you make a keyboard sling. I think this is somewhat typical of the 30-something generation, Josh is also super fast at typing. I learned to wield hammers, climb steel, run hydro cranes, weld and load shoot explosives. So I will be slower in my responses. That said, I did deliberately shift my career focus from field supervision to construction management in 1992. Of course Nate, the—cool older brother, sent me a Mac he had retired and encouraged me to go for it.

But before we go much further—please tell me about your husband, I am guessing he must be pretty smart (like real smart), loves the outdoors, handsome, and probably fairly sensitive?

Now to your questions:

Question 1—What happened to Fouru when you moved to Denver, CO?

Following my struggles in the ninth grade year my parents found a prep school in Salisbury, Connecticut that specialized in helping students in math, English, reading and spelling. The summer program was geared to focus on our greatest shortcomings educationally and help us to overcome them. I can say it did help quite a bit. I learned to speak in front of people without being scared to death, my reading speed improved probably twofold, unfortunately my spelling didn't. It's a ***** when every time you see a word it's spelled differently. When I returned in August 1966, I discovered that my father had sold Fouru and told me that I would have to put my tack, saddle, bridle, etc. up for sale. The only explanation that I got at that time was that I was outgrowing riding and I needed to focus on school.

In late September a lady responded to an ad that I had in the paper that Dad had placed. She came to the house on a Saturday midmorning and as per Dad's instructions, I presented the tack for her review. She barely even looked at the bridle and paid zero attention to a custom-made Steuben jumping saddle. I discovered many months later that the lady—Betty, was the lady that my father had left my mother for. For some time I believed that it was my fault that Dad divorced my mom because I had introduced Betty to Dad while selling the tack. In the years to come, I realized the sale of my horse, and Betty coming to the house to buy the tack was all a complete set up. I'll let your imagination fill the blanks from there.

Question 2—Is she still alive? When you left at 17, did your mother stay with your brothers at that house or did everyone move on?

In August of 1969, my parent's divorce was finalized. The judge split their property/assets etc. 50-50. Of course, this was not what my father had planned. My mother moved back to Colorado, actually Littleton, Colorado, a southern suburb of Denver.

Ed moved out there in early September to attend high school at Littleton High School. I also chose to live in Littleton at my mom's new townhouse. Nate was in college, I think Dartmouth although I could have that wrong.

My mom was a very unique, very intelligent and very beautiful woman. I just looked for a picture of her that I thought I had on my hard drive but it doesn't seem to be where I thought I'd put it. It's a picture of my mother from 1946 or seven when she was in the Navy. I believe she was about 22 or 23 in the picture. She was a knockout. Now that I think about it, I would love to put your picture next to hers at that age. I'm sure we'd see some strong resemblances although you have blonde hair and she was a brunette. I could go on for hours about our conversations together, the things I learned from her and so much more.

Let me say this, I learned four unchangeable, un-negotiable rules of life from Mom:

1. At all times you will be a gentleman; trust me that covered almost everything in life.
2. You will get as good as grades as you possibly can and that ethic will continue with you into the work world.
3. At about the age of 10, I was given a set of chores which were basically never to be added to or subtracted from.
4. It was my responsibility to always look and find something that I could do that would help the family each week. It couldn't be something as small as taking out the bathroom trash nor did it need to be something big as mowing the yard. It needed to be something that would make a difference in a quiet manner.

These rules were non-negotiable. Unfortunately, we lost our mom in June of 1979. Even this past week, when Ed and I were at Nate's house we all spoke with fond memories about Mom. We all still have questions for her and while alive she always had answers, not always ones that we would like but answers that would make us much better men. I would like to believe she succeeded!

Well my young niece, that's about it for these old fingers on the keyboard tonight. More will follow in the coming days. Take care, always travel safely and may the wind always be at your back.

Oh, and the photo of Yen and I is in front of the family house in Kom I Hong, Thailand. We have the east wing of the house for our own area. Very traditional in Asia. The photo was taken in 2009.

Frank

Chapter 7

From: 'Michelle'

Date: Tuesday, October 28, 2:23 PM

To: Nate Brunhoff

Subject: Splish Splash

Look who made an even bigger splash ... How does it feel to be a superstar? ;)

I do have to candidly say that your brother Frank has garnered strong favorability in becoming my coolest uncle. Following his kind invitation to connect, I have exchanged a few emails with him and am so thankful for his willingness to share his life with me. I am trying to hold most of my silly questions for when we get to visit, but there is one that I am very eager to ask ...

Did you go to any Ivy League school?

Hope you are having a good day!

Michelle I

• ◆ •

Earlier this morning, I received a message from Cara, my Google monarch and master searcher of all searchers. Turns out the queen of finding anything, and silent stalker in stealth, found a biography for H. Edward Brunhoff at Dartmouth College on e-yearbook.com.

> *H. EDWARD BRUNHOFF, 1034 Paradise Lake Dr. SE, Grand Rapids, Michigan. President of H Edward Brunhoff Inc. and have been for the past fifteen years. Operation is as a manufacturer's representative selling materials for commercial construction.*

Primarily sales are in fabricated steel. WIFE: Betty (Lawrence College) CHILDREN: Hank, 22; Frank, 19; Ed, 18; Jackie, 16; Jill, 13. Returned from the Navy to Dartmouth and remained until 1947. Spent a year in Cincinnati in Brunhoff Mfg Co. and then moved to Denver to work for Colorado Builders as west coast manager at Ludman Corp. Left to come here and start my own business. Sneaked in all the hunting and fishing possible throughout the country. Spent two years on interviewing committee here and since have not been active. Betty and I were married in Nassau.

It's obvious that my father's family was smart, and following what I've learned about my grandfather, this autobiography is expected and still his character proves disappointing. It's a shame. As alumni of the prestigious Ivy League school, and candidate interviewer, it's pretty obvious he had the pull to get my father into Dartmouth. And also, there she is … Betty. It should start with, *CHEATER: Married to adulterous second wife Betty (Lawrence College).*

. ◆ .

From: 'Michelle'

Date: Tuesday, October 28, 5:07 PM

To: 'Frank'

Subject: Re: The start of a story,

Hi Uncle Frank!

You nailed every quality about my husband. He loves the outdoors, is incredibly handsome, and is very smart. He does not hold a college diploma, he tried that and failed. I always say he went to Western Michigan University for a B.S. degree in business, but instead got his degree in Bull ****.

Charlie is much like his father in that they do not do well with authority. They like to march to the beat of their own drum. His knowledge comes from everyday experiences, news, reading, and much more. He is like a sponge. What I love the most about him is his character. He is goofy, charming, and he can get along with anyone. Wherever we go, I am the shy one and he is always making new friends.

Now to your story.

I am so saddened that your father sold your horse. I can only imagine the anguish that gave you and the anger you felt. You worked so hard to save up every penny and for five long years. I cried tears when I read this and I am so sorry that Fouru was taken from you. Additionally noted is the lady who answered your ad. I am trying to keep myself removed or unbiased, but I keep finding myself getting mad. It is just heartbreaking and it's so much for a young boy to bear. Life is most definitely a journey of ups and downs, joy and pain, challenges and achievements. I am thankful that you did not hold on to those feelings for long. It takes a person of great character to see the silver lining in things even when they feel so tragic. I truly believe that everything happens for a reason. And while you may not see or understand that reason when it happens, it's always with due time that it comes to light.

Your mother indeed is an incredibly strong woman. I already adore and admire her. While I could wish that I had an opportunity to meet her, I am confident that your stories will satisfy my imagination. I have already painted a beautiful picture of her in my head. She taught you many great lessons, especially in encouraging you to do something that would make a difference for the family each week, not big or small—but quiet and impactful. One day when I have kids, I will do the same. She is already having an impact on me and I just learned her name.

I will spare you more of my story until the next time we write. I still have more work to do and don't want to sleep in this office tonight. Please don't feel rushed in having to write your story. Take your time and send tidbits here and there. I am not going anywhere ... and we have the rest of our lives!

Smiles,

Michelle

▪ ◆ ▪

At 7:59 AM, Frank wrote:

Good morning,

I agree with you to a point that life has its ups and downs. My perception of challenges like Dad and Fouru are more Buddhist. We are here to learn and grow spiritually and mentally. Life presents opportunities to grow. If we embrace them we become enriched—if we fight them we become miserable. Change is our constant and once we learn that we will always continue to grow.

One can even reach the point that they can sense a change—challenge—lesson coming. If you can allow that change to fill your being before it arrives it will be like a gentle breeze in your limbs of life.

If you resist or fight, it will be uncomfortable. If you resist too much or refuse to learn, it could break your limbs, i.e. crippling your ability to climb with agility in life.

Imagine a tree that is faced with a powerful wind coming up the valley. If the leaves on the branches and twigs fold and lay back allowing the wind to pass through the limbs of the tree as it bends and bows to the lessons, the tree is strengthened and learns to grow in new directions. If the tree tries to hold firm unchanging with its leaves flat and open to the wind, the lesson could and sometimes does break limbs.

Now on to … Question 3—Do you ever go back to Estes Park?

I have not been back in about 40 years. I know Ed has been a few times. I think of it as a place for young cousins to launch a love for the outdoors. Your great grandfather Palmer created something that four and soon to be five generations have shared. Dr. Palmer, our mom's father, was an eyes, ears, throat and nose doctor. He studied in America and abroad in Venice. There are a few great stories about this guy. Oh, and he always pulled your ears. Not so that it would hurt, just firm enough to let you know that he was paying attention.

Granddad Palmer realized I had pretty bad sight at 18 months and wrapped a pair of wire rim glasses around my little ears—and yes, life was better. I wear glasses every day.

The cabin has been continually upgraded and added onto for the last 75 years. It is a great base from which to explore, hike and camp in the Rocky Mountain National Forest.

More soon.

Frank

• ◆ •

JOURNAL ENTRY

October 28, 2014

"Imagine if a tree is faced with a powerful wind coming up the valley. If the leaves on the branches and twigs fold and lay back allowing the wind to pass through the limbs as it bends and bows to the lessons, the tree is strengthened and grows in new directions."

My Uncle Frank, the younger brother, is wise. He's a man who has grown to defeat his battles of dyslexia by learning to accept the challenges and empower himself to succeed. His writings are profound, meaningful, and captivating. Where I look and see my father's life bound by tall cement walls on each side, Uncle Frank lives in a field of vast land where you can come and go as you please. A place where you are greeted with a pillow to lay your head under the stars and a campfire that burns of conversations throughout the duration of the moonlight. From him, I have already learned so much about my father and my family. And from him, I think I may be understanding my father's tragedies. While a beautiful picture has been painted of my grandmother, she and the kids were betrayed by my grandfather who split the family at a young age for another woman.

It's moments like this, when you hear others' sad stories, that you question your own experiences and whether or not you should consider them tragedies. No life is perfect, and if it were, well, that's not life. How can you feel the joy if you have not felt the pain? Everyone has a story filled with their own tragedies, but it's how you tell it and what you learn from it that builds true character. We write our own stories every day. May I always accept the challenge, grow, and learn. Find the strength of a tree only to bend and grow as the wind blows.

◆

From: 'Michelle'

Date: Wednesday, October 29, 2014 at 6:20 PM

To: 'Frank'

Subject: Re: The start of a story,

I thought about your words last night when reading your message late. The significance of your thoughts at this point in my life couldn't be more relevant or true. In learning my spot or where I fit in my father's life and the Brunhoff family, I need to be like that tree. I believe I, too, will find strength and grow in new directions.

Estes Park sounds like great fun. I imagine the cabin is full of character being that it was built in the 1930's. I gasp that you have not been there in forty years! You must go back and visit soon.

Here's a bit more about me: High School—Some of the most fun years of my life! There was some time that my mother decided to leave town while I was in High School but I stayed ... it was the best decision I made. I was not home a lot as it was and we teased it was just like staying a few extra nights with my friends. Ever since I was a young age, I had always spent my summers away and slept at friends' homes more than at my own. I eventually gave up track and volleyball, and even dance, and worked two jobs to make money during school. I loved sports but they were not what bought me clothes, my car and my freedom.

One of my best friends, Cara, is coming to visit tomorrow so I'll be offline the next few days. I met Cara later in life, following my return to Michigan from L.A. We have been best buds now for five years. She is hilarious, full of wits and smarts. My grade school friends are friendships that will always be important, but Cara is someone I can align with who I am today. She is very creative and has the biggest heart. I have been in D.C. now for two years, so I'm super excited she's making the trip!

More soon,

Michelle

As the days go by, I find myself feeling more and more love for my father. I wonder, is this possible? How could I feel this strong of a connection? Is it an inherent gravitation and admiration that naturally happens between a parent and a child? A connection on a level that is unexplainable, so natural and primal in instinct. Growing up and being raised by a single mother, I tried to look to my mom for grounding, love, and a sense of confidence and belonging. And while I know she tried, she never could satisfy that need. We have always clashed, and even though I have no doubt she loves me more than most things in life, her love has never filled this vast, empty void. It feels like an endless black hole, always longing for his unknown love and a lack of identity with myself and my family. For the many years growing up, through childhood and still today, I have and continue to seek to accomplish more. More education, more life experiences, and always an eagerness for something more, something I am missing. And as the day approaches that I meet him, I am filled more and more with the promise of what I will find and learn.

Undressing to get in the shower this morning, I catch a glimpse of myself in the mirror. Seeing the tattoo under my left breast makes me break down and cry. I've started losing weight, definitely without intention, as Lord knows I need to put on the pounds—not lose them. I'm also becoming obsessively reflective on every thought. The water pours from the spout just as hard as the tears from my eyes. I crumble to the bottom of the shower floor.

I'm a nervous wreck. I've waited my entire life dreaming of this moment. In all honesty, I didn't think it would actually ever happen. Reality is setting in and so are the questions and second guessing. What if he doesn't like me? What if I don't like him? What if it's terrible? I'm mulling over every possible thought and feeling a rollercoaster of emotions.

I eventually gather myself and stand up to turn off the shower, and my tears. I pull my soaked hair into a ponytail and squeeze out the water before stepping out and grabbing a towel. I stare at myself in the mirror again almost in pity, looking at my tear-reddened eyes and frail body. Thank God Cara is coming to visit. I need a distraction, and even if I do find myself still thinking about Dad while we're having fun (which is *highly* likely), it will be nice to have a friend here to share and talk about everything. She comes tomorrow. I'll hardly sleep tonight.

. ◆ .

From: Nate Brunhoff

Date: Monday, November 3, 2014 at 12:37 PM

To: 'Michelle'

Subject: Adventures in So Cal

Michelle

Did Alice send you a pic of the apt bldg depicting which unit is yours?

NB

• ◆ •

At 1:53 PM, Michelle wrote:

I can't believe I get to see you in just a few days.

Alice did send a pic and gave me the address. She didn't mention which unit though, so good thought. Attached is what I have saved on my phone with the address on South Ivy, Escondido, CA.

How are you feeling? Anxious, excited, nervous? Or are you superman? I am feeling a little bit of everything, but mostly really, really excited.

Still dreaming,

Michelle

• ◆ •

At 5:09 PM, Nate wrote:

jeeeeeesssss what if I am a disappointing old codger and Charlie says, "I wonder if this guy knows how to use indoor plumbing ... does he know Call of Duty is not on Game Boy????"

Anyway, your apt is the lower right hand side as you face the building. As noted, the keys to the apt and silver Yaris will be under the mat. There will be a welcoming note on the table without acerbic commentary. A proposed itinerary will follow tomorrow or next to take some of the mystery out of it.

Be assured, we will not be stuck staring into our coffee cups.

- ◆ -

JOURNAL ENTRY

November 3, 2014

Life begins at the End of Your Comfort Zone.

Cara flew in on Thursday and we spent the last few days being girls. It was so much fun! We were singing at the top of our lungs on our road trips to wineries and ghost towns, impersonating strangers when they couldn't see us, wearing horse masks in a department store, and screaming at the sight of weird creatures at the National Aquarium. Our time together has ended, but the memories will live on forever. Before I drove her to the airport, she pulled out a white square envelope with a beautifully written name in manuscript: Michelle. And when I opened the envelope, it read: Life begins at the end of your comfort zone.

So beautiful and so appropriate.

I want this. I have been waiting my whole life for this. And yet through these great words of wisdom and advice, all I can think is my stomach wants to exit my mouth, my heart wants to explode out of my chest, my brain is beckoning me to go into survival mode. Breathe. As the days are drawing near, my anxiety is increasing. I wonder in the flurry of thoughts that exit as quickly as they enter, can I pinpoint what this is? What exactly is my fear and anxiety that is starting to smother my excitement?

There are so many thoughts. Could it even be possible if I tried? I stare at this pen and paper and feel like a moron.

Stop thinking.

Just write.

What will it be like when I first see him; will it be awkward? Do I hold out my hand or do I give him a hug?

Mr. Illusive, who so perfectly avoids every serious question and writes with acerbic commentary, will I be able to learn who you are? Will you answer the mysteries to your riddles and unveil yourself from this ghost wrapping when I finally see you in real life? Will I have to frustratingly keep sneaking in questions into our conversation only to hold my breath and hope I can trick you to answer at least one? Or will I leave with none?

The secret of him is also the hidden symbol I wear on my heart. All these years I've learned to grow to love the unknown and accept the truth that it is me, but now it will all change and with it, so will I.

What if I don't like him? I can't help but fear the possibility. And what will it be like when I see him? Definitely awkward and I'm confident I'll nervously laugh.

He'll probably say something witty to break the ice. And conversation, I'm sure there will be plenty. But if the opportunity doesn't arise, I will be determined to make it happen. I can ask him to go for a walk.

What if I don't learn who he is? This is a truth. And can only come with time. This is only the start of a relationship. I need to recognize and accept just that.

As for the fantasy bubble being popped? It's time to open my heart and mind, regardless of fears and discomfort. The beauty of life is feeling it. I WILL change. And from it, I WILL be a better person. I'll have more depth, more courage, and more knowledge. I will know more about myself as a person, my story, and who I am.

And my fear of not liking him? I will. I do. I already love him. I have always loved him.

· ◆ ·

I can barely sleep at night right now. This morning I woke up early again and nearly tripped over the overflowing suitcases in the hallway. Our bed was a sorted clothing pile last night before I finally gave up and just tossed everything in as heaping piles.

Do I need to worry about first impressions? I don't care who disagrees, my insides scream yes. Someone help me. This is the biggest thing that has ever happened in my life, so I feel like I need to bring the biggest amount of options. I'll admit I was excitedly sipping on wine last night and before I knew it was saying yes to everything. Yes, I want to bring that dress. Yep, I have to have these shoes. Oh, that jacket will be key. Maybe I should bring an extra? Yes, absolutely!

I want to be perfect. I want to be the most beautiful, wonderful girl that my father has ever met. I want him to be proud he is my father. I want him to feel a pinch of sadness that he wasn't hanging out with me all these years because I'm cool and so much fun.

Back in the bathroom, following another morning shower, I grab my toiletry bag from under the sink when a knock at the door startles me. I peek to open the door, not sure who it could be. It's early.

"Good morning!" Charlie's mom, Marie, says all perky and excited, completely opposite of how I feel. I'm filled with anxiety and butterflies that are the size of pterodactyls.

"Just wanted to see how you're doing?" she reads my vibe and softens her tone.

Her sincere concern is almost enough for me to let go and break down, but instead I compose myself. I have to hold it together; even though it's exactly opposite of what I want to do. I cannot let my maxed-out mind and terrified heart break down right now. I have to see this to the end. I am not going to lose it now.

"I'm alright," I respond (questionable for believability) and open the door all the way before breaking and being honest with both her and myself. "I'm nervous. I actually feel the stress in my body, like physically, and it hurts." I show her how I can barely move my neck. It's crazy tense from the stress.

"You have nothing to worry about," she comfortingly tries to remind me. "Are you eating?" she asks as she looks over my body still wrapped up in a towel.

"I know," I embarrassingly admit as I wrap my towel tighter and look in the mirror again at myself.

I haven't been sleeping and I also haven't had any appetite the past few days. I know I have to eat. Let me tell you—it's the worst when you have to make yourself, which is the only option I've had. Out of all the things I've been through, I actually never thought something could so strongly affect me. I have more emotions right now than the ocean has waves, and I'm feeling seasick. I'm grasping onto the edge of reality and saving myself from what feels like drowning in delusion.

I give Marie assurance I'll be alright, and then a tear sneaks into an eye. She lunges in to hug and I grasp her.

"Thank you so much for checking in on me," I whisper, soaking her shoulder.

I shut the door behind her and reflect on the moment. Marie is such a strong woman—self-made, stubborn, but caring, determined, and always beautiful. It was a real challenge to connect with her during the first few years Charlie and I were dating. It took almost two full years until she would finally talk to me without a condescending undertone. It was clear nobody was good enough for her boy. But now, after all these years, we are great friends. I think about our talks now and how well we get along, seeing eye-to-eye on so many things. Who would've thought! But it is still difficult for me to show her my vulnerability. I, too, want to be a strong woman, always.

▪ ◆ ▪

JOURNAL ENTRY

November 5, 2014

My bags are packed. Walking by the suitcases tonight that fill the hallway, I realized this is real.

I've been trying to occupy my mind with pointless things. During the day I've been keeping myself busy with work. Last night, I found all kinds of things that I felt needed to be done to win my father's heart, like painting my toes, plucking my eyebrows, trying new makeup....

The ups and downs are just absurd. One hour I'm smiling, the next I'm trying to catch my breath.

▪ ◆ ▪

ALICE

> Are you packed?
> Are you nervous?
> Are you butterflied?
> :) :) :)

All of the above! It's so silly that I could feel so many ways, so happy, nervous, excited, scared. Pretty crazy to think that tomorrow night I'll be with you. The butterflies are fluttering.

ALICE

What are you scared of?
List 3 things ...

1. Will it be awkward when we first meet? Will I trip? Do we shake hands? Will I get any words out?

2. Will he like me? Will he be proud? Will he let me see who he is, he's so elusive ...

3. I've lived my whole life with the mystery of him. I've accepted that and found peace with it ... now it's so exciting but real which makes it a bit scary. What if I am disappointed?

I've lived my entire life feeling this yearn for him, this insane connection that I just can never explain. I'm also a romantic, so I enjoy the mystery of the unknown. What if that is all it is that I am so enamored with, the mystery? Once I have the answer, will I be deflated? Underwhelmed? Will he live up to all my expectations? I also over-think things way too much. Obviously.

ALICE

Ok, that was more like 25 things. :)

Of course it will be awkward when you first meet but just remember you share a lot of DNA and that will be felt right away. If you trip, just go down like a ballerina and he will think you are so graceful. He is elusive but warm and easy to be around. He is very funny just like you and as I have texted with you I am ever amazed as to how similar you two are. I can't remember how many times I have said to him "she's just like you." And he either responds with a smile or says, "I know."

Of course you love him, he is your father.

Chapter 8

From: Nate Brunhoff

Date: Wednesday, November 5, 2014 at 11:26 PM

To: 'Michelle'

Subject: pizza pizza

If you had a large pizza, extra thin crust, double toasted and extra cheese, what would you and Charlie put on it??

· ◆ ·

I enjoy waking up to see a new message from him. And even though it may be one of the most random, I'm beginning to adore that about him. He is definitely a unique and quirky man. And who else, if anyone, could admire his eccentricity but an overwhelmingly and oddly adoring daughter.

I message him back when I get into the office.

· ◆ ·

At 9:53 AM on November 6, Michelle wrote:

Mushrooms! :)

We order pizza 1x per week and always get extra cheese and mushrooms. Sometimes we get real wild and throw some pepperoni on it. Personally, I will eat just about anything on a pizza, but that is one thing about Charlie, he is deathly afraid of vegetables—except for mushrooms. Vegetables may as well have furry extremities and can bite back. If Charlie sees even a sliver of an onion, he'll freak out and scowl as he pulls it off and lets everyone know how it destroyed his meal (and yes, I 100% secretly mince them and hide them in his meals that receive ravishing reviews from his lips).

Countdown is on! I will text Alice and keep her updated with our flight status and arrivals.

What time should we plan to see you tomorrow morning?

(insert heart filled with butterflies)

·◆·

Hidden in privacy behind the nearly shut door in my office, I hit send and grasp the edge of my desk with both hands. I have only one thought as I push my chair out and twirl with my feet up.... *How* am I going to get *anything* done today?

·◆·

From: Nate Brunhoff

Date: Thursday, November 6, 2014 at 10:32 AM

To: 'Michelle'

Subject: Good Morning Little Wing

THIS IS DAD

Is that scary or what ?

Actually, not. I have an idea. How about if we just pretend this is an audition for a play in which we are assured of getting the parts.

I will be reading for the part of the grizzled old fart, and you—the accomplished and cheerful young damsel. The crowd loves you and I am secretly very proud of you. After the call, we will go grab a bite to eat at a local diner and hang out and talk about how demanding the director (god) was.

Whaddya say?

Good.

On Friday morning I will give you a call at 10:00 am and you and Charlie and I can meet for a brief brunch. Alice will be at Pilates. I will then leave the two of you at about noon-ish to heave heavy sighs of relief while I go get Aunt Maura from the airport at 12:50. We will then meet up at the house at 1:30. From there we are off to the movies at a special theatre, followed by dinner, etc. etc.

Further boring details will be left on the kitchen table in ancient cuneiform which will include phones (again), addresses, and misc. Don't forget to send me your phone #.

Nathan B.

* ◆ *

At 12:17 AM, Michelle wrote:

THIS IS YOUR DAUGHTER

Equally terrifying ?

Good.

Everything sounds great. After the call, I'll throw you a high five and we'll both laugh as if it was the easiest acting call yet. At the diner, I'll give you a big hug and we'll shed a few tears for being such great co-stars. We'll order a double chocolate fudge brownie and delight in its deliciousness as we boast about all of the movies we'll surely star in next, because we finally made our big break.

Then, I'll ask you to hold on, we need to call someone quick to thank ...

Hello, God?

Can't wait until 10:00 a.m.

XO

* ◆ *

Regardless of my distraction, and even my preparations, the phone keeps ringing and emails are flooding my inbox. It's incredibly frustrating. I have zero mental capacity and I worked late nearly every night this week to avoid any stress of work on this trip. I have a sense of guilt, or need, to be caught up in order to leave, but what I need to do is just let it go.

I'm definitely a workaholic and sucker for overachieving. I always justify it with the idea that it *is* how I've made a life for myself—that and I am extremely passionate about my work, no matter what it is I'm doing.

"So, you ready for this?" my boss peeps her head in through the cracked door.

She opens it all the way and I can see into her office as she stands in my doorway. In the distance, hanging on the wall, is a little pink pig dressed in a pink tutu on a calendar. It's become an office tradition, an annual light-hearted gift (pun intended) to poke fun at the aorta of a pig that now lives in her heart following a heart attack she had a few years ago.

"I'm a mess," I admit, raising a hand to grab the terrible kink in my neck. "I've never felt this much stress before. And I didn't think it was possible to be so painful. I can hardly move my head because of the tension between my shoulders."

"You're going to be okay, honey," she repeats what everyone else keeps saying. "You have nothing to stress about. He's going to love you."

Like replay, I assure her I'll be okay. She urges me to leave early, and I urge her in return to call if she needs anything while I'm out.

She's a great boss. A little crazy at times, but aren't we all? I find that especially true for women in leadership positions. It takes a little extra attitude and opinion to be in that role. Maybe that's why I'm not there yet? I smirk to myself by the thought.

I glance at the clock, hurriedly close everything down, and toss a laptop in the orange leather briefcase sitting at the foot of my desk. I swing my purse on my shoulder and grab a favorite worn jean jacket from college, flick the light switch, and close the office door behind me. I hesitate in the hallway and even stop to open the briefcase again to make sure I didn't forget anything. I look around the hall hoping no one sees me and close the case. Then I realize, next time I see this place it will be the same but I won't—I'll be a changed girl.

. ♦ .

JOURNAL ENTRY

November 6, 2014

"Good morning little wing. This is DAD. Is that scary?"

Are you kidding me? Best message from him yet.

Work was a struggle today to say the least. The tension in my neck and shoulders is unbelievable and almost unbearable. We're in flight right now, and I have moved my legs, back, and every other thing in every way—no matter what I do, my body is so uncomfortable and hurts. I forgot how long a flight it is to the west coast.... We've been in travel and on flights now for more than five hours and besides the pain, I am feeling good mentally. My attention has slightly focused to Charlie. I don't think he is used to me having as much care about anyone else and now I have this zoomed-in focus on my dad, and honestly I'm not used to it either. I've definitely never experienced something so overwhelming that I cannot even physically handle it. And now that I am letting the stress of work go, I am seeing his.

The business is crazy busy, he doesn't know these people we're visiting, and he's doing this all for me. I have yet to figure out how I will repay him and everyone else, the world, and the universe.

I am in debt.

I am happy.

I am thankful.

• ◆ •

Finally … the jolt of the plane and the wheels hitting the tarmac wake me up from a half sleep. We've made it. We're in San Diego and it's late! I turn my phone back on and see it's 11:30 p.m. local time, which is 2:30 a.m. back home. We both worked a full day and then rushed to the airport after work. I nudge his shoulder and he wakes with bloodshot eyes. We're both exhausted. Even though he and Alice persistently insisted they pick us up from the airport, I couldn't have *this* be the first time I meet my father. I am now more grateful than ever I made that decision. The moment needs to be better than I being a tired hot mess, and I feel much more comfortable grabbing a cab and heading straight to the apartment they set up for us.

From the airport to the front door of our temporary living quarters in Escondido was just over a thirty-minute drive on the large, four-lane, barren highway. When we pull up to the front of the house, it is large and separated into three different units. The light is on under the front porch and over our door, just as he said, and we find the key hidden under the doormat. In the darkness of the night, I can see rolling hills behind us, palm trees lining the road, and lots and lots of stars. Even in the dark, this town appears to be a cute and quaint suburb outside of town.

Opening the door, we both head straight to the back bedroom to set down our luggage and find the bathroom. On the way, I notice a letter on the kitchen table. Charlie continues, but I stop to pick it up. It has all the "need-to-knows" about the place. A bottle of wine, a wine key, and glasses are all set to the left of the kitchen sink and everything for coffee is set to the right. I check the fridge and it's stocked with everything I told him we liked. From the bathroom, Charlie comes flying out with brand new, plush, bright white hotel robes, both with tags still connected.

We set our bags on opposite sides of the bed and open them to start unpacking. It was kind of our thing (or ritual, I guess you could say). Even if we only stay in a place for a night, we like to get comfortable and "move in." We pull out our clothes and put them in any drawers available, on shelves or hangers in the closet, organize our toiletries in the bathroom, etc., etc. If we're going to be away from home, it's nice to have it feel as much like home as possible.

I unpack before Charlie, reposition and pull tight the string on my comfies and stroll out to the kitchen to crack open the bottle of wine. With a nice, full glass, I grab a seat at the kitchen table to read the letter.

> *Michelle and Charlie:*
> *Welcome travelers of the night!*
> *You are on S. Ivy St. There is no mail box. It is a secret address so that I don't have to empty the junk mail every day.*
> *I have laid in groceries for you. Frig, Freezer and Pantry. If you find it—you are to eat it or drink it.*
> *There is some Stone Brewery beer of different flavors and your opinion is requested. There is also some Red Bull. Wow. That be some nasty stuff there ... Yerba Mate **might** be an alternative ... unknown to me—*
> *On this table is a Jawbone. Pairing for tunes and the phone often is nearly instantaneous—sometimes not ... **but worth it.** **Surprising good audio ... as a phone as well.**
> *The Yaris, out front, has an aux pin-plug w/coiled cable (too early for Bluetooth) between the seats.*
> *You can ...*
> *Plug this into your iPhone*

Turn on the radio
Hit the "Disk/Aux button"
Put the volume at 40 or more
… this will allow you to use Siri for directions and maybe a few tunes if you want.

Please use the park bench in the side yard to smoke. Many of our out-of-town parties are allergic to smoke.

Nathan B

Chapter 9

The alarm went off for the first time, but I've been awake for hours, lying here wide-eyed looking at the ceiling in disbelief of where I am. I'm honestly not even sure I slept. For thirty-three years, I've dreamed of this day. Literally, this is a miracle, a blessing. I'm not dreaming…. I am here.

I've said a prayer. I've said a whole bunch of prayers. As soon as one prayer ends, I put my hands down only to bring them back up again. I'm almost thankful the alarm is going off so I can just get up and try to focus on normal things, like making coffee, taking a shower, and getting ready, instead of lying here thinking, thinking, thinking, over and over and over again….

After making the coffee set out for us by the sink, Charlie took his cup to sit outside on the bench in the side yard that was said to be "designated for smoking." The bench is under a large, beautiful, wispy tree with branches that hang all the way down to the ground. I peek out at him from the bathroom window and he's working away already on his laptop. I admire the tree. It reminds me of a weeping willow, but its limbs stretch as wide as the tree is tall. Its branches drape to the ground with little white flowers spanning the length of every hanging limb. Looking just beyond it, I catch sight of Alice's name and her osteopathic doctor credentials engraved on a wooden sign outside of a building across the lawn. It must be her office. How convenient and cool. Her apartment building is right next door to her office. That has to be wonderful for when helping patients from out of town or to take a break from the workday. Coming out of the bathroom, I take notice to some pictures hanging on the wall in the bedroom. They show the building's prior disrepair, giving guests an appreciation of its renewed state.

Knock, knock, knock.

I was just grabbing some of the water bottles that were placed next to the coffee maker in the fridge when I hear the knock. Confused, I glance over at the clock on the wall. It's only 9:30 a.m. I did notice the mailman walk by the living room window a few minutes ago. Maybe he forgot to deliver a package? I head to the door quickly.

I open it to find a tall man with silvering hair, but notice he's in blue jeans and a white, collared, button-up shirt. Before I can think, he hurriedly steps forward closer to me with a big smile and obnoxiously says, "HI! I'M YOUR FATHER."

Without hesitation, and without a word, I wrap my arms around him and embrace him in a hug. You'd think it would be awkward or uncomfortable, but for the first time in days I feel a sigh of relief and relax my head on his shoulder. Little else has ever felt so right.

With a flushed face and cheeks, I release my hug and just as hurriedly invite him in—reminding him that he was supposed to call thirty minutes out and set a time and place to meet for brunch! We both laugh and are equally awkward. My nerves are running wild, but I somehow have my game face on. No tears are even shed.

"I have something for you," I tell him as we enter the kitchen and I offer a cup of coffee.

He acts slightly awkward, as if the "cat has his tongue," but we don't skip a beat. Either we're moving fast or time is, but his eyes and body gestures show me he's as excited as I am. I pour him a cup and grab the white kraft box off the dining table and hand it to him. He pauses looking at his initials hand-scripted on the top. Still in silence, he opens the lid and pulls out a book. To my surprise, he pulls it up, directly to his nose.

"Old books have a smell, you know," he says, glancing up over his glasses with a tilted chin, revealing a big smile again.

I proudly tell him I had remembered his love of old books from our first phone call all those years ago and how I had found both of the books in the box at a used book store. He pulls the other book out, directly to his nose again. He takes such a deep breath, as though he is inhaling the words right off the pages. And then stories are sparked as each token, so purposefully included, is thoughtfully examined after pulling them each out of the box. Before we know it, an hour has already passed. I reckon the need to call Charlie inside so they can meet and he reckons we need to get on the road to eat.

He shuts the box lid, but I reach out to stop him.

"Wait," I nervously say stopping his hands from closing the lid. "There is one more thing.... "

Of all the things in the box, I was dumbfounded he didn't see this final item. I quickly peer out the kitchen window to see Charlie still sitting under the tree and reach my hand to the corner of the box. Under a white envelope filled with college transcripts, I grab the small round vessel. Contained inside is a red sponge ball. I make a motion for him to hold out his hand and place it in his palm. I read the label to him through what must be a cheesy, super-wide grin, "This is an Emergency Clown Nose."

Looking back up from the label, I see his eyes are big and his reaction a bit funny. I'm not sure how to read him. Then, finally, after an eternity of seconds, he says, "Wow," and then pauses again.

"You know what's funny?" he asks. "I already have one of these."

He reaches over and gently touches my arm to make sure I'm paying close attention.

"I almost wore it over here!" he goes on to explain....

It turns out he couldn't decide. He put it in his pocket, and then took it out, grabbed it again, but then set it down again, unsure if it would be appropriate. As he's talking, he lifts up his sleeve and shows me his goose bumps. All the way up and down, they filled every inch of his arm, down to his hand.

No way. Can it be true? Before I can process any of it, he pulls the clown nose from the vessel and hands it to me.

"Keep this," he says, "and bring it with you—we'll exchange later."

I grab the red nose and throw it in my purse without hesitation. You got it dude! I want to freak out but the bizarreness of it all helps me keep composure. Trying to hold myself together, I realize I'm in another world. It's magic. That moment when you strip yourself of everything you know and go back to being just a girl. When the woods are still a magical wonderland, and yourself just a little starlet, looking up to the trees dreaming you'll grow bigger. I excuse myself and walk out to tell Charlie he's here, and it's also time to go.

I have only dreamed of him until now. For the first time, I can believe without having to imagine. I had prepared myself for the worst, no expectations, possibly disappointment, and yet here I am so satisfied. But this is just the beginning, I remind myself. He and Charlie greet and get ready to go. We still have *much more* to learn about one another.

Charlie and I follow behind his van to a local golf club where he made reservations for brunch. On our way, he calls my cell to make sure we're following closely behind and I assure him we're both admiring his racing skills—the old man drives fast!

- ◆ -

JOURNAL ENTRY

November 7, 2014

"Yeah, go mom!"

Yep, that's a first-ever.

At brunch today, my dad answered every question! It was a picture-perfect setting, straight out of the movies. We shared a mature, quality conversation over a late morning coffee on an outdoor patio framed by a backdrop of lush golf greens, perfectly curated palm trees, and rocky canyons in the horizon.

So, how the story goes.... When he met my mother, he was living high—on drugs and drinking—and saw her at a party (of course, he remarked). He remembers liking her because she was goofy.

He looked at me closely, as if in observation, and said I have her eyebrows ... ? Yeah, umm that's strange. I definitely don't think I have her eyebrows. I'm quite confident I gave him one of my looks after that comment, probably looking at him a little cockeyed.

He told Charlie and me that it was after only three months of dating that mom got pregnant. He was like, "WOAH," that's not what I signed up for. And then he admitted and actually said, "I wanted to terminate you." He realized as quickly as he said it and reached over to grab my arm and apologize. He knew it was a totally inconsiderate thing to say, especially to say it so bluntly, but I appreciated the honesty. I wanted him to be real with me, and I can respect how he felt. We are human.

What I love most is this is profoundly the first time I have had respect for my mother. He said it wasn't even a question for her. She was having me. The deal was that if she did, she would do it without him.

While these two foolish young adults came to an agreement for what seemed to be the best for them, what they failed to realize was that the compromise would affect someone else who would soon feel very differently and have a mind (and thoughts) of her own.

· ♦ ·

After a few hours of downtime back at the apartment following brunch, Charlie and I jump back in the car to drive and for the first time meet the rest of my family at my father's house.

"Are these hills or mountains?" I ask Charlie, who's driving. He looks over to me with a curious gesture before moving his focus back to the hilly roads in front of us. His foot was about as strong on the pedal as my father's going up and down the winding trail.

I have probably dreamed of EVERYTHING, *except* for this. And trust me, I've had plenty of years to dream up and paint multiple scenarios. The streets keep getting smaller and the hillside taller. After a few more turns on side streets, we are now nearing the top of a mountain (or canyon, or hill—whatever they are). Charlie slows down and I see the mailbox number. Can this be real?

The house is ah-mazing. It's *very* big and it's *very* beautiful. It sits at the bottom of a very long driveway down the hillside, and is lined almost perfectly symmetrically all the way down with extra tall and beautiful lush palm trees. At their bases, the drive is lined with shorter lush and blooming purple bushes. The exterior of the home is cream stucco and the roof natural terracotta tile. Enormously large clay flower pots frame the extra large wooden garage doors. The home stands almost as tall as the top of the hilly driveway entrance. I am speechless.

We pull up to the garage to park and walk through a wooden gate on the side, leading to the front entrance. I look to Charlie and say, "I feel like I am in a freakin' movie right now!" Seriously, pinch me. This cannot be real. I just as quickly turn from him, keeping my confidence intact with calm breathing as I move forward with each step. Past the gate, there's more luscious greenery, blooming flowers, a water fountain, and larger-than-life tall columns near the entrance steps. I reach up to knock on another extravagant wooden door and notice how tiny my knuckled fist looks in comparison.

My father answers and welcomes us in. The floors are marble, tables are dressed with unique sculptures, and there are wall hangings and beautiful paintings too large to fit in any room in our home. And there are more columns inside! Gorgeous windows span the length of the tall walls, from the ceiling to the floor, and look out to a meticulously landscaped yard. More lush and large palms, flower beds, and flowering trees are met by an unexpected woodland. There, the bright green grass meets a line of dirt and rock filled with bridges, bushes, and towering trees. The tree limbs are immense and spread so wide that one could imagine the joy a child would have climbing them.

And while you'd think this forest would be bereft of the bright colors that embellish the garden landscape, it has its own manicured beauty that invites you in to a world of imagination and wonder. At its entrance is a pebbled path and an arched wooden bridge stretching across a wide rocky trench that runs full of water during the rainy season. On a wooded and winding walking path, multiple benches are set and sunlight breaks in with bright and narrow beams of light.

My attention is quickly brought back when I catch a glimpse of my father returning down the large front entrance stairs holding a red, foam ball in his hand. I laugh and grab mine out of my purse, and then he places his hand in mine.

"You keep mine and I'll keep yours," he says.

Charlie and Alice make us pose for a pic, and we both throw our clown noses on. We settle at a table in a kitchen nook nearby and are sipping distilled mineral water and nibbling on fresh fruit when Great Aunt Maura arrives. She comes blazing in like a force, with her strikingly white hair and ice blue eyes. And as quickly as she parks her suitcase, she opens it up and hands us both a framed image of herself captured in stylish, reflective blue shades in the sunshine. Once she settles in, Great Aunt Maura pulls out a yellow folder filled with pictures and printouts of the family lineage and history. While she thumbs through it, I manage to squeeze in another question when I catch Nate looking over at me.

"What do you do?" I say looking at him inquisitively, knowing it's such an awkward and untimely question.

"I'm a property manager," he says, tilting his head, looking me in the eye with a coy smile. "When the hot water heater pilot goes out, people call me and I tell them to take a cold shower."

We both laugh.

He continues to share that he manages all the properties they own. He also cares for their estate and the six cats, but of most priority is Alice's office. He handles all the business affairs, including legal work, for her practice.

◦ ◆ ◦

JOURNAL ENTRY

November 7, 2014

There were a few moments today that I looked at their seemingly rich life and wondered what the purpose was for me only to experience this until now. I look at this beautiful home, almost picturesque. A driveway lined with palm trees, large beautiful clay pots that are the size of my door back home, and such a grand entrance with large pillars and a wooden door fit to welcome a giant....

But I have to remind myself that I enjoyed my childhood and this is not who I am. I can appreciate my upbringing because it helped shape me into who I am today and the life I have and love. I, too, have a rich life ... not with all the palm trees, marble floors, and large columns, but one rich in gratitude and deeper meaning.

Chapter 10

With the first day lit up like a birthday cake, it is now day two of three and this morning I have time alone to bond with Alice. She picks me up in her convertible, a gold Lexus, and warns me of the workout I am about to experience. Already on the short drive to Pilates, I'm starting to think that while my father may keep many things hidden from me, when he does share, his words tend to hold weight—she is impressive, funny, and intelligent, but also very sweet, composed, and considerate … and competitive.

We start the Pilates class with a fairly easy flow, getting warmed up to music doing stretches and getting familiar with our benches and weight pulls. Nearing ten minutes in, I am already starting to sweat and am running out of breath. Alice takes every opportunity to look over at me and playfully give an "I told you so" with a laugh. How is she not even sweating? She's kicking my ***.

The class winds down after quiet meditation, and I watch Alice quietly clean up her station and start a conversation with the instructor. I find more towels to dry off and try to wring out my clothes. Eavesdropping, I can't tell whether they are really good friends or if Alice just frequents this place a lot. I am going to guess the latter. Alice calls me over to introduce myself and, to my enjoyment, again teases me. I present myself proudly with a sweat-soaked body and looking like a drowned Vanna White. I thank the instructor for the workout and admit to Alice that she was right.

"Did I work up an appetite?" she asks.

"Yes, my whole body hurts and I'm starving!" I laugh, shaking my head.

At a café called Broken Yolk, we meet Alice's sister. She's equally beautiful with natural fair skin, a kind smile, and dark brown hair. They both are carrying large designer handbags and flashy iPhones, but what's more entertaining is their candid banter (especially with the Canadian accents they never left behind). They are raw and honest with one another, and as they carry on I think perhaps one may even consider them a little crass; classy, but crass.

Dried off and returned to a lowered heart rate, I'm feeling fancy with a veggie stuffed egg white omelet sitting in front of me, sipping on champagne and orange juice in a crystal glass flute. I might as well be the poster child of "rags to riches," rocking questionably smelly and tight yoga gear with tousled hair. We toast our mimosas and dig in to our plates, or maybe it's just me digging in because I just used every ounce of energy in my body for that workout. I need something to help me recover. I keep working on this mimosa, but surely not even that can prepare me for what's next.

A few exchanges of hugs and goodbyes, and Alice and I head back to the car. The plan is to drive to the apartment so I can shower, grab Charlie, and then he and I drive back to the house for the rest of the day's planned activities. Since my father has not spent many years with Great Aunt Maura, he's going to spend some QT (quality time) catching up with her and we'll all meet up later. What isn't in the plan is my seriously sore behind and what Alice shares with me before pulling in the drive.

I knew my dad's mom, my grandmother, died in 1979, but nothing more. Alice confides that she thinks she knows why it took my father until now to meet me. He had a very troubled family life, most especially with his own father, that only worsened into his adult years. It turns out my grandmother didn't just die of natural causes—she was shot and killed; murdered in her own home as she sat in a chair in the living room—and the family is convinced my grandfather had something to do with it. It's still an open case, unsolved, in Arapahoe County, Colorado. Deputies found her with her head covered in blood and no signs of life, sitting cross-legged, holding a partially smoked Golden Light cigarette in one hand and a television guide on her lap. A pair of blue shoes sat on the floor in front of her. She was fifty-seven years old and died from a single gunshot to the head. The bullet entered above her left ear and exited above her right eye. The weapon used was most likely a Colt revolver or Garate Anitua, says the report, but no casings were found inside or outside the apartment.

Alice says the kids, my father, and his brothers, have always blamed their own father for their mother's murder; not by his own hand, but by a hired killer. He was questioned and interrogated by none other than his best friend, a cop. Coincidentally, a court hearing was scheduled that same month, in June 1979, for the divorce settlement of over $30,000 in alimony that my grandfather was charged to pay her. Even more ironically, my grandfather too ended up passing a few years later from a stroke—or was it guilt?

At the time of my grandmother's death, my father had just recently married. Alice says his wife desperately wanted children, but my father wanted none. The cumulating stresses ended their marriage only six months later. To cope, he took up drinking, which is still a natural solution for anyone who grows up in Northern Michigan. He meets my mom at a party, and the rest is history.

My eyes well up and my heart is now bearing more pain than my backside. I feel terrible for him, my grandmother, and the family. I can only imagine. He was already terrified to be a father.... He loses his wife because he doesn't want kids (and she's demanding it) ... then he loses his mother to what he believes is his own father's doing ... and *then*, just when he feels at the bottom of it all, he tries to run and escape from life with drugs and alcohol but God has different plans and surprises him with what, of all things, me—a daughter. He must have been terrified.

I start to wonder if it's been my grandmother whom I have felt with me much of my life? When I was younger, the feeling was stronger and much more present. I have never seen or had a vision of an angel, but I have always felt a "presence" with me—like that of a guardian angel. It's a loving and protecting presence that could be described as a dream or imagination perhaps, but I always felt it had a hand in giving me the strength, guidance, and hope I needed in my life. I believe miracles do happen, and surely right now this feels like another unexplainable gift.

The rest of the day, Charlie and I find ourselves having a great time bonding with Alice. The city is going through a three-year drought, but is still beautiful. The natural landscape has a sort of whimsical character about it, which makes it not surprising to learn that the author Theodor Seuss Geisel, better known as Dr. Seuss, was inspired by and perfected his craft here as a children's author. But what *is* surprising is that even amidst the drought, it is still deceivingly lush. Most areas are a mix of native spiraling trees and blooming bush, and there are many homes and communities invested in the care of their landscape; and it spreads farther than "one block" (eh-hem, Beverly Hills, clearing my throat). Those homeowners who decided to part with grass have tastefully crafted a landscape to adapt to the dry and hot climate.

In Balboa Park, the first garden we walk through is a Japanese garden called Zoro. But "there's nothing here!" we joked, calling the garden "Zero." As we move on, we discover stretches of the park that are indeed beautiful and vast and embark on a long hike filled with more conversation. When we return to the main entrance, we find a table at a small café and quietly sip on coffee and people watch (arguably more entertaining than any of the gardens we saw).

A few hours later we reunite with my father and Great Aunt Maura in the Plaza where we find them seated at their own individual small bistro tables with graphite pencils in hand, drawing on sketch paper. The setting is outside an open, French-esque café and near the Plaza entrance where a roundabout circulates entering traffic. In the center of it all is an impressively large bronze sculpture of a man on a horse. He appears to be some kind of a war hero with a sheath and shield, or maybe a medieval knight? He's holding a flag affixed to a long, sharp spear. My father and Great Aunt Maura both appear entranced, intensely looking back and forth between their selected objects and their canvas. Maura is an artist, which is apparent as I watch the strokes of her pencil on the canvas.

Our arrival starts the countdown to the day's next planned activity, and shortly thereafter, we're all in line to watch an illusionist inside the Plaza theatre. The show begins with a spotlight on stage and us seated in silence in the audience. The entertainer enters on stage with a chair and a microphone, no props. He challenges us to think about reality versus the internet. He poses the question, is reality not good enough? Does the internet provide us with the correct answer to every question? Does it correctly define our existence and situations better than what we can in real life? Life isn't cut and dry, but the internet is: question = answer. Life is more like art; it's an experience, and every object can be drawn and question answered uniquely—not universally or unanimously the same.

When he starts doing his magic tricks, I am mystified. I struggle to understand how he is pulling it off—he's good!! He's making a case good enough to question, is this real or magic? Is it possible? Nah. But with all things considered, how he opened his act does pose a good question that now has me thinking … what is my reality? How quickly *do* we just believe what we see as truth? Why *do* they say ignorance is bliss?

The show was great. The entire day has been great, and it couldn't possibly get better; but when we return to the house, I am shown that it quite possibly can. I enter right behind my father and we're both greeted by a man whom I haven't met. His look is a bit gruff but manicured. The gentleman is dressed in a chef's white top hat and messy-upped long apron. The aromas from the kitchen smell delightful and with a kind smile, he offers to help me remove my shawl and then hands me a glass of freshly poured champagne.

Following a quick cocktail hour of socializing, we're directed to the main dining room. I hadn't even noticed the room before, as it sits obscured by the staircase in the main entrance with a hidden hallway from the kitchen. A large dining table made of thick, clear glass and held up by carved marble stone is dressed in formal white china, fresh flowers, and candlelight. The room is decorated with more oversized artwork and features a wall of windows to the backyard gardens. The chef pulls out my chair and offers to take my emptied champagne glass, then pours me a glass of wine. We enjoy an evening with more service, glasses of wine poured, and every course hand-delivered by the chef—a four-course meal made to Charlie's and my likings, based on a list of items gathered by my father in email prior to our arrival.

I feel like I am having an out-of-body experience. I'm living the pages straight out of a storybook. And yet, what I want to know and make sure is that this *is* real, that he *is* real. While all of this is over the top, beyond expectations and making me feel so incredibly special, the only thing I really want is my father, and that is all. All this preparation, activity, and fun *is* amazing, but all I need is him—nothing more and nothing else. I'm praying tomorrow will give us the time … for just him and me.

* ◆ *

JOURNAL ENTRY

November 8, 2014

At the dinner table tonight, we were drunk on wine and filled with the most delicious food served to us on fine china and by an in-home personal chef. Paper rice spring rolls filled with sprouts and cucumbers, tossed in olive oil; endive points filled with Indian hummus and accompanied with sliced chicken and tomato, adorned with a rose tomato peel. My favorite, a salad of buttered mushrooms lay atop sweet potato spaghetti, morels, lobster mushrooms, and others I can't even remember. The main course was salmon and asparagus topped with cilantro béarnaise and served with a delicious cauliflower soufflé. Lastly, an avocado ice cream and chocolate mousse was paired with sliced pear and raspberries. Each plate delivered was followed with silence then a symphony of "ohs" and "yums."

In between courses, the conversation got better and better, too. At one point, Great Aunt Maura asked me what I thought about my father and me meeting now after all these years. My response was there patiently waiting, right at the tip of my tongue, and rolled out without hesitation. I, of course, had always hoped for it to happen but shared what I think is the most interesting fact that it's happening now, meeting him at the age of thirty-three, which was the age of my father when I was conceived.

Later in the evening, after a few too many glasses of wine, I also decided to divulge the most embarrassing part of it all.... I told them about the tattoo!

It was an attention-getting, conversation-starter to say the least. My face was flushed and Alice, the caring and protective doctor that she is, asked me to be sure she sees this before I leave to make sure it's okay, being that it is ink tattooed directly over my heart.... I put it on my heart and hid it under my breast, so it is small.... I assured her I will let her see it before I leave.

- ◆ -

After writing in my journal and before I fall asleep, I send my father a text.

> So, I was just thinking ... tomorrow morning we will be at a restaurant on a beach, no? Maybe you and I could go for a walk after breakfast? Just a short one. Whattya think?

Chapter 11

Pinch me. I have found him and lost him before; in fact, twice now, but one by my count.

The first was that time in high school when Lo and I found him and my step-grandmother, Betty, on the internet. That she hadn't spoken to my father in years makes sense now; she was the woman who had lived next door and had an affair with my grandfather while he was married to my grandmother and had three children, including my father. Plus, she too was married.

I remember speaking with Alice all those many years ago. She had such a kind heart even back then; you could hear it in her comforting voice on the phone as she explained that my father too was expecting my call and had given me his email, suggesting that I write him. In hindsight, that was probably the worst advice anyone could have given me as an untamed writer looking for an outlet. But when his "new" email address didn't work, I had promised myself I would never pursue him again. I held true to that promise for fifteen years.

The second time you might say I "lost" my father was years later. After college, I moved to California to start my career and had way more fun than financial success. Working on the 26th floor of a high rise on Wilshire Boulevard, across from the infamous tar pits of L.A., you'd think I'd be a young go-getter making all that cash, but yeah … nope. PR, better known as public relations, doesn't make beans in the big cities, not unless you own the agency or are at the executive level. Truth be told, they have a genius business philosophy. They recruit all young talent who are smart, eager, and cute or funny. Regardless of your skills or personality, it's all man-eat-man business structure, churn and burn. I only landed the job because of my persistence. I did enter the PR agency above entry level and had my own office with a door and a view from the top. Yet, I made only enough to afford to split rent with three girls in a one-bedroom apartment in West Hollywood. All our single beds had to be staggered in height from the floor to fit. One was in an actual bed frame (mine!), one was just laid on the floor, and the other was a handy Home Depot concoction mastered one night with nails, 2x4's, and plywood.

I lasted a mere two years in L.A., only making enough money to make ends meet and go out to the clubs, and of course buy cute outfits to do so. The lifestyle swallowed every penny I made, plus savings. Never meeting any guys who were truly good people was also disappointing. Thankfully, I did meet the greatest group of girls. We called ourselves, "Hot Legs." A group of runners brought together by complete randomness, a Craigslist post, back in 2004, with a query to form a running group. We became really good friends, all brought together from across the U.S. with only two things in common: 1) we just moved to L.A. and 2) we liked to run. Some of them I am still close with today. No matter where and when we have the opportunity to see each other, it's always so great to reconnect. It's such a random and crazy stroke of fate that all of our lives were brought together in this one spot, in the big city of L.A. I can honestly say they are one of the few things I treasure most about that time in my life; it was their friendship. We were lucky. And we had such a great time together.

Just like time, we all move on. Once I had my fill of the fun and crazy, free-spirited life, I moved back home to the Midwest to get grounded and figure out my next chapter in life. My first night home I had dinner with my mom. I had already lined up a job and apartment before returning home, so she met me in the building I was moving into. After only the first thirty minutes, one cocktail, and an appetizer, she dropped a doozy—one of a lifetime—on me. To this day, I still struggle to find forgiveness for her in my heart....

"There's something I have been meaning to tell you," she said. And I honestly didn't think much of it. Her life problems are countless and I have always heard about them and have had to deal with more than a fair share of them. It's usually never anything that is "life-altering," mostly just something to make you feel really bummed and worried. After time, you just get numb to it.

"Oh yeah, what's that?" I asked.

"Your father contacted me," she said.

"WHAT?" I choked on my glass of wine and set it down so hard I almost broke the stem. "When, why!?!"

I was dumbfounded, filled with bewilderment and also a bit scared with a sense of excitement, and then super irritated. This was something she's been meaning to tell me? I looked at her piercingly. This better be good.

"Well, it wasn't actually him," she said in a voice that sounded annoyed. "It was his lawyer."

"When was this?" I asked, quietly screaming with elegantly disguised anticipation.

"It was a few months ago now," she said and took another bite of the appetizer and flushed it down with a sip of her drink as if it were nothing. Either I was hiding my internal freak-out incredibly well, or she really was not in touch with reality. She took another bite of the appetizer and said nonchalantly, as if it would have no impact on me, "But from what his lawyer said, he lives out there in California."

Are you KIDDING ME!? I couldn't believe it. I couldn't explain the beginning or end of the emotions I felt. It was a swirl of anger, excitement, confusion, resentment. She had said enough. The fact that I was just living in the same state as him, that is clear on the other side of our country, DO I EVEN DARE ASK HOW LONG SHE KNEW? I was living there for two years. How is it possible that it didn't cross her mind to tell me? She not only waited to tell me until I moved home, but she waited until the actual day (my first day) I was home. Like what!? This woman, I do love her, but the way her brain works continues to leave me absolutely perplexed. She is my mother, but this was too much. It hurts my brain just as much as it does my heart. Selfishness is such a terrible character trait and sadly can consume your good. In fact, it is the worst; the absolute worst.

So, the new version of the story goes…. My father was trying to leave the country and travel overseas, but because he never paid child support the courts would not authorize his passport. His lawyer reached out to my mom to request that she clear him from any ill will, but she decided (now) that she was owed all the money he never paid….

I didn't want to listen to any more of it.

I grew up learning to care for myself at a *very young* age. I never had a babysitter and inherently always fended for myself. When I came of an age that I could make my own means, I wanted a better life, so I made it happen. I started babysitting in middle school and at the age of fifteen I was an officially paid member of the work force. My senior year, I worked two jobs, giving up sports. I bought my own car when I turned sixteen, and I bought my own clothes, shampoo, shoes, lotions, and perfumes, anything that I wanted or needed. Most of my adolescent years were not spent at my house with Mom, but at my friends' homes. I spent summers away and during the school year, my friends' parents invited me in for sleepovers throughout the week. My friends' families were so amazing, and so kind to always accept me and share themselves—at times, as though I was one of their own. They have no idea how ever grateful I am, and how much of an impact it had on my upbringing. Because of them, I was surrounded by love, laughter, family, and teachings.

No one ever stayed at my house. At two different points in life, my mom, brother, and I didn't even have a place to live and again, my friends' families took me in. It is truly because of them—their graciousness, warmth, acceptance, selflessness, and so much more—that I am who I am today. So, again, to hear my mom say that she was owed money touched a very large nerve. How is it that money is most important when my father reaches out?

Okay, fine. I am always willing to try to put on the shoes and understand the other side. And I get it. She raised me on her own and it was hard. But she also made the decision to do so all those years ago, so why now did she feel owed? She made it; she did it. And I turned out pretty okay! Why not uphold that pride?

But nope, you know what it is? Money.

Because what's left after you remove the money from this conversation? … Oh, me? Does she care how I feel about this all? I mean, I'm pretty sure I'm an important piece in this puzzle. She really couldn't even ask me nor have any concern for my thoughts? Or maybe it's because she knew my answer would have been immediate and irrefutable: we don't need the money, and we don't want any money. What we need is for him to be a father. Tell him the only money you expect is for him to buy a plane ticket and meet his daughter.

That night was the first and only time I have ever closed the door on my mother, and I hope it is the last. I couldn't help it. I was so disgusted. Did she really think this was all about her? She made her decision a long time ago. I never had the chance.

When the door shut, I dropped to the floor. Right there in the entry of my new apartment, I collapsed. I hadn't cried that hard in many years. I had just moved back home and was immediately slapped with the reality of remembering the worst of what I had left behind—pain, sorrow, and hard times. I remember waking up the next morning still crying. My heart was just broken and I was so lost. As soon as I could gather my wits, I went looking through all the cardboard boxes for those notes, printouts, and family names, from when I had found and contacted him back in high school. After a few hours of opening and closing boxes, mindlessly and madly multi-tasking and setting items in the vicinity of where they should go in the apartment, I found it: a yellowed manila file folder with the original copies printed that summer at the energy company. They still show the date, 9/9/98, in the footer on the first printed page and the handwritten contact info for my dad, his brother, and my questionable step-grandmother.

After all the years, I reached out and called once again, dialing the number for his brother, my Uncle Ed. He answered and he spoke with me. But he equally devastated me. He told me my father wanted nothing to do with me. He sounded very upset and was rather mean, and he let me know very clearly that my father was very upset. I could barely choke out any words through my tears, "I'm sorry, I'm so sorry," I remember apologizing over and over again. This is not what I ever wanted. "I knew nothing of any of this!" I promised him.

I begged and pleaded, asking him to please let my father know I didn't want any money and all I've ever wanted was just to meet him. With annoyance, he complied and hung up. I remember feeling the loss of my father, once again, and that I had no control. It was one of the hardest days of my life. And that's when I promised myself again. I swore from that day forward, I would never ever try again.

Chapter 12

After the delicious meal with the in-home chef last night, I wake up hungry, wishing this apartment was a hotel with breakfast served. I throw on the hotel-like robe my father so proudly purchased (and bragged about to Great Aunt Maura and Alice yesterday) and make a cup of coffee. Sliding on a pair of flip flops, I grab a light cardigan sweater and walk out to the weeping willow-like tree between the apartment and Alice's office.

As I approach it, I pause, look up, and admire, while stopping to take a sip of coffee. I continue my stride in, sliding my right hand along each hanging branch to gently move it out of my way. The tiniest little white flowers fall in my hands and also from above into my hair. I take a seat on the wooden bench that Charlie had sat on the morning before and move about the little white rocks at my feet. This is my last day. This is my chance. I need to seize every moment, every opportunity, and make it last. Because, what if I never see him again? I must make this count.

Before we left for the trip, I decided on five questions I'd most like to have answered. The goal was to be realistic about how much I can learn in our limited visit:

1. Are you sick?
2. Where did you go to school?
3. What's your profession?
4. Who is Mary Palmer?
5. How did you meet my mom?

I rattle them off to myself and celebrate having an answer now for most!

He did go to college. Several times in fact. He first went to Northern Michigan University (NMU) for law, and said it was horrible. The town was sleepy, empty, and so very cold. It was filled with desolate landscapes and snow that came down sideways. There was nothing more to do than drink with friends, and that's exactly what he did. He drank himself right out of school. When he was ready to try again, he was ready to be more serious, and that's when he went to Dartmouth.

He continued to study law at Dartmouth. He didn't share much more than admitting that he managed to flunk himself out of school again. The story included a tale of rolling up joints and filling them into a plastic baggie, and then lighting up before class and staying high all the way through.

Then there's his mom, Mary Palmer, her death still an unsolved homicide in Colorado. Shot in her home, sitting in her living room chair, and found by her neighbor the next day.

Last night at dinner, the family talked about Grandma Marti again. I learned that's what they called her ... not Mary, Marti. They shared how much she changed following the divorce, especially once she left Michigan and moved to Colorado. She had become so paranoid that she wouldn't leave the house.

Agoraphobia, they said, is what she developed. She never went outside, not even to get groceries or the mail. The logic and circumstances are enough to question. Why was she *now* so fearful? Surely, only she knew of things they do not and likely would have kept things, especially terrible things, from the kids both to protect them and help maintain a relationship for them with their father. I wonder. Was she scared to leave the house because she was scared of him? It seems like a question worth asking.

According to Alice, these were times of trial and challenges for Dad. He tried to get his head straight after all those years of drinking and flunking out of both NMU and Dartmouth. When he gets married, he's finally putting his life back on track, but his new wife *really* wants to have kids. She wasn't willing to wait, and he wasn't about to abandon an opportunity to get a degree. Then, his mom died, possibly at the order of his own father; you surely can't help but have sympathy and understanding for his return to a self-destructive path filled with loss and resentment.

There he was, without his wife, and without his mom. Then, can you imagine, he gets news of me!? Surprise! While I can't agree he made the right choice, it's not surprising that he chose to run. He packed up and moved to California.

It took some time after the tragedies, but he did finish school. He also reconnected with Alice, who was also living California. Alice was attending med school, and he was working on his law degree (again). They had met and dated in New Hampshire, both attending Dartmouth.

At the time, Alice was eighteen and he was twenty-two. He had given her friends a ride and she left her notebook in his car. The rest was history. When they reconnected, it was 1986. I would've been five and he was thirty-nine.

The true irony, however, is that after all that time he spent to right his life and get a degree in law, after a mere few years working in the practice he realized it was not what he wanted to do.

Today, the only practice he does in law is for Alice. And because of the loss of his wife, mom, and father, I would argue he was never capable of opening his heart and fully loving again. It very well may be why he and Alice never married. She would say otherwise, but I can see how much she loves him. I believe she made the decision to live as partners only because that is what he wanted.

When my father shared stories of his short days as a lawyer with Charlie and me at brunch the other day, he prefaced with what he *thought* life would be like as a lawyer. His briefcase would be made of fine Italian leather, hand-stitched and tossed on the end of the couch while he sat comfortably in his luxuriously rich and comfortable leather chair, feet propped up on a large mahogany desk. A lamp with a base of gold and dark green glass shade would dramatically cast light on his monogrammed notepad and draw shadows on the ceiling-high, built-in bookshelves behind....

The wind suddenly gusts and rustles a low hanging limb that brushes my hand and reawakens me to the coffee that sits in it and is getting cold. Still under the look-a-like willow tree, my bum is starting to get damp from the morning dew. I check off the questions on my father-to-ask list. There are two left: Where did you go to high school? And are you sick? I prioritize them in more obvious order and take the last gulp of coffee before returning inside to get ready for the day.

We arrive to the house around 9 a.m. for our breakfast reservations at Marine Room in La Jolla. High tide comes in at 10 a.m. and we hear it is a spectacular event. The famous restaurant is situated on the edge of the cliffs, its westernmost side covered in thick glass from ceiling to floor, acting as an aquarium to the ocean seaside. The entire family is out for the special occasion. There is an endless morning buffet of renowned delicacies. I don't catch a glimpse of any fish through the glass, but I do catch my father sneaking bacon onto his lap! When I giggle, he shows me the little desserts he has hidden in the pocket of his suit jacket too.

Halfway through breakfast, the fog starts to roll out and gives way to a bright and beautiful sunrise on a crystal-clear ocean-scape. It's surrounded by the large rock cliffs of La Jolla and crashing waves that the tide has brought up to the wall of glass in front of us. It's a very cool place. It's old and dated, but has a gaudy charm. It admittingly also has an odd smell that I have a "fishing" sense is from the ocean. Without a doubt, the place is rich with history. At the clash of another wave on the glass, we tip our mimosas in cheers to the unique experience and fine cuisine.

I think again of my questions and pause to take a moment, reflecting on it all. We all have a story. Would you read yours and love it? Would you want it to be your story? He knows he shouldn't have that bacon, but what price will he pay? Will he get to enjoy every savory moment of those desserts hiding in his pocket, or will it give him pain, hurt his health, or leave him with regret? Every story has an ending that we can read in a book, but not in life. The only ending we know is what we can do. I hope he enjoys every moment of that delicious bacon and dessert.

After breakfast, we drive the narrow streets of La Jolla and head downtown. We find a space to park and take a shortcut to the cliffs, sneaking through a grand hotel filled with fabulously rich people. They were beautiful, all the women and the men. They carried Louis Vuitton leather and wore elegantly revealing clothing. I catch myself admiring a couple in particular at guest check-in and run into someone. I'm nearly knocked off balance. Maybe they didn't see me? Am I invisible in this land of only the finest? The gorgeous, tall woman with blonde locks flowing down to her designer jeans and fabulous pink heels hurriedly walks away holding onto a dark-haired man, large in stature, exceptionally good-looking, clean, and very well dressed. He carries on his shoulder a stylish canvas bag filled with what you can only imagine. We finally exit the foyer and come out on the other side of the hotel where we see the oceanside below the cliffs, and seagulls everywhere.

They are huge, both the cliffs and the seagulls! I have never seen a larger seagull, no exaggeration. We enter a grassy area and Alice reaches down to pull off her shoes and carries them at her side. I admire her. She can get her feet dirty and enjoy the earth touching her toes. She's comfortable and just as natural as the waves that break at the cliff's edge. Wallowing in admiration of her confidence and carelessness, my heart starts pounding at the walls of my chest, trying to escape the discomfort of talking to my dad. I need to find the courage to get the answers (and the one-on-one time I so desire). With every step, I feel the excited anticipation and walk a little closer to him. And then as soon as I get close, my nerves crawl up my feet and snatch my tongue.

We walk the grassy knoll until we get to the cliff's edge and stop alongside a wooden fence that frames the blue and aquamarine-colored water below. I pose for a picture with Charlie when my father quickly slides in. He smiles and grabs one of my sides, and then Great Aunt Maura slides in, too.

I'm feeling excited about the photo. I'm also beating myself up for not having the courage to ask him to walk alone with me or ask any more questions. On the way back to the van, we pass a small French boutique. Charlie stops us girls and I look at him with surprised eyes. What is he up to? He tells us to go inside and check it out. Of course, this is a great idea!

One of the first garments I see, I slide my hand to the price tag, which reads $1,149, and ever so casually slide my hand away and turn to find the sales rack. Thumbing through the sale items, and price tags, I find a few contenders. I pull each one out and hold it in front of me, looking in the mirror to imagine how it would look if I actually tried it on. This place is too fancy for me. I am feeling intimidated. If I find anything, it has to be worthy of paying a crazy price but it will always remind me of this trip.

Like a sommelier who swirls the glass and takes a deep sniff before a taste, I sway a shirt back and forth and turn from side to side. I place it back on the rack and slide down to one more. It's an elegant piece and as soon as I hold it up in front of the mirror, I know it's for me. It's a cover-up made of thinly knit blue silk and gold threads, simple and sparkly. It's beautiful. It has a single and simple tie, high up on the waist line. The tag reads MES DEMOISELLES, PARIS. *Mes demoiselles* means "my damsels." The price says $400 with a red line and a handwritten $45.

When we get back to the house, I slide out the new cover-up from the tissue and put it on. Looking in the mirror again, but now with it on, I tie it at the waist and smile in reassurance of finding a special piece—and a good bargain. I catch a glimpse of the clock behind me. It's 8:30 p.m. It rushes over me that the day is already almost gone. I grab my cigarettes and head to the garage to have a smoke and figure out a plan.

Walking past Alice and Charlie in the garage on the way out, I hear laser shooting and both of them yelling behind the Atari Centipede arcade console. Outside I find that it's not only late but is also already getting dark. The sun is setting. I look up through the tall palms at the edge of the drive and see a bright moon and even a few stars. I realize I can't ask him to go for a walk now. The door opens behind me and it's Great Aunt Maura. I smile to her, as I anticipate a good conversation, but then it clicks … he's in there, right now, alone.

Just as quickly as I had lit my cigarette, I put it out and excuse myself from Great Aunt Maura, who convinces me it's no worries as she had just stepped out to enjoy some fresh air. I hurry back inside with zero plans. But when the door closes behind me inside the house, I feel immediately defeated by the silence. I freeze. What do I do now? Where is he? I start checking all the rooms. The kitchen, the living room, dining room … he's nowhere. He has to be upstairs. I approach the banister from the side and lean up, grabbing the railing with my hands and peeking over to look upstairs. I see a light on in his bedroom. Now I'm really torn with conflict. I can't just walk up to his bedroom and "surprise" him. What if he is in his undies? Unlikely, but still I'd prefer not to risk it. Do I yell up from the bottom of the stairs and say "Hey!"…?

Nah, that's impolite.

Maybe yell up "Hey, Nathan!"…?

No, what if he finds it rude that I call him by his first name? He has been introducing me to everyone this weekend as his daughter.

I'm now nervously walking back and forth at the bottom of the stairs, and finally just do it. I blurt it out. It's quick, awkward, very deep (surprisingly), and throws the two syllables together into what sounds like one muffled word, "HEYDAD!"

His response is immediate. His attentiveness is also a bit surprising. He hurriedly rushes out of his room and down the first few stairs. When he sees me, he stops and asks, "What's going on? What do you need?"

I wasn't prepared for this at all. I stutter out of my now fully flushed face, "Oh, hi … I was just wondering, um, where you were. And uh, maybe … hey, would you want to talk?"

"Of course!" he says without hesitation and continues down to meet me at the bottom of the stairs. He looks over to the large library, just behind us and past a row of columns, and to a velvet, crescent-shaped couch in front of the fireplace.

"Shall we sit there?" he asks.

I head to the couch so quickly that it has to be more than evident how nervous I am. The couch has an extraordinarily high back with pillowed pleats fastened by fabric covered buttons. It's worked with brightly-colored threads, silk pillows along the entire back of the seat cushion, and a light cashmere cover across the edge of one of the low profile arms. Everything is so perfectly arranged, I wonder how long it has been since anyone had last taken a seat there. I move the pillows to the side and plop down with an exonerating exhale. *Here we go!* I begin wrapping one of the ties from my cover-up around a finger, nervously twisting it before he takes a seat. I decide to go right in for the kill, asking my most important, #1 question....

"Are you sick?" I abruptly say with no appropriate or polite lead in.

"Yes, I am," he says assuredly.

He leans in close with confident eyes and warmth. He explains that he has been suffering from colon cancer for the last six years. His last surgery was exactly that, the last. He has been cut open and stitched back together too many times, and they have nothing left to stitch back together. He is essentially inoperable. His last options are chemo and radiation or to try and beat it organically. He opted for the latter and feels confident under Alice's guidance.

It's all starting to make sense! The enzyme specialist, who just moved to the area and stopped by to meet me the other day; the hidden desserts and bacon in his pocket; and the time I saw him walking up the stairs one night with a pot of coffee.... Now I know that was for his daily enema. He explains that the stacks of short books on the counter today from the mail are what he reads to occupy his time during the process. And the small scratch that kept reappearing above his lip was a symptom from the disease, too.

"Are you in pain?" I ask.

"No, none of my symptoms are painful," he assures me.

Everything makes sense now, but my biggest fear is now true. I just found him, and I may just as quickly lose him (again).

"I just care about you a lot," I say, but really I want to hug him.

He promises everything is going to be okay and that Alice is very intelligent and knows what she is doing.

"I'm not going anywhere," he says. "But if I do, I will always be with you on the other side."

"You will?" I ask, surprised. "Can you make sure I know?"

"Yes, you will know it is me," he says.

Chapter 13

When Charlie and I return to the apartment, I pull out the bottle of white wine from the fridge and take a seat at the small kitchen table. The table was already set with my wine glass, a writing pen, and my journal, and I was ready for a night of writing. I pour and fill the glass three quarters full, take a sip and then a deep breath.

Charlie is sitting in the living room watching TV. I have so many emotions and need to write, but first, not in my journal. I need to write a thoughtful note; one to Nate, and one to Alice. I rip out a page from the journal, accidently tearing into its side. I crumble it and toss it in the trash. I pull out another page and it tears out clean. I grab the pen and address it to Alice. And after a few sentences, I begin to cry.

My note to Alice takes much longer to write than expected, and I find myself struggling. I had hoped my words could leave with her my overwhelming thanks, but instead the page is capturing the tears and smearing the ink.

What if this is the last time I see him? I can't help but spiral. What an incredible weekend of memories I have been gifted with. This was it; this *is* my dream come true. Ever since I can remember, I have wanted to meet him. And since I've been older, I've worn his tattoo on my heart. Now, the tattoo will mean something different than it had before. Now, I can say "dad" and I can place with it a face, a smile, and memories. The symbol will always be on my heart, but now I can wear it proudly and am no longer ashamed.

I can tell that Charlie is starting to get annoyed when I look over to him in the other room. I just ended the letter to my father and am still the same mess as when I started. Even I didn't think it would take this long to write the notes. Charlie rises up from his chair and walks into the kitchen, asking again if I'm almost done. I apologize to him once again and promise him, I am almost done.

His mood this time, though, is very different. I can tell he is upset. I walk out to the living room to sit with him. He mutters something under his breath that I can't quite understand. My brain is a pile of spaghetti, tossing around guesses as to what's bothering him. Maybe it's stress from being away from the business? Maybe it's the emotions of the weekend? But can he really not be here with me in this space right now? I'm having a hard enough time of my own. Do I really need to take care of him too?

He grabs my journal and whips it across the living room, hitting the lamp and wall beside me. I watch him throw it with such intent force that I immediately react in prayer. It knocks the lamp shade off and sends the lamp falling to the floor—CRACK! The light bulb breaks and, in a snap, a brilliant blue light fills the room and we are both silenced. As quickly as it flared, the light is out and we find ourselves in the dark. It was clear; it was just as shocking to him. I unthinkingly walk over to him. He reaches out and pulls me in close and tight. We both cry.

· ◆ ·

JOURNAL ENTRY

November 10, 2014

Last night I cried myself to sleep.

I put Dad's red nose in the palm of my hand and prayed in the dark until I had no more tears.

When I woke, my hand was still clenched. When I opened it, his red nose was still there.

· ◆ ·

Climbing out of my father's van in front of American Airlines at the entrance for airport departures, I set my luggage curbside and hug him goodbye. I hug him tightly as though it may be our last, not knowing if I would ever be able to hug him again. He's a little stiff but returns the tighter squeeze and then I feel him turn his head. "I am very proud of you," he says quietly in my ear, "and so glad to have this time to know you."

I squeeze him again tightly. I look over to Charlie. He sees my tear-filled eyes and grabs my hand, and I grab my luggage with the other. We walk to the automated entrance door, and while every part of me wants to turn around, look back, and wave goodbye, I just couldn't do it. I just kept walking. I had to be strong.

❖

From: 'Maura'

Date: Monday, November 10, 2014

To: 'Alice', Nate Brunhoff

Cc: 'Michelle'

Subject: What an amazing weekend!

You are the most wonderful hosts—you have planned everything imaginable to entertain, stimulate, distract and please us! Thank you for everything ...

I can't tell you how much this weekend has meant to me, with the glorious reunion—no, meeting, I should say—of you, Nate, and your daughter, getting acquainted with you makes me sad that I spent so many years not knowing you, and so happy that we can finally be kindred spirits. Alice, I am blown away by your skills and love this connection we have found. I feel great today, still tall and straight and flexible. Our yoga teacher could not make today's class, but I'll show 'em all on Thursday!

With much love and joy at finding you,

Maura

❖

On November 11, 2014, at 10:40 AM, Nate wrote:

I just got back from a trip among the stars. A parallel universe. It was wild. I found a daughter that was really smart and graceful and funny that I instantly liked. She was attached to this really nice guy, Brutus, that escaped from a Popeye cartoon with hands the size of a first base glove. There was also an elderly woman who kept beating everyone at a dice game claiming her Neptune in her Jupiter. There was another girl too, called rabbit, that seemed like an old friend to my new daughter. She kept calling me dog even though I was not at all furry or on all fours. I think it lasted a lifetime of three days. Totally weird but seriously wonderful.

I'll be right back ...

. ◆ .

On November 11, 2014, at 7:50 PM, Michelle wrote:

No worries, NB-3. Ironically, I too experienced a land in the stars. I laid to sleep on Wednesday and did not wake until today. You wouldn't believe that I met my father, Darth, and learned my real name is Lukelle. It felt as though I knew him all my life. Our conversations were enlightening, set atop large ant hills along the ocean's coast and I was guided by both a beautiful angel and galaxy queen who has lived hundreds of lifetimes and accomplished that of ten in one. My adventures were totally crazy and as awesome as any place I'd ever call home. I didn't want to wake up, but I'm glad we are here now reconnecting.

It appears that we didn't miss a "beat" ...

. ◆ .

I've been home for three days now and I'm feeling ready to finally tell my mom. I fear the possibilities of what her response may be. It's been five years since we last spoke about him.

We had our first fallout over him when I moved home from L.A. in 2005. That was the night we had dinner and it ended with me slamming the door in her face. The next time was nearly four years later, during a birthday party for my close cousin. The family threw a big party with an over-the-top bonfire and live music at my aunt's house. Charlie had just proposed a few months earlier and I hadn't yet shared any news about our wedding plans. It was a cool summer evening and the fire was our light through the night. We all enjoyed plenty of drinks and dancing. I was standing on top of a small hill in the yard with my mom and cousin. We were overlooking the party, looking down at everyone dancing to the band and enjoying the night, when Mom brought up my engagement. I told her nothing was concrete yet, but that we were having a destination wedding. As soon as the words escaped, she about choked on her drink and then froze, staring at me intensely with extra wide eyes. I knew it would not be a good time to talk to her about wedding plans, but her reaction was also unexpected. She looked awkward, like a terrified Madonna striking a pose. I immediately wanted to walk away. I assured her we would still have a very small, intimate wedding at our local church (holding back that the only reason we are doing this is to ensure it will be legalized), but when she finally opened her mouth again, it reminded me of every reason I chose to plan our wedding to be destination.

"Oh, well," she said in slight disgust. "That's just too bad." And then in a deeper tone with concerned eyes, she reached out her hand and laid it on my arm. "I was going to invite your father to the wedding."

I remember having the taste of disgust in my mouth, once again. She went there; she played the father card! It was either the booze or my disbelief, but my quick reaction was a nervous laugh followed by an annoyed, "MOM." I knew she read what I was saying with my eyes, like "You're kidding me, right?" And, "Of course, Mom, that would be the *perfect* time to meet my father for the first time." Maybe he could just walk me down the aisle, too! Needless to say, that conversation ended just as quickly as the last, but this time I wished I had a door to slam in her face again.

I shake the memory from my mind and stand up to push the chair from under me and go to close the office door. It's near the end of the work day and I need to put my thoughts together without distraction. I flip off the switch to the florescent ceiling lights. The office becomes softly lit by a floor lamp in the corner and decorative table lamp on the desk. I open an email and start writing a new message to my father.

◦ ◆ ◦

From: 'Michelle'

Date: Wednesday, November 12, 2014

To: Nate Brunhoff

Subject: Ask Oreo

I think I may be ready to tell my mother that I found you. I do still have a tiny fear that by doing so it may put our relationship at stake—and that is the absolute last thing on earth (and in the galaxy) that I ever want to do. I am still feeling cautious as I don't know exactly what happened before and I am wondering if there is anything I should know or be concerned about before embarking on this journey.

Awkward!

◦ ◆ ◦

On November 12, 2014, at 10:10 PM, Nate wrote:

Worry not little wing.

You are your own woman. You have proudly come of age and you are your own person.

OUR relationship is our beginning this last weekend and rolling forward. If your mom has issues—then they are squarely between her and me, with no nuance and must be kept in that category.

If she feels she needs to yell at me for whatever reason, then she should yell at Me. Not you. Anything that approaches tension, moral, ethical, judgments, etc. must be directed to ME not you ... and I am going to enlist Charlie in this to encourage you not to get sucked in to some mother daughter drama destined to go nowhere.

You had NO part in the brief relationship between me and your mom.

You had NO part in the decisions made 30 years ago. You are bullet proof if you use the magic words, "Talk to him."

If she contacts me, I am going to empathically and immutably at inappropriate times (so she gets it), "You will leave Michelle out of this."

I'll stand behind you and protect you.

Does that help for starters??

NB

• ◆ •

"Worry not little wing," his words keep echoing in my head. "I will protect you."

My mind blanks out for a moment and I go back to another memory....

It was fourth grade and we had been living in a new house for only a short while. The first time we made the drive up north to look at the house, I still remember how beautiful it was. I had never seen a house so big and so pretty. In the city, we lived in a townhouse. This land was far away and close to Grandma's and Grandpa's. It was set on a lake with the only close neighbors hidden by the surrounding trees and forest. One tree in particular I loved was a large weeping willow down at the water's edge. While living there, it had become my nature-made tree swing. You could grab a clump of the long branches that reached to the ground and go running off the side and swing out into the water and drop. The stairs there were carved into the hill from the lake up to the house and made of real railroad ties, maybe a good twenty or more. Each side was filled with trees that stretched up higher than the two-story home and a sprawling beauty of lilies and ferns below. In comparison to our place in the city, it was a beautifully unkempt mansion surrounded by wildlife and adventure. I was looking forward to meeting new friends, and I had already spent most holidays and weekends visiting Grandma and Grandpa here growing up, either at their house or down at the lake property. This town, for me, already held most of my best childhood memories, and it was kind of neat to live where my mom grew up.

A few months after the move, I remember sitting on the couch, looking out at the lake through the big picture window in the second family room, the room without a TV. I was used to being able to go knock on any number of friends' doors to play, because most of them lived right next to me. The few new friends I had made at school now lived too far away to walk or even ride my bike. Bored, and unentertained by the gloom in the sky, at some point, I left the couch to take a seat on the floor and in front of a large bookcase. I remember it being filled with stacks of old family photo albums, lots of books, and a bunch of random small boxes that had not yet found a space in our new home. There was really no rhyme or reason to the organization, and I had no idea what most of it was, but it was an adventure I needed for the day.

At the bottom of one of the lower shelves was a large thin box that did not perfectly sit in its stack. It was square and made of a material that was linen-like, a faded pastel pink. When I pulled it out, I found it was labeled Baby Album. I assumed by the color that it was mine, and was pleased when I opened it to find that it was. I thumbed through all the pages with intrigue but I had no memories as it was from my earliest years. At the end of the album, inside the back cover, was a pocket. It kind of looked like a pocket you see at the library with a checkout card. Tucked inside was a browned, folded piece of paper. As I opened each fold, I couldn't believe what I ended up finding. It was my birth certificate. My eyes did not scan for a single moment, but instead focused on every bit of detail, every letter and every number without any urge to move on until I was fully satisfied with every detail consumed. I read line by line, learning for the first time where I was born, who my doctor was, what time, and then … there it was, his name filled in below "Father's Name."

And now here I am, more than two decades later, nervously about to tell my mom that I not only found him (once again), but have been talking with him, *and* I flew out to meet him.

The phone rings and Grandma answers, "Hello-oh?"

"Hi, Grandma."

"Oh, hi," she says, always with the "oh" drawn out and "hi" ending up-tone.

"Is Mom there?"

I hear only crackles of silence on the other end. I'm flipping nervously around my fingers the keyring dangling from the ignition on the dash. My car is still parked in the lot at work. I thought maybe I would need more time to make this decision after letting my father know, but now it's quite apparent that his response lit a fire in me. His words became my motivation and the self-assurance I needed.

"Hello?" Mom says.

"Hi! How are you?" I ask (we *are* classic).

"Oh, I'm alright," she sighs and then continues. "The car has been breaking down again and I can't get anywhere. Your brother is supposed to come over tomorrow and fix it. I'm just hoping I can afford it."

"Mom, that car is a money pit," I remind her. "Just like every car."

"I know, but it's all I can afford."

"I know.…"

"How was your trip?" she asks.

"It was okay. Well, actually, I have something really crazy to tell you.…"

"Yeah?"

"Mom," and then I pause. "What I'm about to tell you is something I never thought I'd ever say."

I take a deep breath and then slowly exhale, trying to relax. I turn the radio all the way off.

"Michelle?"

"Mom, I met my dad."

I audibly hear her gasp. And then I can hear her start to cry.

"You found him?" she asks. "Did you meet him in California?"

"I found him this summer, but I kept it all secret. I didn't … " I pause again, trying not to say too much until I can gauge her reaction. "I didn't know what would happen or how you may take it."

"Oh!" she pipes out quickly. "I am so happy you found him!"

"Really?" I ask for reassurance. "You are?"

"Of course, I am!" she exclaims, muffled by a growing sob. "Michelle," she reminds me, "you've been talking about him ever since you were a little girl!"

The next thirty minutes turn into one of the best conversations we've ever had. It was truthful, sincere, raw, and full of emotion. We shed tears and even laughed together—and that hasn't happened in a long while. When we end the call, I am almost in disbelief. Her response was not what I expected. I am feeling a sense of peace with her of which I've never felt before. Can I finally put to rest all of our discourses?

Like the little ten-year-old girl that I was, sitting on the floor with my newly discovered treasure and his name on my birth certificate, I can remember the confidence I had then in believing. I am ready for it. I am here to live it, breathe it, do it and own it, know it, and not ever give up. Like Ernest Hemmingway wrote, "Try to learn to breathe deeply, really taste the food when you eat, and when you sleep really to sleep. Try as much as possible to be wholly alive with all your might, and when you laugh, laugh like hell. And when you get angry, get good and angry. Try to be alive. You will be dead soon enough."

Chapter 14

Today is beautiful but really cold. It's a fall morning in D.C. and the leaves are sparse on the trees. Most of them are on the ground in colorful heaps, but others are still left dancing in the sky and blowing in the wind. I'm bundled in tall boots and a considerable layering of clothing. I have convincingly mastered the technique, growing up and surviving the cold winters of Northern Michigan. On the way out the door, I grab a favorite fur-lined coat, and a big knit scarf made of colorful yarn with big pom poms. Charlie's mom Marie and I are heading into the city.

We have one destination and it's just northeast of Capitol Hill, off Sixth Street and north of Florida Ave., D.C.'s hidden Italian store, A. Litteri.

We park in the alley and combine the lists of ingredients we each can recall by memory for Grandma JuJu's homemade spaghetti recipe. As we near the entrance, I'm a few steps ahead, so I pull open the surprisingly heavy painted door. I also have to pull them closed behind us. We're greeted within inches by a sales rack that extends high up to the ceiling from the floor, followed by incredibly narrow aisles with unreachable shelves that are only accessible by a wooden ladder on tracks.

Like a miniature maze, each corner you turn opens to a new hidden alley. Even after visiting a handful of times, I still find myself surprised by how much this tiny store holds. There's an entire aisle filled with bags and boxes of pasta in every color and shape imaginable. And there's a full row of balsamic and olive oils, and another with sauces and tomatoes; there's alfredo and marinara, pumpkin and vodka sauce, whole, peeled, crushed, and paste tomatoes, all in cans artfully stacked with colorful Italian labels.

We navigate our way back to the six-foot deli counter. Behind it stands a handsome young man with messy, long black hair and dark brown eyes, wearing a dirty red apron. He asks for our order and we point to the sweet and hot Italian sausage links, ordering six of each. While we wait, I grab a large twelve-ounce tub of fresh Romano and then a long, old-style baguette from under a sign that says it was freshly prepared this morning. Marie throws in the basket a jar of spiced olives and a few bottles of red wine. We grab another basket and fill it with tomatoes and pasta and check out with two cardboard boxes brimming full.

We're laughing now, walking back to the car, and talking about how awesome the rest of our day is going to be. Preparing this meal is just as much fun as eating it. It takes many hours and fills the house with amazing aromas, along with good conversation quenched with rich, red wine that so smoothly warms your soul.

We talk a lot about my father, the trip, and his sweet lady, Alice. I can't talk or think about them enough, so it is a very welcomed and exciting conversation and day. Later in the evening, there's a text message from Alice.

ALICE

> Your dad and I are wondering what you are doing for Christmas? We would like to fly you out again. You've spent every Christmas with your other family, how about this one you spend with us? ☺

This is exciting—my father wants to see me again! But then, I feel a pit in my stomach. Can we do Christmas?

The holiday is our one big trip to Michigan every year to see all our family, including my mom and best friends. Christmas is my absolute favorite and it's such a great time spending it back home. The ground is always frozen and covered in white snow that glows from holiday lights hanging in the trees and on house eves. All bundled up in furry boots and fuzzy hats, you feel as cozy outside as in the living room where you can find wood burning in the fireplace. As a family, on Christmas Eve, we line up the street with paper bags in the snow and light luminaries with everyone in the neighborhood. You can find every street full with families as the sun sets and the last bags are lit. Then, at night, all that lights the town are the glows from Christmas lights and the luminaries that line the roads. As if God brought down the sky for a night and lit the stars in our yards, the moment feels like magic and lighting the luminaries is one of my favorite holiday traditions.

It's time to prepare the table. The homemade spaghetti and sausage dinner is almost ready after cooking all day. I share the exciting but confusing news with Charlie. He can sense my struggle and suggests we pay for our own tickets and just go another time. We could always visit for New Year's, but I do a quick look online after the table is set and see those tickets are running $1,000 plus each. It's too expensive. Charlie suggests February when we will be in Vegas (I am there for work and Charlie is flying in to meet me for his 30th birthday). I agree, it's a good idea. We could take advantage of already being on the west coast, tagging on to the tail end of that trip, and then we would have more time to plan and budget for it too.

Pathetically, I yearn to hang out with my dad every chance I can get. I want to wake and sit in his kitchen with the sun pouring in over the hillside and sip our coffee over small talk. I want to spend the day carrying wood he needs to build a new bench in the backyard. I want to go for walks in the hills and read Shakespeare while he explains what it all means. I want to be his best friend. I want to make up for all the lost years. I want to be his daughter.

Then, Charlie changes his mind, saying, "Let's just do New Year's."

"Yesssssss!" Let's just do it. I excitedly look up from cleaning the counter to see Bernie perfectly perched, sitting in a chair at the dinner table with his head just above a plate. Charlie is oblivious, sitting next to him with his elbows on the table and hands up to his face, his eyes illuminated by his phone screen.

"Bernie!" I yell out after a giggle. "Get down from there!"

I dry my hands and grab my phone to snap a photo. Bernie has been with us for eight years now and has never done this. I share the pic and the good news with Alice. We're going to spend New Year's with them in San Diego!

Dinner is just as wonderful as the good news. The family's Italian recipe is the kind of delicious that is impossible to replicate without the special ingredients, hours of preparation, and love that goes into it. After cleaning up, we all move as slow as sloths with our overfull bellies to the family room to find a movie on TV. While they all scan and play movie trailers, I'm still hooked to my phone when I find an email and photo that comes in from my father.

. ♦ .

From: Nate Brunhoff

Date: Sunday, November 16, 2014

To: 'Maura'

Bcc: 'Michelle'

Subject: I wanted to share

this Garry Winogrand photo with you. After all these years it is still just incredibly powerful. You can put it on your desktop screen and blow it up to see the amazing composition. Three high-steppin girls, dressed to the nines, arriving on sunbeams. And there to the left, a chair ridden child with a cup for pennies between his knees. He is not in the sun. He is oblivious to the beautiful girls passing him by.

· ◆ ·

I am mesmerized by the photo. At first glance, it captures the mystique glamour and show lights of Hollywood. Then, your eyes settle, and you begin to notice everything else. All that hides outside of the lights. That is the true Hollywood I know. You see the little boy on the bench with his mother. He's looking over curiously to watch the girls walk by. But will they notice him or the poor man in the wheelchair right in front of them? Will they stop to offer him help or share a warm "hello"? Or will they be too preoccupied with their own lives and walk right by?

I witnessed this every day living in Hollywood. The only thing beautiful about that boulevard is how raw and real it is. A mirror of our own infatuation with things that don't really matter, our trivial downfalls and devastations. It's the place where the dream of fame and fortune is mostly fake and the only stars you see are on the sidewalks covered with dirt, trash, spit, and gum. The less fortunate are the only ones here that greet you on the street, asking you for change to spare or dressing to impersonate the famous for a $5 photo op.

The photographer, Garry Winogrand, truly captures the moment. These high-stepping ladies are real women and not actors, and so, too, is the boy who looks over with compassion. The "chair-ridden child" has his head sunken in his lap and is ignorant of the beautiful ladies walking by and so likely oblivious to anyone who may care. He is hidden in the shadows and yet the light is there; it's so close—a metaphor of Hollywood.

Life is hard, and even for those more fortunate than us. What we all have in common is we are all born and enter life with a choice of what kind it will be and what we will do with it. It is up to us to choose. And regardless of our paths, we each have a story, our own struggles, a life to live. How would you answer if someone were to ask, "How do you live yours?" With a sunken head? Or living vicariously, watching others? Or ignorant of others who need our compassion?

I hope to live in reflection. While I may strive to be perfect, I am not and do not always make the right choices. But I can always reflect on every moment. It is surely intended to be collected and refined. Maybe next time I can get it right or possibly even better. Like Frank Sinatra sings, "The best is yet to come."

· ◆ ·

From: Nate Brunhoff

Date: Sunday, November 16, 2014

To: 'Michelle'

Subject: Yeah tho I am emotionally secured to the dock on the bay

I have begun the book on Shakespeare which you so generously gifted me. Rarely if ever does one find amazing fluid and beautiful prose. It is clear Schoenbaum has been steeped in all manner of Elizabethan literature and yet has escaped the perils of scholarship.

Thank you for your kindness. This is fantastic text!

NB

· ◆ ·

After seeing this email, I can clearly see that he is engaged right now. I'm going to try to see if I can catch him live and send him a text.

· ◆ ·

> So glad you like the book and can't wait to see you again. Thanks again for hosting us for New Year's!

DAD

It's all good. Now you will be able to experience just how BORING we are.

Orange juice and bridge, anyone?

DAD

How about a little afternoon shuffleboard?

· ♦ ·

There's no doubt spending New Year's with him and Alice will be one of the best possible ends and beginnings to a year—even if that entails trading crochets and yelling at the TV. I upload the Garry Winogrand to my saved photos and close the phone, nudging Charlie with my foot. We wish everyone good night, fold and throw our blankets in a wicker basket by the couch, and call Bernie to head upstairs to bed.

Chapter 15

"Click." My lap belt snaps into place and I feel, oddly, the opposite of déjà vu. The navy-blue seats, narrow windows, and a tiny sprocket blowing air in my face is starting to feel more like a regular reoccurrence these days. Between travels for business and going home to see family in Michigan, meeting Dad in San Diego, or other personal adventures, I have been flying the friendly skies more frequently than ever. Now, yet another business trip to Denver. Last month Charlie and I were in Tampa with family for my 33rd birthday … and now that I think of it, I wish I was flying to the Sunshine State to play on the beach and enjoy cocktails and dancing at night. The morning of my birthday was like every other and I had walked out of our hotel room in my pajamas to have a cup of coffee with the girls outside. Our hotel was on the beach and our rooms were on the second story balcony. We were just a few doors down from each other. But that morning, I opened the door and walked into a big bundle of birthday balloons and wrapped presents. I couldn't believe my sleepy eyes. It was a really great birthday....

"Please buckle your seatbelts and turn off your electronic devices," a woman's voice interrupts on the intercom. "We're about to take flight."

A child cries from a row outside of first class and someone starts banging their knees into the back of my seat. I grab my coffee from between my legs and carefully squeeze it into the magazine pocket hanging on the back of the seat in front of me. I pull out my hot pink headphones, a *National Geographic* magazine, and three tabloids (always a guilty travel pleasure). Channing Tatum is starring in a new blockbuster, *Foxcatcher*, based on a true story, Sir Mix-A-Lot reveals that Jennifer Lopez was the inspiration for his hit "Baby Got Back," and Matthew McConaughey takes front cover of *People* magazine with a story about ten moments that changed his life—just seeing his face changes my life; so gorgeous.

"Captain says our flight will be three hours and thirty-four minutes," the voice on the intercom interrupts again and then continues with the usual set of instructions on how to use the oxygen mask and the floatation device under the seat.

"Would you like any snacks or something to drink?" the flight attendant says rolling and parking the beverage cart between seats.

I wonder … they can put a video screen in a headrest, plug outlets and charging stations in the seats, and connect to WiFi while in the air, but the flight attendants still deliver drinks and snacks out of an ancient and wildly oversized ice box?

She is in her mid to late sixties and still as charming as I imagine she would have been in her young twenties, when it was elite and popular to be an attractive flight attendant. Her pale skin is barely touched by age and elegantly painted with powder and light pink blush. Her golden blonde hair is tied up in a bun, giving her passengers full view of her ice blue eyes and dark eyelashes. She hands me a mini bottle of red wine. I crack open the seal and pour it in my plastic cup, selecting "shuffle all" on my iTunes. Sinatra is conveniently the first to serenade me with, "Come fly with me, let's fly, let's fly away."

We land a few hours later and I take the thirty-minute cab ride into the city. After check-in and dinner with work colleagues, I crawl into the pressed white sheets. I grab the dark chocolate wrapped in a Ritz Carlton gold foiled wrapper from the pillow next to me, turn off the bedside lamp, and roll to my side to watch the city lights blur into the night.

• ◆ •

JOURNAL ENTRY

November 21, 2014

Just before I left, I had texted my dad about my upcoming travels. He responded, "This is wonderful and cool in the extreme. Don't forget to send material to my email cuz I seldom carry my phone."

"Ok, I'll be sure to send you some material today," I texted back.

I sent him some "material"—as identified in subject line, and my email contained an image of swatches of material (colorful fabric).

It's my last day in Denver and he surprised me with a text this morning, "It's Friday, you may go home now...."

At this point, it's becoming rare not to have communication with him in some form, whether serious or funny (and mostly funny). His text was an awesome surprise. It made me smile.

· ✦ ·

I wish someone knew the secret to slowing down. I would indulge myself in every moment, not working.

Three nights, conferences, meetings, and dinners.... it all becomes one big blur, but my time in Denver did not prove to be unvaluable. I gained interesting insights on the hot new topic of "Big Data." It has become the latest obsession in marketing. The concept is most easily explained as the collection of customer demographics and insights to create a more customized, personal experience with a company. Our lives are consumed with technology and online experiences, and everyone's trying to capture pieces of our digital footprint. From a marketing standpoint, the challenge is how to collect and use this "data" to build a better relationship with our customers, helping to tailor their experience and break away from all the noise (or clutter). I still believe it's important to keep the most simplistic and traditional methods at your core—knowing and understanding your customer and showing them you care. They are not just a number, another "eyeball," or a statistic. We should challenge ourselves to learn and understand our customers on a real level, give our company a personality (a friend and a heartbeat), help them relate to us, and talk with them, not at them.

I finish packing my clothes back into my suitcase and snap a photo of the cityscape from my window. The sun is just rising. A foggy pink line separates the sky from the city below. Coors Field is to the left, high-rises made of glass stretch the skyline straight ahead, and a large cloud of smoke billows from a smoke stack in the distance. It's quite a spectacular view.

I grab the last of my things, including the manila envelope of the writings I received from Great Aunt Maura. I attach the pic of the city skyline to a text to my father and write, "View from my room this morning. Just finished reading the autobiography by Great Grandpa. He's so cool."

What a heritage, to be able to claim Edward Brunhoff as my great-grandfather! He was a world traveler, an inventor, a linguist, successful manufacturer, and an extremely respected citizen of Cincinnati, Ohio. He met and was acquainted with King Kalakaua and Princess Liliuokalani of Hawaii. Among his inventions were filing systems, self-feeding soldering irons with the gasoline in the handles, cigar cutters, and gate latches. I love to think there's a connection between his inventive business sense and my drive and ability in marketing.

Chapter 16

I arrive back to D.C. late, but it's Friday and there's still enough time to drop off a bag and pack up another to head to the cottage for the weekend. I fill a rinsed coffee tumbler with red wine and throw my briefcase in the back of the truck with hopes to catch up with work after being out of the office. I can't count the number of times I have attempted to catch up on work while I am at the cottage doing nothing, but to no avail, I have yet to open my briefcase while there. Maybe this time will be different?

As soon as we turn on the cottage street, Bernie's head perks up from napping and he starts whimpering. How he knows is a mystery. We turn on the gravel driveway and the cottage is lit up like a Christmas tree. Ah, my happy place. I love escaping the busy life.

A pair of old tennis shoes, cowboy boots, and a mess of work boots are lined up outside the door spotted with dried dirt and mud. Marie is already passed out on the couch with a half-filled glass of champagne sitting on the kitchen countertop behind her. We make our way down the hallway and unpack a few new things we brought in the room, adding to the already filled dresser drawers and closet. We have a few hours to unwind and both put on our comfies. I fill a glass with wine, grab a beer for him, and we head out to the garage. We pull out a few folding chairs stacked behind the smoker and open them to sit facing the woods and catch up on our week spent apart.

The entire weekend flies by fast, as we spend our time antiquing, cooking big meals, playing games, and sipping on tequila. It was successful fun and relaxation, and arriving back in the city, I laugh pulling out my briefcase … which I once again never opened.

After unpacking all travel bags, including from the trip to Colorado, I put a load in the laundry and pull out my laptop to start checking work emails. Starting from the most recent, I begin working away, reading, responding, and deleting, when I come across a new one from my father with a subject line that reads "Grt Grandpa B." Intrigued, I set aside work once again this weekend.

· ◆ ·

From: Nate Brunhoff

Date: Sunday, November 23, 2014

To: 'Michelle'

CC: 'Alice', 'Maura'

Subject: Grt Grandpa B

Yes, GGB was an awesome character. What is little known about him was that, in between gardening and inventing, he maintained a garret apartment for trysts. His favorite tryst was with a poetess named Alice Cary of Cincinnati, Ohio. Alice Cary (April 26, 1820 – February 12, 1871). http://en.wikipedia.org/wiki/Alice_Cary

You will recall GGB invented the cigar cutter. The story tangential to this is that the mayor of Cincinnati, Harry L. Gordon lived next door to GGB. http://en.wikipedia.org/wiki/Harry_L._Gordon

Gordon's Mulberry trees were as notorious for dropping berries on GGB's land and sidewalk as Gordon was known to be disdainful and arrogant. GGB repeatedly attempted to get an audience at the mayor's office to discuss the matter but Gordon refused to see him unless he "dressed up" and made himself presentable. So GGB took two Cuban cigars and sewed them, as epaulettes, onto a brown shirt and marched right in on Gordon demanding that he remove the overhanging branches or he, GGB, would cross-over and do a "self-help." Gordon was so incensed by this breach of conduct that he hired German labor (insult) and in two days erected a brick wall, using discarded broken brick. GGB retaliated by planting female Ginkgo Biloba trees at the wall so the orange-like fruit would fall on the Gordon side of the fence. The fruit of this tree smells somewhere between bad B.O. and sewer gas. http://temple-news.com/lifestyle/these-smelly-trees-force-you-to-leave/

GGB was also known for his wry if not questionable taste in literature and art, and was often given to writing off color lyrics; "There once was a toad name Maud," etc., etc., etc.

But, another unspoken adventure is this;

Late in his career he wrote a book of which there remains only one known copy written by Alice Cary under their pseudonyms. I hesitate to share it with you because of the Dad/Daughter thing and because it may disclose my own sense of dubious sophomoric humor, not to mention the response from Alice; "OMG! Omg! OMg!" ... and all that ...

How tedious.

Nonetheless

Have a nice day,

Dad

◦ ◆ ◦

I am sitting at the far corner of the large dining room table audibly laughing all by myself. I read his email again, and again. I clicked on the links and researched more. The patches of these missing stories from Great Grandpa Brunhoff's autobiography are so interesting. Can it be? I start to envision the theoretical tales and unwind into my own adventure. I ignore the rest of the emails and, instead, spend the next hour adding untrue tales that one may dare to believe for good entertainment.

◦ ◆ ◦

On November 23, 2014, at 7:03 PM, Michelle wrote (reply all):

Great Grandpa Brunhoff, what a character he was. I can envision myself as him, sitting in a big leather chair with my feet propped up on a rich, mahogany desk. I light up a cigar and invite my guest in.

I'll take notice to a loose string on his pressed uniform and casually approach him to release it with a quick snap of my impressive cigar cutter. As his questions close, I'll disclose that a frightening Chinese crested dog has been running rampant on our streets pretending to be a rat disguised in a wig and creating fear in the hearts of children. The creature has trespassed my land and crapped in my beautiful garden every day until that smelly Ginkgo tree appeared. The convincing tale will reveal that this tree, which is native to China, is more than just a curious botanical anomaly but is a sacred manifestation of yin and yang and a symbolism of longevity. The hands to end this tree's life will also bare [sic] the same fate.

Besides his scandalous endeavors hiding trysts in the attic (geez oh peetz, I hope Great Grandma found out and beat the **** out of him!), I am so captivated by his smart and mischievous ways. A witful and charming man, he is adventurous and enjoys a life living on the edge not one within the confines of political correctness ...

I knew it. Oh ye who writes, "I am emotionally secured to the dock on the bay," jump ship and get your *** out here to sea!

xoxo,

Little Wing

· ◆ ·

I'm really starting to enjoy exchanging emails with my father. He inspires me to think "outside the box" and write more creatively, with intent and purpose still, but with a sense of entertainment for those reading. It's not writing for myself in my journal, nor is it writing for a professor who torments you all semester to write "how they like it" to get the A you know you deserve—the reason I changed my degree from Journalism. I was over it. I did it all through high school, and had started it all over again in college. I couldn't imagine living the rest of my life writing only how others thought I should, with every boss (or editor) having a differing opinion on what style they "think" is correct. Writing is an art. It should be a very personal thing. It's a personality. It would be better to learn how to hone in and perfect the writing style that is true to you, instead of trying to change it into something that aligns with someone else's.

The next morning, I find myself still reflecting on our stories while getting ready and making coffee before work. Maybe this is, or will be, the one thing I learn as a daughter from her father, how to write?

· ◆ ·

From: 'Maura'

Date: Monday, November 24, 2014

To: 'Michelle', Nate Brunhoff, 'Alice'

Subject: Grt Grandpa B

I am really amused by what grandfather is becoming! Shall I tell you my memories of him? He died when I was about 3 or 4, so not much remains. He had a conservatory/greenhouse room in his big Victorian house, where he grew exotic things, like huge sweet lemons and very big leafy things and some flowering things that must have been orchids. One did not cross grandfather. He was severe and had a temper, but he was also kind and loving. When big events came along, he was the one in charge. (I get this from family lore, maybe from my father.) He was one of the founders of the Cincinnati Philharmonic Symphony and every year (in Avondale section of Cincinnati) he gave a very big party to honor the musicians. At the house was champagne and at the gazebo in the garden was beer. There was music hired for the occasion. He did all the planning. Grandmother was expected to buy a beautiful gown and come down the curving staircase for her grand entrance. But nothing more was expected of her. We had lovely Christmas dinners at their house (in the village of Wyoming), another very large Victorian house. The huge tree was decorated with the old fashioned large, heavy ball ornaments and candles were lit on the branches weighted down by heavy balls. They had a cook, serving maid, house maid, laundress, and gardeners.

So Alice Carey did not show up, nor his authorship under pseudonym! He sent each of his 6 daughters on an extended European tour after they finished their schooling.

I would not find it hard to believe any of these stories about him (as evidence, you cad, you, Nate) and I think he would love them too!

Love and hugs,

M

⋅ ◆ ⋅

Wait a second.... Is he really that full of hogwash and completely made up that entire story? Even all the background links! I am laughing and shaking my head at the same time. Unbelievable, he pulled one over on me.

. ♦ .

> Wait a second ... was that whole email about GGB fiction?

DAD

Yes. It fooled Maura too. I didn't catch her in time and she sent it off to Jenny.

ALICE

Yep. Your Dad is a weirdo. :) :) Aunt Maura relayed the whole story to family. She cracked up when he told her he made it up.

> OMG you had me fooled. Oh you are good. Crafty ...

DAD

Thank u

. ♦ .

I respond to Great Aunt Maura's non-fictional email to thank her for the factual story and also share a bit of history on "how I found on my father" (insert evil laugh—muah-ha-ha-ha).

. ♦ .

On November 24, 2014, at 5:12 PM, Michelle wrote (reply all):

Thank you, Aunt Maura, for the FACTUAL information. I will add these notes to my biography file and pull OUT the latter.

While we are all together though, this may be a good time to share some interesting history I found on my father.

NATHAN H. BRUNHOFF ('48)

Nathan is a large, green, physically intimidating Ogre who has lived mysteriously in Escondido, California for the past 59 years. Much of his childhood was remiss, and in true Ogre tradition, Nathan was sent away by his parents on his seventh birthday. The years that followed he was spotted traveling alone being screamed at or teased by passers-by. After scaring away the angry mobs, he finally had arrived to his new home, a swamp. Though surly, misanthropic, and venomously cranky, underneath the thick, mucus-colored skin, Nathan was as peaceful and loving as a bunny and didn't want to hurt anyone. He just wanted to live his life in solitude and be left alone.

When Nathan finally broke into adulthood, he unfortunately did not mature and was still found constantly scaring off villagers "roaring" at them. He became more insightful and practiced the study of the nature of onions and their layers. The community became to know him as the Ogre who lives in the big, green murky swamp. It contained small and big ponds of muddy water along with geysers that squirted mud a mile high.

In present day, Nathan still has a problem socializing due to the fact that he is an Ogre, but the human society has since come to learn, understand and accept Nathan for his indifferences. Ogre Nathan is now recognized as a folklore hero and people travel from near and far to see him, disturbing him even more.

Tedious, indeed.

It makes me want to "SHREEK"! ;)

. ♦ .

On November 25, 2014, at 11:42 AM, Nathan wrote (reply all):

Dear squirmy scum:

Thank you for your exposing expose. I'll have you know I spent years, yeah, nay, decades keeping the infant population to a minimum in Escondido — especially those with shingles. Now I shall have to find another swamp bridge under which to live and play old Joan Baez tunes (insert link to "500 Miles" video by Joan Baez).

Yours truly, working for scale,

NB (Troll in Residence)

Chapter 17

Thanksgiving always ends feeling fat. For Charlie and me, it's not only a weekend to stuff our face but also our wedding anniversary.

Our love has never been perfect, but I guess that's the beauty of it? It's true, it's real, and at times it has hurt very much. We have always said to one another, "So stupid much," because it feels like love makes you stupid, that and I do love him "so stupid" much.

We have been together for nearly ten years now, married for four. We arrived at the cottage on Wednesday and both surprised each other with small gifts that were EXACTLY the same—a card, new music album, and some candy, mine savory and his sweet. We reminisced on that day we said "I Do" in Puerto Vallarta (with a donkey's vibrant, low and long "hee haw" interrupting the pastor and us as we exchanged vows).

For some reason, we were meant to be together in this time and space. For better or for worse was our vow, and while I arguably would have admitted it may be for the worse, it didn't matter. We were in love and we got married. How can you not believe that true love will always win? That's where my heart has always been.

In the movie *Her*, actress Amy Adams says, "I think anyone who falls in love is a freak. It's a crazy thing to do. It's kind of like a form of socially acceptable insanity."

The weather at the cottage this weekend is cool, but not chilly enough to stop us from having an outdoor campfire. Looking out the window down to the lakeside, Marie and I catch Martin lighting a fire. He's wearing his favorite old fleece-lined flannel jacket, a tattered ball cap, and rugged leather boots. We prep some cocktails, top off a full shaker for shots, throw it in the cooler and fill the rest with beer, wine, glasses, and snacks. We dress ourselves warmly and walk down to the beach.

The stories around the fire are always my favorite part of the day. Tonight, Martin tells us about his recent travels to Africa. His current contract work is to help the tribes of Kenya understand what kind of systems their government (or what we would call our local police) can set in place to prevent the tribes from continuing to steal cows from one another. It seems very third world, unreal and un-relatable, to hear that there are native tribes fighting like teenagers and sneaking out in the midnight hour to steal cattle. However, the tribes' attempts are getting more and more violent, he says, and also less discreet. The health of their culture and humanity is at an all-time low and it's impacting the survival of the tribe families. They hope that using the technology of drones will provide their government with remote-controlled, monitoring flying devices that can easily travel to the remote areas and help capture the thieves where and when they are least expecting it, from high above and with video surveillance.

After a few hours of storytelling around the fire, the dark of night rolls in with the moon and stars hidden behind in a thick, wet fog over the lake. Back in the house, we had lit another fire in the fireplace. At each side is a set of wet boots and work gloves from Marie and me working in the garden earlier. There is also sour dough bread which is now rising, placed carefully in front of the fire in a thick metal tray. There's something romantic about the scene that warms my heart. My phone dings and I find a message from Uncle Frank saying, "A very Happy Thanksgiving!"

I click open the notification to see what he sent and find the greeting was not just to me but to the entire Brunhoff family. Wow, very cool. Does this mean I'm official, part of the family? It's signed with "Roasted nuts and toes," so I quickly chime in and respond all, "and warm buns!" with a photo of the bread rising in front of the fireplace.

◦ ◆ ◦

JOURNAL ENTRY

November 30, 2014

I walked outside tonight for a breath of fresh air when I looked up to see a net dropped in the sky above. The stars were glowing bright in a cloak of angel dust. I stood there for moments mystified by the magic under the moonlight, before I turned my gaze down to the lake.... Then, falling right in front of me, twinkling and lit only by the stars and moon, was a single, small, and perfectly shaped brown oak leaf that elegantly twisted and danced before it finally dropped at my feet.

When I leaned down to pick it up, I was reminded we can gracefully enjoy the fall.

· ◆ ·

It's Black Friday today and Marie and I decide we're going to partake in the festivities country-style. Instead of trying to beat off the crowds for the best deals at the mall, we'll be spending our day fighting off scavengers, driving from town to town hunting for antiques and treasures.

Just south on Route 1 to Richmond we find a treasure trove. It's a huge, old, white plantation home with green trim and metal signs that take up most of the road side. It's set in about a mile from the highway and has a large collection of discolored, rusty, wood and metal objects spread throughout its front lawn. A sign saying "Squashapenny" hangs above the house entrance. We park the car and make our way through the maze of objects in the yard.

Inside, many aisles are filled with old advertising pieces from Virginia-owned companies. Out of curiosity, we inquire with the store clerk and learn every company in Virginia that is 50 to 100 years old has a stake in their merchandising. While it's fun to browse the advertising knickknacks and carnival of colors, it really is *cold* in this store. The only thing that heats the entire place is a cast iron wood stove set in the middle of the first floor. It's impressively large and stands much taller and wider than I, but the radius it heats is arguably small. I stand close to it and keep my backside toasty while looking around the shelves nearby. I start to feel inspired, and I wonder … if this store is dedicated to the history of Virginia's local companies, maybe there's an antique store that carries items from Great Grandpa B's company in Cincinnati, Brunhoff Manufacturing Company.

I can't find much interest in any of the antiques the rest of the day. The sun is setting when we pull back in the driveway and the dogs greet us as soon as we open the truck doors. I can't imagine being so ridiculously excited every time someone comes home. Even if we're gone for only a few moments, how do they have *so much* joy *every time* we return? Crazy dogs.

Only a single site (or posting) populates my search results for items connected with Brunhoff Manufacturing. It says, "Art Nouveau Metalware Coin Tray (or Ash Tray)" with a description of, "Est. 1930's, made of pewter featuring a woman with swirling hair and adorned with a lizard at its crest." I click the link to see an image. It is very retro, appears Greek, and is stamped with the company name and numbers 303. The numbers remind me of my age (33). I hit "Add to Cart." In checkout, I have an opportunity to leave a note, so I type, "Please ship with care. This is a special gift for my father whose name is Brunhoff. ;) Happy holidays!"

Two days later, I receive an email from the company.

. ♦ .

From: 'Bridget'

Date: Monday, December 1, 2014

To: 'Michelle'

Subject: Vintage Brunhoff Coin Tray - Order #1272408

Hello Michelle,

Sorry for the delay in responding to your order, but the Thanksgiving holiday meant more time with family, less with my shop. Thank you so much for shopping at Refined Vintage. I hope your Dad will enjoy using the vintage metal ware coin tray. It is very unique, it is so cool that it has his name on it, any relation to the manufacturer? Will he be using it as a coin or ash tray, or purely decorative? Just curious. Don't worry it will be wrapped very well , it is a heavy metal, it would take a lot to damage it. Your order will be shipped today Dec. 1, 2014 ...

Thank you once again for supporting small business owners in Michigan.

Kind Regards,

Bridget

. ♦ .

On December 1, 2014, at 12:26 PM, Michelle wrote:

Hi Bridget,

This may sound like a fictional story, but I promise you it is very true. I most recently found and connected with my father and have learned that the founder of Brunhoff Manufacturing is my great grandfather—my father's name is third generation. I love antiquing and this weekend I had visited a shop in Virginia that was filled with old manufacturer merchandise native to the state ... this is what gave me the idea to see if I could find something connected to the old family company. Your piece is the only one I could find online. It will make a perfect gift for our first Christmas together!

The happiest of holidays to you and your family!

Michelle

· ◆ ·

On December 1, 2014, at 7:12 PM, Bridget wrote:

Michelle,

Your story touched my heart.

I am so happy that you found this Brunhoff item for him, it was discovered at an estate sale. It was unusual and I was intrigued by it. I wonder if he will be able to tell you more about it. It was very difficult to research, not a lot of information about this particular item, but I shared what I discovered in the listing. Now that I know your story, I am sure he will love this special gift. I hope you all enjoy a beautiful Holiday season. I will be sure to contact you if I discover any other Brunhoff items. Thanks so much for responding to my email, I love selling vintage and when I get to know the whole story it's the best!

Take care.

Chapter 18

I haven't heard from him (my dad) since Thanksgiving and am worried. Ugh, I hate it. I can't help but have fleeting thoughts of despair. I am nervous with his illness and my confidence is being tested. I know as soon as I hear from him I will be fine again.

I am constantly thinking of him. It's quite atrocious, really. For every minute of a day, he consumes at least half. And often times, it's followed with my own discourse on the day's conversation. Do I love him or am I in love with the thought of him? Is this an obsession? Quite convincingly it is feeling like one.

I've lived thirty-two years without him. Thoughts of him then were fewer and farther between and made up of only dreams and an unreality. Now he is here, and I'm filling in the lost pieces of my past, consciously working double time trying to make up for the all the years lost. Those feelings are compounded with the enjoyment of finally having a father. I really hope that as time builds, I can let go a little and it will feel less overwhelming.

In comparison, I talk to my mother only once every month. The love and appreciation is there—she's my mother—but you sure won't catch me daydreaming about what she's doing and wondering when I will hear from her again.

· ◆ ·

From: Nate Brunhoff

Date: Tuesday, December 2, 2014

To: 'Michelle'

Subject: Shakespeare Classes

Teach you Bard? Yes of course. Please set aside a decade or two.

The easiest and fastest way to find the humor and beauty of the Bard is to go to plays—wherever you are. Here in San Diego we have the Globe Theater.

Here is a good quick review to stun your friends and intimidate your enemies: http://en.wikipedia.org/wiki/Globe_Theatre

Unlike the sonnets, the plays are Performance. Sonnets are to be read. In our digital age, we have come to expect everything to be on video, a performance. When sonnets are embedded in a play, the play stops dead for the recitation.

Always see a play first. Then read the annotated text. Then see the play again. Merchant of Venice is most often taught because the plot and language is most accessible. The histories are most difficult ... esoteric. The tragedies are brooding and dark and not much fun.

When you or I or anyone watches a Shakespeare play, the first 15 minutes are lost. It takes that long for real people to switch gears and begin to hear the language. But it's all there.

The other advantage of a performance is that we, the audience, can pick up clues from the body language of the actors as to the intent and content of the language, and the plot.

A well-acted comedy is still, centuries later, very very funny.

There are almost zero DVD performances of Shakespeare and most that I have are really tedious tiny stage performances. I don't know why.

I hope you and Charlie have a really good xmas.

See ya'll in a couple of weeks.

* ◆ *

On December 3, 2014, at 8:45 AM, Michelle wrote:

Morning,

I hope you and Alice had a nice Thanksgiving holiday. And how was Sir Chef? Was he as spectacular as our evening with him in November? I'm still salivating over that strange bowl of delicious mushrooms that came in shapes and sizes and tastes that we had all never experienced before.

I am recovering from our fun holiday weekend of eating and drinking, playing Yahtzee and dancing to my new Taylor Swift CD. She indeed took a turn from her country roots but I'm liking it.

As for Shakespeare, I was not aware there are comical plays. And who wouldn't enjoy those far more than what school teaches? In one ear and out the next is how I learned the ones they taught. The text and language is so foreign and no one took the time to help me understand the meaning of it all.

What I had envisioned was you sharing a few favorite quotes, or short stories, with me. My novice attempts to decode the text to be slashed up by your red marker. I have never known anyone with such great knowledge of Shakespeare, and ... I would love to take advantage of this opportunity to learn a little.

But then again do we need a decade or two? I hope you're planning to hang around for a long time. I'm cool with taking forever.

xoxo

- ◆ -

On December 3, 2014, at 1:35 PM, Nate wrote:

blip.

Have you ever been lost in a new city or new place and you suddenly decide to put your brain on auto pilot (get out of your own way) relax and bingo you have found your way?

The same is true with the language of Shakespeare. It was meant to be performed, meant to be heard. So when you attend a play you can relax and listen. Don't decode it. "Get out of your own way" and you will hear it. Even though it is a different language it is not that distant. For example, if you were to take someone from the Louisiana bay and put them in the same room with someone from Maine ... same language but it will take a while before the one can understand the other. Don't THINK about it. Step aside and let it flow and you will hear it.

Coming back to a play on paper, after you have "heard" it—seeing it in text will make sense because, like music, it is in your head. Now you can read the annotations and see the subtle and patent puns and see the etymology of the language. The plot will lift off the pages.

Remember, Shakespeare was intended to be performed. He was the YouTube of his time and it still works. So, don't take it seriously. Just kick back and let it flow.

West Coast Dude

(pat the bear, kiss Charlie, dance the dance)

‹ ♦ ›

It's Friday night. Thank goodness. It's been a week and my wine is poured before I even take off my coat. After a few sips, I pull it off and toss it on the chair. I start pulling the groceries picked up on my way home out of their paper sack. All picked fresh for tonight's dinner. We're not going out, and it's one of my favorite nights in. I turn on some Sinatra, light a few musky scented vanilla candles, turn the fireplace on, and pull out a cutting board to begin laying the groundwork for a delicious meal. Little do I know, I am in for a surprise and an acorn squash is going to get the best of me.

I chop the mushrooms first, and then try my best to not touch the garlic while mincing it. I hate the way it makes my fingers stink. I throw them both in a sauté pan coated with olive oil and top it with fresh parsley and onions before turning the stove on to medium heat. I throw my hands under the running water behind me and slide my fingers that touched the garlic on the sink's stainless steel. It's an old trick to get rid of the garlic that otherwise sticks to your skin. I'm not sure how it works, but I'm sure thankful it does.

The filet is marinating while I prepare the vegetable. With my left hand on the acorn squash, I pull a large knife from the wooden block with the other. I tip the point of the knife towards the cutting board and pull the knife back and down, hard and fast. The stalk unexpectedly snaps and sends the acorn squash flying like a bomb—and without warning, I "punch" the empty cutting board. Reacting quickly, I try to catch it, to prevent it from breaking the glassware or hitting the floor and exploding. All the while, completely missing the trickles of blood I am leaving everywhere. I look astonishedly at the saved acorn in my hands with triumph, but feel immediate defeat once I notice the disturbing mess of blood all around me. In horrified panic, I set the squash down and rinse and wrap my hand, grabbing a soapy cloth to wash it up.

Mess cleaned and cuts tended to, I finish the rest of dinner. The stupid squash ends up taking nearly an hour before it is finally cooked all the way through. With the rest of the dinner sitting at the table, I pull the squash out. It looks like a golden bowl of butter with maple syrup and cinnamon glazing its sides. I scoop the squash out of its shell and into a serving bowl. Everything looks beautiful and perfect. It just took way too long (and nearly killed me)!

Waiting for Charlie to come down from upstairs, I sneak a spoonful in my mouth and, "ACK!" I can't believe it. It's sour and chalky! It's a bad squash....? You have to be kidding me. Ugh.

Marie walks in and catches the look of horror and disgust on my face. I fill her in on the wartime events with my squash and she gets a good laugh. She comforts my humiliation with a story of her own, the "killer avocado." In a similar turn of events, while living in Abu Dhabi, she attempted to split an avocado in half with a knife as she always does. She was in a hurry but had also cut *many* avocadoes in her lifetime. She picked up the side with the pit into the palm of her hand and with the pit facing up, she dropped the knife, but the knife slipped and dropped right into her hand. Instead of stabbing the pit to pull it from the avocado, she stabbed her own hand! Her battle ended with a visit to the hospital.

With a bit of salvaged dignity and only a "dinged" hand, I'm able to enjoy the rest of dinner with Charlie.

On Saturday morning, I wake to a drizzly patter on the window pane. It's dreary and cold outside. Marie and I decide over morning coffee that we'll warm up our spirits with a drive to our favorite Amish bakery, a booth at the Hughesville Market in southern Maryland. It's nearly a two-hour drive with traffic both ways, but absolutely worth it for possibly the best rolls and baked goods I've ever had.

Great, the booth is open! The Amish woman is dressed in all black and wearing a white bonnet that holds back her long, graying hair. She's placing more baked goods out on a table in front of her booth, hidden from the rain under an awning. We share our excitement and pick up speed walking. I want to run and hug this woman, I am so happy! There are fresh rolls, loaves of cinnamon raisin bread topped with icing, baked pies of almost every flavor, double-layer carrot cake, banana cake, tubs of homemade butter and jars of jams, trays filled with chocolate sweets, and so much more. We load up four grocery bags full and thank her for making such delicious goods that we drove so far for.

On our way back to the truck, we stop at a few other shops looking for treasures. The final booth we stop at has an old pin-up girl sign that reads, "Gals no shirt—Free Drinks." Marie thinks it will be fun to pin it up at the boat house with all her other signs and grabs it. We walk up to the counter when "Grammie" encourages us to walk around and she shows us *everything* she has. She is full of personality and (very obviously) wearing a big blonde wig. She is making us laugh with her charismatic, shameless, and comical banter. She insists that we call her "Grammie" and tells us she is 104 years old, but in fact there is no way this is true. I admire her wit. I mean, why not? I think I'll do the same when I get "that old."

• ◆ •

JOURNAL ENTRY

December 7, 2014

In a truck filled with delicious home-baked goods and special treasures today, Marie and I told stories and laughed a ridiculous amount of times on the way home from the farmer/Amish market. It was a great day. We found ourselves with an unexpected adventure.

And when we pulled in the drive and started to unload our purchases, the best treasure of all came from the mailbox. The gift I had found online for Dad had arrived! The antique pewter coin tray is even cooler in person. It's in near mint condition, and it's really heavy in weight, slightly larger in hand than I expected too. My favorite is when you flip it over and see the company seal imprinted in the metal, "Advertising Specialties. The Brunhoff Mfg. Co. Cinti O."

I hope he loves it.

Chapter 19

From: 'Jenny'

Date: Sunday, December 7, 2014

To: 'Michelle'

CC: 'Maura'

Subject: Family

All the family clan plans to be there for our get together on Jan 11.

We'll go to the Lake Barcroft house.

JENNY

* ◆ *

On December 8, 2014, at 7:25 AM, Michelle wrote (reply all):

Fantastic news! Thanks so much for doing this, Jenny. I'm so excited! Do we know what time to plan on and the home address? Also, should I bring anything?

Curious ... you say "all the family clan" ... How many of them are there?

Michelle

* ◆ *

On December 8, 2014, at 2:32 PM, Maura wrote (reply all):

6 children and 4 spouses. Judith is a "thalidomide" child (she's 43 now), severely retarded and deformed, and very sweet! She has a long-time caretaker named Isabel. Judith actually owns the house and Sarah and

Don live there and take care of the premises. Judith loves to swim, so there is an indoor/outdoor pool and then another pool down near the lake. The home is in Falls Church just outside of Washington, D.C. in Virginia (on Lake Barcroft).

While Jenny is at work on Monday and Tuesday, Jan 12 and 13, I'll be hanging out at her apartment. I wonder if you'd have time for lunch one of those days?

Have fun in Escondido for New Years!

Lots of love,

Maura

· ◆ ·

I hadn't heard from Jenny since we met in Old Town, Alexandria, but Great Aunt Maura had made mention of a reunion of sorts coming up in January. She also said she'd be in town before an astrologist conference in New York. She promised Jenny would contact me to let me know the dates for the family get-together, so I was thankful to hear from both of them again.

I'm nervous but excited to meet more family. It's nuts that they live here in D.C. and I am here, too. I Google the address. Their home is only 15–20 minutes away. I'm familiar with the area because we do a lot of home sales in Falls Church at the real estate company where I work. It's also close to our main office in McLean, where I'm headquartered. Also crazy, I had no idea (nor can I picture) there's a lake there—it must be hidden! And knowing what I know about the real estate in this area, the price point on this home has to be ridiculous, especially on a lake.

After work, Charlie and I jump in the truck for an evening drive. Sometimes we do it just to get away, but this time we're going to check out the area and see if we can find this "lake." Then we'll grab some dinner from one of our favorite spots on the way home. I pour a roadie (wine in my coffee tumbler) and throw Bernie in the back before Charlie pops it in drive and turns up the radio.

At a stop light, I pull out my phone and scroll through the latest alerts. I had been so busy with both work and the company the past few days that I hadn't checked any messages. Oh hey! Maybe I am finally over the butterflies and can now have a (somewhat) normal relationship with my father. I last messaged him a few days ago about a really strange dream I had. I rarely ever remember my dreams, but this one I did and he was in it. It was so vivid. Every detail I can still see and play like a movie reel in photographic memory.

I was in a train station, or some type of subway-metro stop, that was open to the outside but covered by large, industrial roofing and rows of train tracks running parallel to my right. There were lots of people, they were blurred, and then a boy approached me claiming to be my brother. He looked awfully familiar and his name was Charlie. I must point out that this was not odd at all in my dream. I learned that he was another estranged child of my father. Then my father arrived and the awkward introductions were exchanged. I pulled him aside and asked how he had found a son and how does he know it's his child? Of course, he riddled himself out of it, even in my dream. Then the boy, Charlie, started acting rude and naughty with both us and nearly everyone around us. My father pulled out a broken cigarette. It was broken in length, but also had a crack as if it had snapped right above the filter. I watched him bring it up to his mouth and wanted to scold him, but I never did. Instead, I furiously watched him try to light it, repeatedly, over and over again. He hadn't realized the butt was snapped and cracked from the rest of the cigarette and that it would be nearly impossible to light. He continued and ended up lighting the lighter on fire and burning the plastic. A thick film of ash and black soot covered his face. Then, a loud RINNNNG ... RINNNNNG ...

The ring is what startled me awake. Charlie changes his alarm ring tone nearly every month and he always picks the most obnoxious, ridiculous tones, thinking it will help wake him up. It never does and it *always* wakes me up!

"It's going to be right around here," Charlie says at a stoplight that just turned green.

"Whoa!" I see the results of my search for local real estate for sale.

"What?" Charlie asks, looking around cautiously, lightly stepping on the brakes.

"No, sorry," I apologize for startling him and look back down to my phone. "It's the home values of everything around us right now. They are all multi-million dollar homes."

We're both familiar with Michigan where homes on the water are everywhere, and many of them are very large in size and beautiful—what we call McMansions, but the price tags are small. We throw our heads back, looking out our windows in disbelief.

In a similar light, I can't help but continue to be shocked by the wealth that seems to come from my father's family. I recognize, again, that I'm grateful for being raised humbly and that I can appreciate the comparably smaller things in life. I'd also like to hope that I would still feel the same if I was raised with marble floors below my feet.

We drive by the home and it's nice, from what we can see from the road. Modest and classy, it is a decent size home on the waterfront. It's a traditional home, not "exceptional." D.C. in general is an old city, as is this area, so the homes can often reflect dated eras and old money.

On the way home, we stop at Jersey Mike's. As soon as you step in the door, the smells flood in and so do the memories of summertime. Nearly every night, after our summer softball league, Charlie and I would stop here to grab a sub and fries. We both grab our sodas and wait in line to get called to the counter.

"Hey, want to sit at the bar and have a glass of wine and a beer while we wait?" I ask Charlie after we place our order.

Normally he'd say no, but tonight he actually agrees! We used to do stuff like this all the time but now we rarely have a night out with just us, ever since we moved in with his parents. It's nothing special about this place or the night, but it's just sitting here in this moment that I feel happy. It's always the little things. We enjoy our drinks and original Italian subs with oil and vinegar and cracked pepper.

⋅ ◆ ⋅

From: 'Michelle'

Date: Wednesday, December 10, 2014

To: Nate Brunhoff

Subject: You're so quiet over there ...

How are you doing? My dream freak you out? It was pretty scary! LOL ;)

Thinking of you ...

⋅ ◆ ⋅

On December 10, 2014, at 8:22 PM, Nate wrote:

Oops. No, no, your dream did not freak me out in the least. In fact, I liked it.

One of my tenants broke the lease and did an NSF on me after I cut her a break on the deposits to help her out. I cut her a break twice on seriously late rent (two months) to help her out, put in new sink faucets, two air conditioners to make her comfortable, new blinds in the bedroom and more ...

So now I have to put on my legal beagle hat. We've had this apartment building for 15 years and I have never had a problem.

I told her not to **** with me ...

And I have been pinned down by Nazi troops here in the small village of Bahhiteme AND I have had to spend time consoling Alice when she gets 7,000 or less on Wurdle [sic]. A living LifeTime movie.

Not to mention ... well, just stuff I guess. I promise not to be so self-centered ...

NB

＊ ◆ ＊

On December 11, 2014, at 10:55 AM, Michelle wrote:

No, no—please, be self-absorbed.

I know now that if I don't hear from you in a few days, I don't need to be worried or that you've fallen somewhere and can't get up. But I did want to make sure all was OK. Now if a few days pass, I can know you are off screaming in landlord land telling residents, "BITE ME!" This is far better than anything I imagined.

That woman sounds like she is in a very unhappy place in life. It's too bad that she can't recognize your helping hand. Thankfully, Karma is a beautiful thing. It will all work out. It always does.

Sending good thoughts your way—for today to be a good day.

xo

＊ ◆ ＊

And then there are the not-so-little things....

A black Mercedes with tinted windows and shining chrome trim pulls up in front of the townhouse. I finish the last hit of my cigarette while the driver pulls to a stop and opens his door. A sharply dressed man wearing an all-black suit, black collared shirt, and shining shoes, steps out and walks towards Charlie and me. He has a handsome smile on his face. He greets each of us personally, with impeccable manners, and then grabs our suitcases only to reel them to the side. He walks us both to the car and opens our doors, then goes back to grab the luggage to stow it in the trunk. I see him struggle a bit with mine, watching in the side mirror. I'm terrible—I packed *a lot*. I have with me all my best jewelry and attire, and I pulled out extra cash today to go shopping in the city. We're celebrating our four-year wedding anniversary (together now for over nine years) and are staying in Georgetown. We've explored this part of the city together many times now, and it's one of our favorites, but this will be our first overnight stay in downtown D.C.

Seated in the luxurious, large-stitched, black leather seats, we pop a champagne bottle and pour our glasses to the rim. By the time we arrive downtown, we both hug the driver goodbye as though he's already a good friend. And with our suitcases in tow behind us, we look at one another as though we're giving a high five.

"This is our time!" I exclaim in excitement, throwing my bags on the bed. "We can do WHAT-EV-ER we want.... sooo exciting!"

Our room has a full kitchen, a living room, and a bedroom. I pour a glass of wine, looking around, take a delighted sip and realize, I miss this. Our home in Michigan was so nice and it was all ours. I could decorate and set and move things as I pleased. I could walk around naked, sing and dance, whatever I wanted, whenever I wanted. It was all mine and I could be me.

I sneak away into the bathroom to throw on some sexy lingerie and then quietly tip toe back to the doorway of the living room where Charlie is sitting. He notices me right away and runs towards me as though he had never seen me dressed in a sexy ensemble. He picks me up and carries me to the bed. I love him so much.

We spend the next few hours in the room having fun before heading out to walk the now darkly lit streets of Georgetown. A few blocks away, we find a quaint French restaurant called Petit Plats. We both agree, this is the place, and walk in to get dinner. We order deliciously expensive and smooth, buttery red wine and excitedly comment on nearly every bite of our filet mignons. It is absolute decadence. We order chocolate crepes to-go and take the long way back to the hotel, walking through a park under the starlit sky, feeling the energy of the city.

The next morning, I open my eyes for the first time and look over to the alarm clock on the nightstand. It's 11:15. Charlie is still sound asleep. I avoid waking him and quietly roll out of bed to get in the shower and start getting ready for the day. He sleeps until nearly one!

"Our batteries should be recharged now," he says rolling over and then grabbing me at the bedside to pull me back into bed.

We lie there wrapped in each other arms without an agenda and without parents downstairs. I'm not worried about the business and am not thinking about work. This is our weekend.

We start at a cute café, continuing conversation from last night, and then spend the rest of the day walking around and exploring. We go shopping, we watch the baseball game on a rooftop bar, and then we find ourselves on another late-night walk to find dinner.

I open up tonight, finally confessing to him the emotions I have been experiencing, the rawness and embarrassingly vulnerable feelings I've had during this time of finding and exploring a new relationship with my father. It has all been a bit overwhelming. Of course, I throw in a validating excuse for my own redemption, but it's Charlie's response that melts my heart.

"Michelle, it's awesome that you have so many unbelievable similarities, but this trait is YOU and has been YOU your entire life," he adamantly reminds me.

One of my most unshared and favorite self-realizations during this time of discovery with my father has been gaining a new understanding of where my "drive" comes from—it's a self-motivation and hunger to always do more, want more, work harder and give my everything. It's been my belief that it's the only honest way to find success. And I've always just believed this, self-taught not taught, that true success is only accomplished through hard work and appreciation. Considerably different as compared to my own family.

Can it be true? I am on this journey with a mission to find out more "about me," but am I getting so wrapped up in this that I'm actually losing sight of what I already know, which IS "me"?

From: Nate Brunhoff

Date: Monday, December 15, 2014

To: Michelle

Subject: Yes. I am alive.

I may not smell as tho but I am.

I have survived The Attack of the Lutz. She dragged us around to movies and beer joints and scored heavily at Farkle which seems to be a better game than its cousin Yahtzee. I have brought on board some poker chips.

She will be back.

I think we have a good plan to bore the * * * * out of you and Charlie, but it will be enjoyable to see you suffer in the midst of entertainment.

I concede I am not always a great pen pal and am working on that personal short-coming.

Dad

◦ ◆ ◦

On December 16, 2014, at 10:21 AM, Michelle wrote:

laughing

The apologies are absolutely unnecessary! But if you want to feel bad and write more ... well, you will never hear me complain. I still want to know everything. You know, SUPER important stuff like: What's your favorite color? What's your best talent? Do you wear crew or ankle socks? What would you do if you could be invisible for a day? Do you pick your nose with your finger or a tissue?

Farkle is fun! And I can't wait to be bored as * * * *.

I am getting super excited!

xo

◦ ◆ ◦

JOURNAL ENTRY

December 18, 2014

Apologies? I find it humorous that my dad has been apologizing lately for being a "bad pen pal." Be self-absorbed, I wrote him back. I do mean it with all honesty. Of course, there are parts of me that want to say, "Don't be self-centered!" It is a talent he has mastered very well in his life. Ouch, harsh, but it does make for a giggle, because it's true!

I have to smack the palm of my hand and remind myself that we both have our own lives and while this is exciting, it's important to shift some of that focus back on ourselves. We had lives before this and will continue to, regardless of all that has happened. As much as the greedy little child within me wants more, I am finally recognizing I need to take a step back and appreciate what it is and not what "I may want."

Chapter 20

I couldn't sleep last night. I woke nearly every hour in anticipation of going home today for Christmas. I'm so excited to see all my girlfriends and spend the holiday with family. It's my ultimate favorite. Charlie got home really late again last night and hasn't even packed. All my suitcases, a few bags, and three totes full of presents are in the hallway and ready to go. I turn over and grab my phone to check the clock again and it's (finally) 7:00 a.m.

I'm over the tossing and turning and pop up out of bed. Charlie is still knocked out, lightly snoring but I'm not going to wake and bug him just yet.

In between coffees, and last-minute packing of random items I don't need to bring but keep throwing in my bag anyways because we are driving and I can, I keep peeking into the bedroom and obnoxiously checking on him.

"Babe ... " I quietly whisper loud enough to hopefully wake him from his slumber.

I get nothing, so I continue on only to check back obsessively a few moments later.

"Babe ... " I intensify my whisper and finally see movement and his eyes open.

"It's ten after eight," I tell him.

With each time update, he acknowledges me now but is not getting up. I keep pretending that I'm doing him a favor and he keeps pretending that he's not getting annoyed.

At 10 a.m. we're *finally* on the road. I practically had a coronary.

Our road trips are also my very favorite. The music, the conversation, the random stops and sometimes adventurous exits, the snacks, the dreaming of our future, the company, my job, and finding our new home, and listening to our favorite murder-mystery shows and podcasts.... It's always a full, fun day of whatever the adventure brings us riding in the truck cab together.

"Where's the snow?" I question loudly as we cross the state line.

It's just before 6 p.m. and the blue and white "Welcome to Pure Michigan" sign welcomes us across the state line. I can't believe it. There's no snow. There was even snow in D.C. this morning. After last year's torrential pounding, setting records and "sucking souls" as they joke, it's surprising there's not even a single trace.

Around eight o'clock, we come turning in the drive. It's dark as night with no moon and Christmas lights are all that light the house. Charlie can't put the truck in park fast enough for either of us. We both jump out to hug everyone already standing in the driveway. Everyone helps unload and grabs our bags and totes filled with presents. Our first night home is always serendipitous. After ten hours on the road, we are still up and ready to have fun.

Wine and spirits are already out on the counter, snacks on the buffet. The mantel in the living room is glowing from the Christmas tree brightly lit in the corner, and brighter than the fire below. Our holiday ornaments are set out in boxes with our names, ready to be opened and put on the tree. Every year they wait for us and we get to pick our spots on the tree. It's been a tradition since our very first Christmas together, nearly ten years ago now. The rule is no one can hang your ornaments but you. Charlie and I usually have a good fight over the best spots on the tree.

"Unbelievable!" I yell at Charlie.

He took my spot again. Front and center, his ridiculously cute second grade picture is pasted in the center of a cut-out Christmas tree and is hanging in front of my ornament, again … every time. I swear that mischievous, tiny, and adorable smile in the picture can still be found on his face today.…

                          • ♦ •

From: Frank Brunhoff

Date: Monday, December 22, 2014

To: (all the family)

Subject: May this be among your best Holidays

With the Holiday season upon us, it is a wonderful time to remember all those wonderful people that have touched our lives. A time to promote the positive things we have in the world and inspire discussions about family, friends and all our neighbors of all types close and far.

For myself, it is a season that I try to envision ways to bridge gaps. I also look for ways to expand what I give to others that are less fortunate and look at what I may contribute to the health of our nation, the people of the world and our fragile environment.

May all your dreams and wishes be fulfilled this year and in all the years to come.

Frank

◦ ◆ ◦

Busy, busy, busy. The holiday is so busy. I stop to look at myself in the mirror and decide how best to make myself look more well-rested. Ugh! I rub on (supposed) skin tightening serum, curl some locks, throw blush on my winter-white face, down a cup of black coffee, and then layer up my clothing. I close the truck door right on time … 10:30 a.m. I wish Charlie was with me, but it's "too early" for him. I kissed him goodbye while he was sleeping. He didn't know and I wish he did, but I honestly don't care. If I were to wake him up only to feel pressured to make sure he is enjoying himself, I'd much rather he just stay in bed. It's worth the humiliation of me showing up without him and giving a random excuse why he's not there.

First stop is a get-together with some of my family. My cousin just returned from Afghanistan and her older sister is pregnant and engaged. It's been a while since I have seen both of them and walking into the bar, I feel excitement.

The Corner Bar is famous for its hot dogs and its eating contest. I find my way to my cousins sitting at a large round table in the middle of the restaurant. The walls are lined with small gold plaques and every name of those who have conquered the challenge. The top winner in the Hot Dog Hall of Fame is Tim Janus, "Eater X," with a record of eating 43.5 world famous chili dogs in four hours.

Some of us ordered brunch and others breakfast. I snatch up the last deep-fried pickle and dip it in a tub of ranch before the waitress takes it away. Below her reach, my cousin is pulling out a white business envelope from her purse and starts snapping it in the air, in her hand like the streetwalkers of Vegas. Everyone looks as she announces that what lies inside reveals the gender of the baby. While her older sister could barely keep her cool, her fiancé was going insane. He wants to know so badly. The official reveal is in a few days, but my cousin couldn't resist taunting them.

I'm thankful this holiday brought us together again but just as quickly as I arrived, I am back on the highway and heading to my next date.

> We are going to surprise everyone on Christmas Day but I want you to know ... It's a boy!

Aw, reading the text from my cousin, my heart is so full it could burst! I also notice I am running behind and whip into a grocery store. I race through the aisles throwing things in the cart. I hit up the veggies, chips and dips, crackers, cheese, and wine.

I spend the rest of the day with my girlfriends. My favorite day of fun with the girls comes and goes with no loss of memories, so fast that I can't decide if I am so incredibly happy to have seen them or sad that it's already gone.

I give my body a big stretch, still lying in bed, and rub my eyes. It's Tuesday and we're heading north today to see Mom. Charlie's coming with me today. Mom and Grandma are the only ones he'll visit, sometimes I think deservedly so. My family is so small and so divided. When you visit with family you should feel warm, soul-filling love, and comfort, but too many times in mine can you be disappointed.

It's been a few years now since Mom lost her house. She rented the place for more than fifteen years. So through all the years, it did become home. When she told me she was getting evicted, I couldn't believe it. She told me she hadn't paid rent for an entire year. I remember wanting to scold her but held it in mostly because of her tears. But a whole year.... How could she be surprised. Right? She *had* to have seen that one coming. Mom ended up getting a-n-o-t-h-e-r storage unit and moved in with Grandma. The good news, (yes, thankfully) is Mom and her boyfriend finally did move out of Grandma's this year and have a new place on the water.

We pull in the drive at the new house, but they're not here.... Typical. She's late, as always. The place is cute though, small but cute. It's kind of what you'd describe as a lakeside shack? There are a few of them down here at the bottom of the hill from the road. In its heyday, I imagine this was a desirable lakeside "cottage" to rent in the summer and experience Up North on Croton Pond. You'd surely miss its hidden drive if not for the sign on the road that reads "Castaway's Resort."

Mom's place is the third and last building, all the way down the drive and on a peninsula with the most waterfront. Four vintage, metal patio chairs line the front of the small home topped with a flat, metal roof and awning dressed with dangling icicle lights. The spot is the most attractive on the property.

Mom and her boyfriend finally pull in the drive, after we've waited nearly thirty minutes, and I can't help but say something.

"It's okay, we're used to it," I quip following her apology.

Inside, the house is exceptionally small. The entire place could be considered a single room but is portioned into tiny spaces to replicate what you would expect in a real home, including a tiny kitchen, small living area, a bathroom and two micro-size bedrooms. One bedroom can fit only a single bed and the other that has a stackable washer and dryer acts as a closet. All that fits in the living area is a chair and couch. The narrow kitchen has a single set of cupboards, a compact fridge and stove, and small tub for a sink. This is simple living at its finest, but there is something sweet about the quaint quarters. You can't argue. It's in their price range, on the water, and I know they'll have fun and enjoy it here.

We exchange gifts and drinks and then jump in the car to take them to the Driftwood, an old-timey bar on the water just a few miles down the road. Mom and I order fried chicken gizzards, a glass of wine for myself and a gin martini for her (keeping it classy). The boys head over to the other side of the bar to play shuffleboard while we get caught up on family and life. In between visits, we really don't talk much. We exchange text messages here and there, but rarely ever a phone call. I'm not sure which of us is to be blamed.

"Glad to see you all invited me … " says a raspy male voice from behind me.

I turn around and do a double take! I haven't seen him in years and there he stands, my brother. He's an awkward but tall and handsome man with sandy brown hair, green eyes, and a distinctive mole that sits high on his right cheek. He's dirty, however, and unkempt. His old tennis shoes are faded in color and breaking at the seams. He's wearing dirt-stained jeans. His flannel jacket is filled with holes and is missing a large section in the bottom left corner. I can't tell if it was torn or burned. With teary eyes, I stand to give him a hug.

"Oh man," I whisper to him. "It's been at least five years."

I reach back up just as quickly and give him another hug. He was driving by and saw Mom's car in the parking lot. He's not much of a talker, so I have to ask all the questions, prod and encourage his responses. I ask him if he's heard the news about me finding my father, because we both have different dads.

His eyes widen and he mopes out a quick and careless, "Nope."

And then I realize and ask, "Have you ever met your father?"

His response was just as quick and unemotional as before, "Nope."

Getting annoyed, I throw him back a fake smile and notice the time on my phone. I call Charlie over from the shuffleboard table and let him know we need to go. If we still want to visit with my Grandma, we need to (and should) leave soon.

For whatever reason, Charlie really likes Grandma. I struggle to understand it, but I also appreciate it. Grandma always shares stories that only Charlie can ever get out of her. And this visit is no exception. Grandma tells Charlie about how she first met Grandpa. I remember reading my grandma's journal a number of years after Grandpa had passed. She had shared it with the family to read. I always thought it was odd and was disappointed by her harsh words and unhappy memories. It seemed as though she wanted to convince the family that my grandpa was a bad man—a once handsome aircraft mechanic who had "tricked" her to moving to the "resort" life in Newaygo.

I didn't know him well, my grandpa. I was either six or seven when he died. He wasn't a typical grandpa, but I had always liked him a lot. He was funny, always ready to crack a beer and a joke and even I knew this at a young age. He'd always hang out in the basement, the oldest section of the house. His chair was a leather high top bar stool that sat just around the corner of the stairs coming down. Next to where he sat drinking beer and smoking cigarettes was an old wall phone with a jack and mile long cord that drooped down to the ground. The basement was his garage because they didn't have one. It was also where they lived until he finished building the rest of the home upstairs. You could try as hard as you could to sneak down the stairs and scare him, but he always knew and was prepared to scare you first.

Way past our hour visit, Charlie and I get back in the truck and head to Lo's. The welcoming committee is the same every time we pull in their drive. Their black lab comes galloping towards the truck and Lo comes running out the front door yelling, "Woooo!!!"

It's party time! We unload our overnight bags and get settled in for the night. Charlie heads out to the pole barn with Lo's husband, while we girls pull up to the kitchen counter on bar stools. She already has a glass of wine and a shot poured for me, a beautiful display of snacks and, as always, a delightful smelling lit candle. We start catching up, take a shot, and turn on the music. It is such a fun night, as it always is.

Following a long night, I wake early to open the curtains in our room. There's still no snow. We have one more gift to get and need to tackle our last-minute shopping. Charlie and I pack up our things quietly and I leave a note on the counter.

When we finally pull back into the drive in the city, it's already nearing one o'clock. We walk in and are greeted by an excited, yapping Bernie and are told we have only two hours to be ready for our next holiday party. This is exhausting.

After spending the past few days, house to house and party to party, I am boycotting on Christmas and staying in all day at home and in my pajamas.

∙ ◆ ∙

On December 25, 2014, at 7:12 AM, Michelle wrote:

MERRY CHRISTMAS!!!!

I'm up sitting at the tree waiting for everyone else to get up.

I am so thankful for you. Super duper Merry, Merry Christmas to you and Alice.

Xoxo,

Michelle

∙ ◆ ∙

It's the day after Christmas and our last full day in town. And, of course, it's jam-packed again. Thankfully we did get a restful day yesterday. First up, coffee at 8:15 a.m. at Starbucks with my first boss and life-long mentor. I met her at the start of my professional career after college and have appreciated our continued friendship throughout the years. Then, another coffee date at 9:30 with an old friend and her little girl. At 11 a.m., more family. Then, later, at 2:30 p.m., a hair date with my "sisters," so we can get fancy for dinner and dancing in the city tonight. The salon is small but is reserved only for us and we walk up like a mob of gangster beauties. If we were in New York or L.A., we would arguably be show-stoppers, but in Michigan there are so many beautiful people, we are just another group of pretty girls.

Back at the house, the boys are all dressed up and looking good. We enjoy pre-dinner drinks and hors d'oeuvres followed by steak dinner. Before parting with the parents, all the "kids" get together and strike a pose in the middle of a moonlit street under high rise buildings for a picture to remember the special evening.

We wake the next day with groggy eyes that later become tear-filled when we have to pull out of the drive. The truck is all packed up again, this time with all the gifts we received, and now we're heading back "home." It's warm outside and there's still no snow. Everyone comes out to the drive to send us off. We hug, cry, and wish we had another day. It's been seven days, and it feels like we just got here. I never want to go, and this is always the worst part of the trip. This is home.

· ✦ ·

From: Nate Brunhoff

Date: Saturday, December 27, 2014

To: Michelle

Subject: Weather and Cheese

This is not your doin' ... bring your mittens. The chance of rain—insignificant. Chance of frosty little digits—a little more. Chance the weatherman got it wrong—99%.

NB

· ✦ ·

On December 27, 2014, at 3:54 PM, Michelle wrote:

Oh boy! That is definitely not my doing. Looks like it is going to be a bit chilly during our visit but will still be nicer weather for us AND it's been warm here. We are back on the road and should get home around 1am tonight. I can't believe we never saw a single piece of snow anywhere on the ground. And gas was under $2—crazy!

xo

· ✦ ·

We arrive back in D.C. just after 1:00 a.m., and when we pull in, we leave everything in the truck and walk straight inside, up the stairs, and fall into bed. We're both absolutely exhausted, and it doesn't end.

The next morning we wake to another Christmas celebration. It may be possible that I'm getting tired of having so much fun. I would love to just sleep right now. I need a vacation from my vacation. And we still have more exciting holiday plans ahead of us. Our flight to San Diego leaves tomorrow at 4:30 p.m.

I am holding a secret from everyone, including Charlie. After our trip to San Diego, on our last day, starting the New Year, I am going to quit smoking—cold turkey and after fifteen years!

· ◆ ·

On December 28, 2014, at 3:50 PM, Nate wrote:

I think you will NEED to bring your imported Belgium Versace Lamb Skin driving gloves with the hand-stitched Yak thread, Kevlar palm pads and baby rabbit wrist trim. Or any gloves.

If I were you, and/or Charlie, I would want to take one of the cars one afternoon and hang out for several hours at the boardwalk in Pacific Beach, aka PB, where the crowd and menu is 25-45. This is Southern Cal.

Old farts guard the pets and tv while the children explore the new frontier.

Interested?

· ◆ ·

On December 28, 2014, at 8:28 PM, Michelle wrote:

Ummm, yes. I have never heard of such gloves, but I am positive I need those in my life.

It would also be really cool to check out PB. Maybe Charlie and I could go for a late breakfast but I will remind you that we really do like old farts. Stinky as they may be, they can be pretty hip too.

Honestly, we are up for anything! Everything sounds great! Can't wait to hang out with you!!

xo

♦

On December 29, 2014, at 11:36 AM, Nate wrote:

Good. Excellent.

Please mention this to Charlie if you haven't already—so when things move at a glacial slide, take the car and your iPhone and off you go! Early is really good because the boardwalk becomes filled with bizzzzzare costumes, roller skates, bicycles, and folks sitting in cafes doing munchables. You will want to walk or ride and be a Lookie Lu.

Have a chance to spend with JUST Charlie? We will stay home and pull ear hairs and marvel in monosyllables about your (plural) spunk.

Big Daddy O

♦

On December 28, 2014, at 8:28 PM, Michelle wrote:

BIG Daddy O!

Hahaha. Love it.

Holy crap.

Tomorrow.

To-morrow, tomorrow, I love ya, tomorrow ... You're only a day away!

xoxo

Chapter 21

ALICE

Are you going to be hungry when you arrive in San Diego?

Ya we'll be hungry, but snack stuff, nothing crazy! We just landed in Texas ...

DAD

Snacks probably mean something different to us. Clue?

Magnesium and calcium

or maybe a glass of wine with cheese and crackers

Are you guys scooping us from the airport?

DAD

I am. Alice was going to stay home and make some magnesoli with calciumski sauce.

> We are boarding soon. I'll give you another update when we are about to take off.

> OK, new update, we don't board for another hour ... put us in around midnight. You both just relax. I'll keep you posted but we will take a taxi.

ALICE

> He said he is picking up his daughter no matter what time she gets in.

⋆ ◆ ⋆

We *finally* land. I reach in my purse and pull out my phone to turn it back on. The screen lights up to show that it's nearly midnight in San Diego (which is 3:00 a.m. our east coast time). I text Alice and Big Daddy O and find out he's already here, waiting in a cell phone lot to pick us up after we get our luggage. I'm a little nervous, but nothing like last time. As soon as I open the car door and see his face, my apprehensions dissipate. I start to vent about the horrible delays with our connection flight and, before he puts the car in drive, he opens the center console and reaches in, pulling out a metal corkscrew wine opener. He hands it to me with a smirk and points to the cup holders; both the one in front of me and the one in back, by Charlie, are holding empty wine glasses. Then, he reaches down to the floor and pulls up a bottle of wine from under his seat. "Help yourselves!" he says, and we all start laughing.

Charlie and I head straight to the guest bedroom in the far back corner of the house and lightly unpack, enough to just get settled for the night. In the room are our robes from the first visit laid out on the bed and mine is now accompanied with a large pair of brown, furry moose slippers. The thoughtful touch warms my heart and makes me laugh.

Per our instructions, we return to the kitchen and find my father flipping eggs and toasting English muffins. A plate full of sliced cheese and crackers is on the island along with two mugs of hot cocoa. We grab all the goods and take a seat together at the table in the breakfast nook.

Our mouths quickly open to eat and drink, and yawn. We feel drunk on being tired. With our bellies full, we stumble down the marble hall and pass out in bed.

The next morning, I slip out of bed and close the door behind me without waking Charlie. I've been awake since daybreak when the morning light first hit the cracks in the blinds. I am up, but I don't think anyone else is. It's silent in the house. All you can hear are the light smacks of my bare feet against the cold stone floor.

I need to decide what day I'm going to quit smoking. I could quit tomorrow on New Year's Day, or maybe I should wait until we leave? For precautionary measures, it may be best that I consider option two and avoid any opportunity of turning into a raging witch on visit #2. I am not sure how things will go or how I will deal. I've never tried to quit before, and I am doing it cold turkey.

Approaching the kitchen, I can hear coffee brewing just as Dad said it would be, as it's set on an automatic timer. I grab a coffee mug out of the cupboard and help the door lightly shut, so as not to disrupt the silence in the house, turn around, and *scream!*

I nearly drop the cup. Dad was up, and he snuck in on me. He's standing just a few inches from me with a big cheese-eating grin on his face.

"Ahhh," I grab my chest to make sure my heart doesn't expel from its cavity. "You scared me!"

I fill the cup with coffee and then smack him on the shoulder for scaring me. I hear Alice in the living room. She is also up, sitting quietly and giggling over our morning exchange. I grab a seat on the floral upholstered chair next to hers and set my coffee on the table between us. She lets me know she's not feeling well and wants to be 100 percent for the festivities planned this evening, so she suggests she stay back from the activities today. Dad joins us, taking a seat on the couch and kicks up his feet.

"Are you ready to go racing?" he asks.

"What do you mean?" I ask, returning the question. "What kind of racing!?"

Charlie wakes up and we get ready for K1 Racing a few hours later. At an electric indoor kart racing venue, we are given required racing gear, including gloves and helmets. Charlie is pumped and slaps my helmet. And as soon as the flag is waved, we are running and jumping in the karts. I hit the pedal and don't ever let up, including around corners, keeping it down while pressing the brakes. I leave Dad in my dust and am about to lap him. Oops! I bump him as I pass!

I'm determined to beat Charlie. I keep passing him but then he comes out of nowhere and passes me again. On the last corner, I'm passing Charlie again. It's a heated race to the finish and he is right on my bum. He tries to hit me, but I keep my wheels straight … and I win! I beat both Dad and Charlie!

On the drive back to the house, I think about all our holiday adventures and am feeling a little bewildered we are here again—add the fact that today is New Year's Eve. This year has been one of the best. And, it's already a great day so far too. Back at the house, we enjoy light fare paired with good conversation and then separate to our quarters to get refreshed, dressed up, and ready for the evening's special dinner.

We meet back in the kitchen at 5:00 p.m. Before we leave, Dad presents Charlie and me with a "taste testing." However, it's not food. He has purchased multiple fifths of very nice vodka and starts pulling them out from a cupboard and onto the counter. He is curious to know which one will stand up to the palette when it comes to price versus brand. We are equally entertained and excited to be participants. He pours four shots, one each of Absolute Elyx, Belvedere, Grey Goose, and Absolute Platinum. He labels the napkins 1 through 4. Both blind folded for the testing and not knowing what the other is selecting, we both pick the same: #3. Grey Goose wins the smoothest vodka taste test.

We pile in the van again, but this time with Alice and all dressed up wearing our shining best. We head to Brigantine for a celebratory New Year's Eve dinner. The restaurant overlooks the Del Mar horse track. It's a warmer evening in Escondido on a soon-to-be January day, so we opt to sit outside on the enclosed deck with space heaters where we can view the horse track.

We order Brig classic calamari and crispy Brussels sprouts to start. Charlie gets the New York steak and I order macadamia crusted mahi-mahi. Everything is so delicious we barely have time to talk between mouthfuls. It's rare to see all of us with completely wiped clean plates. Dad comes over to our side of the table, which is a cushioned bench. Alice grabs her phone and we all smile for a pic.

As the clock hand spins and the digital clocks tick, it's only a small distance between now and 2015. I'm still holding on to my secret, and am feeling more and more determined to do it. I am going to quit smoking. After all these years, I am doing this.

Chapter 22

Happy 2015! It's New Year's Day and I'm up early ... again. I grab a cup of coffee and find Alice in the living room wrapped in a blanket sitting in her chair. She's still not feeling well. I had wondered yesterday if she had stayed back to give us time alone, but now I know she really is feeling under the weather. I feel horrible that she cannot join us again today. Being sick is the worst, such an inconvenience.

Today, we are riding Segways. Ironically, when Cara was visiting us in D.C. in November, we were walking the Mall to the Washington Monument and saw a group of tourists on Segways. She clamored about how much fun they would be, and I was very adamant that I would never be caught dead on one, and ESPECIALLY wearing a helmet. Now, here I am downtown San Diego watching a video about how to control and safely ride these things ... and picking out a helmet!

Helmets are safe and important 100 percent of the time, but they are also usually uncomfortable and not cute 75 percent of the time. There's a bright pink one, so I snatch it up and reluctantly put it on, looking in the mirror. I just don't like helmets. Why do they even have this mirror? Do people really feel the need to check themselves out putting on this hideous gear? I mean, I am looking, but I would much rather not be.

Helmet on, I hop on the Segway and quickly jump right back off. These things have some surprisingly serious power and I am intimidated. The machine operates based on your balance and movement, and it can take you by surprise. I hop back on and work with the instructor for the next five to ten minutes to get the feel for how my body movement can move the machine.

Zigging and zagging through the streets of downtown San Diego, we are off and segwaying to Balboa Park. After crossing a bridge, we enter through two large stone columns connected above with a bridging architecture. A large centerpiece sits in the middle and is adorned with ancestral crests. It's explained by the tour guide that these are the gods and goddesses of the land and ocean. The park entrance is grand. We also learn from the instructor that the port of San Diego was one of the last to be developed on the West Coast. It took some convincing and eventually old money was brought down from San Francisco to start building what exists today, including the 1200-acre park. And it was not only the trees within the park that they funded and planted, but trees through all the streets of San Diego. They planted 100 trees every year in the park and 300 more in the city.

Dad is riding behind us and keeps sneaking up on his Segway saying, "I want to go faster!" We can also hear him echoing and mimicking the instructor's directions.

"Up here we will make a right," yells the instructor loudly so that everyone can hear, "and be careful of the bump."

"AYYEE—YOOOO," yells Dad from the back.

After a day filled with entertainment, including Dad's idiosyncrasies, we meet up with Alice at the movie theatre to watch *The Gambler*. The movie rocks me. My stomach is still churning, and my common sense has me infuriated. I love a good movie, but I just spent nearly two hours watching a man destroy an absolutely incredible life (comparative to many). The character quickly transpires from a decent man who could have it all to the world's dumbest loser. And then you watch in agony every dumb decision he makes. He is raised with smarts, wealth, and education, and yet chooses greed and wastes his life, destroying everyone in his path. And over what? The dream of winning it big.

After swallowing the movie over a much better glass of wine, dinner follows with champagne, pajamas, and games back home. It was an ultimate New Year's Day. I finally fall asleep in the early morning hours snug tight in Charlie's arms.

The next morning the sun is shining through the blinds again, waking me only a few hours after we had fallen asleep. As tired as I am, and considering the excitement of our last day here, I still can't fall back asleep. I get up to meet Dad and Alice in the living room again, to enjoy a cup of coffee and learn about today's adventures.

Today we are squeezing it in. I wake up Charlie and we both shower and dress in hiking gear. Dad hits the gas pedal in the van and like a roller coaster we fly up the tremendously steep eighty-five degree driveway, backwards. Impressive is an understatement. I witnessed him bring the trash up the other day doing the same thing, driving backwards. With one arm out the window, he held the trash can and gunned it up the hill with his other hand on the wheel and head turned to see behind him.

For the next thirty minutes we drive to a small, dusty town called Ramona. When you hit the first stoplight (one of only a few), a large sign sits on the corner. It has a brick base with large, oversized gold letters that read "Welcome to Ramona" and display of a rusty metal horse, all framed by a wooden arbor and set against a desert landscape behind. Just before we hit the second traffic signal, Dad flicks on the blinker and we take a right. The next few miles are winding up mountainous terrain. Every now and then the road has a bend where you can see above and below the trees, revealing how high up we are. A final turn on a private drive brings us to the tippy top of the foothill (what feels like a mountain). Dad parks next to a silver Airstream. It's set atop a landscaped area with an enormous boulder on the backside and a small fireplace in the front. The scene could easily have come from a Hollywood movie screen.

We jump out to discover the land and then tour the Airstream. It's in great condition but the décor is dated. We help Dad with a few tasks, including getting the fire pit ready, and then set off for a hike. The path we follow quickly gets lost and overgrown and prickly brush grabs at our legs and ankles. We climb up on a set of large boulders, nearly twelve feet in width and at times almost triple in height. We reach one that is perfectly set on the edge of a foothill and nestled under the limbs of an aged tree. A small wooden bench swing is hooked to one of the tree's larger limbs. Alice looks over at me and asks, "You ready?"

We both jump on and before I say anything, she pushes us off the boulder with our feet are dangling high in the air and over ground far, far below. "Wooo!" we both scream in delighted laughter.

"Do you think Charlie and I could stay here for a night next time we come stay?" I ask Dad.

I dream of Charlie and me sitting at the fireside, enjoying the stars with a nice glass of wine and conversation. We're so close up here you could almost just reach up and grab one.

"Of course," he says.

On our way out of town, we grab a late lunch at a small mom-and-pop dive restaurant. A bowl of homemade chicken noodle soup and a side of fries satisfy my grumbling belly. Charlie brings up our plans to go to Harrah's Casino tonight. He's been planning to surprise them and treat them to dinner. A few weeks before we left, Charlie received in the mail a special discount membership card from one of his friends in Las Vegas. He said his friend is a DJ for one of the casino's parent companies and he can send the VIP cards to friends and family. Harrah's is a new casino in San Diego and part of the same chain, and with the membership card, we get a $100 credit towards dinner at the casino's finest, four-star restaurant. We have been treated to so many great dinners, entertainment, and activities; it will be so nice to treat them back.

Dressed again in our finer attire, we leave the car with a valet when we arrive (Charlie says it comes with the deal). We step out and the large, glass doors open to the casino, and all you hear is a ruckus of dings, rings, and bells. I'm not interested to play, but I'm glad we're here and able to treat Dad and Alice to a nice dinner and magic show.

We check-in at the restaurant and find out we have some time to kill. Alice suggests walking over to the craps table and watching others play. I like the idea and nod in agreement, but Charlie stops and pulls me back.

"What's wrong?" I whisper.

"It's rude to watch over the shoulders of other players," he says.

He would rather go on our own and play a few games. I agree; we have been with Dad and Alice the entire visit. I yell out to them walking ahead of us and say we'll just meet at the restaurant in thirty.

I watch Charlie lose $200 in a matter of minutes and about mess my pants. He drops another hundred-dollar bill in a random slot machine that we are just walking by. Then again, I watch him do it again. Another hundred-dollar bill disappears in less than a minute. Well, I guess we are on vacation, I think. But, when he puts in a *another* hundred-dollar bill into another machine, I ask him if he has lost his mind, and in all seriousness.

A waitress thankfully shows up and we get drinks instead of starting an argument. She walks away and Charlie points to two open slot machines and gives me money. We spend the next twenty losing and winning, getting excited and then bummed, and drinking endless free drinks.

The VIP treatment is no joke. At dinner, the manager greets us at the door, seats us, and then gives us a complimentary calamari appetizer. Throughout the meal, we are constantly checked on and treated as though we are someone of significant importance. Alice snaps a pic of Charlie and me sitting together in the opposite booth from her and Dad. It's a quarter to nine, so Charlie quickly reminds us the show is starting soon and signs a slip with the casino card. At the theatre entrance, we are escorted to front row seats to watch the Masters of Illusion.

I poke Charlie in the leg and whisper, "We're so going to get picked on!"

Chipper Lowell takes the stage and the entire room fills with loud laughter that never disappates. And just as expected, halfway through the show, Chipper calls Charlie to the stage. Charlie goes up and stands in the bright light, and Chipper asks random questions while he prepares his next trick. Charlie stutters in every response, so noticeably that the entire audience laughs every time. The short skit was all a bit awkward but it was Charlie's five minutes of fame, and is nearly all we talk about the rest of the night until we get home.

It's been another eventful day and we're all quick to go directly to our rooms and take off our shoes as soon as we get home. We all stagger back and meet in the living room in our pajamas. Dad has a movie playing and Alice gives Charlie and me ice waters with a bowl of fresh fruit. I don't last more than fifteen minutes into the movie. Charlie wakes me after everyone has gone to bed and carries me on his back to ours.

What time is it? I wonder. The morning sun isn't peeking through the blinds. I roll away from Charlie and grab my phone from the night stand. It's 6:10 a.m. Today is our last day. This is also my last day smoking! Agh ... I grumble in silence. I remind myself, it's time. I slide out of bed, zip up a hoodie, and slip on flip flops. I quietly creak open the back door that leads to a private patio connected to our bedroom. I wipe off a cushion on a wicker chair and sit down, picking my feet up and pulling my knees to my chest. I take in a deep breath, seeking to appreciate my surroundings. A thick layer of pollen has dressed the ground, everything is neon green, and the air is crisp and fresh from morning dew. It's a refreshing smell like that after a rainfall or fresh snowfall. And like the tree at Dad's apartment that dropped tiny white flowers on my hair, the tree above is percolating tiny green flowers into the stillness of the morning air, less even a tousle of wind. I enjoy my last morning smoke and slip back in just as quietly through the creaky back door.

I start pulling our things together and pack up all the memorable trinkets collected on the visit, including our race sheets, tickets from the magic show, and my new sparkly blue blouse. I try to enjoy the day, but all I can think about is, this is my last coffee with Dad, this is our last ride in the van, this is our last lunch, and this is our last movie—which actually was the best of the trip. The movie was *The Imitation Game*. It's an excellent mix of history, thriller, and mystery. After the movie, we head to Ocean Beach to grab one last bite to eat.

At OB Warehouse, we're waiting for our food to be served when I finish my martini and have the gumption to finally share the news. I reveal my secret and tell everyone that I am going to quit smoking. Dad and Alice are full of excitement and encouragement, and Dad recognizes me for my bravery to quit cold turkey, especially for the first time. Then, surprisingly, Charlie starts vocalizing his doubts in me, for the first time.

I've already been picking up on Charlie's attitude, but it really sucks not feeling his support. Dad gets up to find our server to put in another order of celebratory beverages and Alice goes to the restroom. In the safe space, Charlie starts a fight. I beg him not to do this right now, asking repeatedly, over and over. I don't know what is going on with him. He buttons it up just before Dad returns to the table. Charlie's actions surprise me, but also don't, sadly. I know we're both exhausted from all the travel and days packed with activities this holiday.

Back at the house, we put on our pajamas early and curl up on the couch again. I wake in the late night hour to Charlie nudging me to come to bed. My bare feet softly smack the marble tile floor down the hallway for the last time. We sneak out onto the back patio before bed. I sit there again, on the same cushion with tiny green flowers still dropping onto my hair. This is my last cigarette—my last cigarette <u>ever</u>.

Chapter 23

The last question on my list (I proudly remember) is the final unknown and unanswered from my "priority" list: Where did he go to high school? It's early morning, seven o'clock, and very brisk outside. Dad and I are in the van parked outside the garage at the bottom of the palm-lined, rollercoaster of a driveway. Charlie is standing outside smoking and no one knows yet that I haven't had one. The bags are all in the back and we're just waiting on Charlie to finish so we can go.

"I swear he loves to test me when he knows we're running late," I nervously say looking over at Dad. "Hey, I forgot to ask you. If you grew up in Ada, then where'd you go to high school?"

With a bit of a quizzical face, he responds without hesitation, "Ada township was very small back then and didn't have its own school system," he explains. "This was well before Amway was founded. Us kids either went to East Grand Rapids or Forest Hills back then. They are both neighboring school systems. But my first two years, I went to high school at a private school in Delaware."

"That must have been hard," I interrupt, failing to follow up with an explanation why. It would suck being separated from everyone you grew up with to start high school.

Again with a perplexed face, he assures me that it was not a problem. "I was happy to pack my bags and say bye to my folks," he laughs.

Now it is me that has the perplexed face. I wonder how he wouldn't miss his friends and family. His upbringing and challenged relationship with his father starts becoming clearer.

"So, when you returned?" I continue.

"Oh, yes," he says, "Forest Hills. I finished my last two years at FHHS."

Charlie opens the door and slides in as quickly as the stale smoke and swoosh of brisk air that hits my face. Then, the car, just as quickly, goes into reverse and flies up the driveway backwards.

"Oh baby," I say and grasp the sides of my seat. "Here we go!"

Dad laughs and says we're late and cutting it close. I turn in my seat to give Charlie a playful but damning eye. Dad is racing down the highway like we are in go-karts again, weaving in and out of traffic the entire way. Sitting at a stop light, a train crossing light starts flashing and dinging. Dad says we're only a block from the airport now. He hits the van into reverse and covers an entire block backwards, then another, and another. We went backwards down the road for four blocks. He turns, runs a red light, and we beat the train!

"That was awesome!" I shout in laughter.

A few moments later, we're parked curbside and pulling out our luggage. "Give me a hug," Dad says, handing me my last bag. With tear-filled eyes and looking down so he can't see, I throw myself at him and squeeze him tight. I hate leaving him. "Now this side," he says pulling me in again just as soon as I finally let go. "And again on this side," he says pulling me back one last time before he puts his head just to the left of mine. I can't help but laugh this time. I squeeze him tight.

Charlie and I walk away with our luggage to the check-in counter, and this time I turn around to look back, but Dad was already gone. Charlie turns to me and says, "Did you see he was crying?" I nod and smile. I was encapsulated in the moment. I didn't need to worry this time. It's not goodbye.

Following our normal routine, we check-in and I walk with Charlie outside to find a designated smoking area for one final cigarette before going through security. He hands me one.

Already ... he already forgot.

"No, thank you," I say with a scrunched forehead. Did he not think I was serious?

He gives me the same playful but damning eye back, "Are you sure you want to quit today?"

He gets me thinking.... Traveling is so stressful, maybe I should wait until I get home....

"Thing is," I think aloud as I am realizing the truth, "No day or time is going to be good."

I grab and squeeze his free hand and he says, "I'm proud of you."

That's all I've needed to hear.

◦ ◆ ◦

From: Nate Brunhoff

Date: Monday, January 5, 2015

To: 'Michelle'

Subject: Smoking

Rumor has it that you are going to quit. Serious kudos. Not an easy project but I personally think that you have the character.

I do have a thought that may be helpful. In reality you have to demonize the cigarettes, the cigarette company, because they are in fact evil. They live on the dark side. As you struggle with this you should in fact get pissed at them. For decades they have cajoled with advertising and connived with science to capture and enslave you. I am not kidding. This is serious * * * *.

 · ◆ ·

On January 5, 2015, at 12:04 PM, Michelle wrote:

Indeed it is true. Saturday night before we went to bed was my last cigarette. I am only on Day 2, but this is much easier than I had anticipated. I didn't know if I would be twitching, yelling, screaming, crying ... I have never tried to quit before for the simple fact that I couldn't bear the thought of being unsuccessful. I had seen my girlfriends quit and fail for years. I knew I had to do it when I was ready.

There were a few moments that I anticipated a freak out—like not having my cigarette into work this morning with my coffee—but it really wasn't as bad as I thought it would be. All it is, is a decision. The want goes away as soon as you make the conscious decision that you want it to. Easy peasy. You just have to put your mind to it. It's almost like reconditioning. Proving to myself that the ride to work in the a.m. can be just as enjoyable with just coffee and music, and not a cigarette.

Funny you say that though, as I have been getting mad at cigarettes this past year. I was starting to feel like they were in control of me (sneaking out at a work conference and then layering perfume and trying to hide the smell, feeling like I don't like it but I need to have it). I yelled at Charlie's cigarettes last night and said to the box, "You do not control me * * * * * *—I control you!" LOL

Kudos can come at the end of week 1 and again at the end of week 2. I don't feel worthy of any yet ... it's only Day 2. ;)

XO

· ◆ ·

On January 5, 2015, at 8:31 PM, Nate wrote:

Rock on. You have the character ...

· ◆ ·

From: 'Michelle'

Date: Friday, January 9, 2015

To: Nate Brunhoff

Subject: 6 Days

One more day to go and I will have a week down. I was told I have "the will power of an Ox". lol

Charlie suggested we see a movie this weekend! :) I'm wondering if you have seen any good ones since we left?

Hope you are having a good week!

Happy Friday,

Xo

P.S. My calendar reminded me that it is your brother Ed's birthday today. Alice had given me your birthday as well as your brothers—I had asked for the dates back in October when you all sent me birthday wishes. If you speak with Ed today, please give him Happy Birthday wishes from me as well.

P.S.S. Sunday at 3pm Charlie and I are meeting Great Aunt Maura and Jenny in Falls Church at the family home on Lake Barcroft.

· ◆ ·

On January 9, 2015, at 12:20 PM, Nate wrote:

aYO! 6 days! I understand. Totally. Awesome. Totally Awesome.

⋅ ◆ ⋅

JOURNAL ENTRY

January 11, 2015

One week down! And a lifetime to go. Geez, that sounds daunting. Baby steps. Little triumphs. I made it a whole week without a cigarette. If I can make it one week, I can make it two weeks.

I thought my morning coffee and driving in the car without a cigarette would be killer hard, but really the hardest time is at night. Thank the sweet Lord I can still sip on my wine while making dinner. I just can't wait until I can STOP thinking about the stupid things. That's the most annoying part about all of this. Hopefully one day I'll just forget that I ever even smoked.

Great Aunt Maura arrived in town yesterday and is staying for a few days with her daughter Jenny before taking the train up to New York for an astrology conference. I'm excited to see both her and Jenny again, but also this time to meet more of the family. Today we are meeting relatives and descendants from my great grandpa's family.

⋅ ◆ ⋅

Passing the same homes again we had seen on our investigative drive to the family residence, we're still in awe of the grandness and beauty of this hidden lake community. We pull up to the all-brick, ranch style home and park on the side of the street. A long driveway winds down the hill and wraps around the side of the garage, continuing down to the water's edge. We walk down to the grand, double wooden door entrance. I feel my nerves starting to jumble. What are they going to be like? What if I don't connect with them? Will they be stuffy? Will I feel welcomed or will it be awkward?

Dingggg … dongggg….

The old tune of the doorbell can be heard ringing inside the house, and then one of the double doors open. There stands a beautiful tall blonde with striking blue eyes. She is maybe in her late fifties or early sixties and looks incredible for her age. Her smile is warm. Her bright presence, soft spoken words, and welcoming tone immediately comfort us. She glances at Charlie first with a kind "hello" and then over to me and says, "You're definitely a Brunhoff—come on in."

One by one, we're introduced to everyone inside. We quickly learn that Sarah, who met us at the door, is the oldest sibling. She and her husband, Don, a former NFL player (who unquestionably looks the part), live in the home and care for Sarah's sibling, Judith, who Great Aunt Maura had mentioned is mentally disabled. There is a brother, whose name completely evades my memory nearly as quickly as he is introduced. He is very kind and most reflects the German heritage. He has a stocky, tall build, wispy blonde hair, and ocean blue eyes. Another sister approaches us with her lesbian partner. They are nice, and I can't stop staring at their matching butch haircuts. A third sister walks in the side door of the kitchen, coming in from outside. She is the most proper and elegant, and seemingly opposite of the rest of the family. Her hair is long and dark with a patch of gray in her bangs. She could be a stand-in for Cruella de Vil but is kinder and more attractive in appearance. Charlie and I spend the next twenty minutes chatting with her over a glass of wine. She's an artist and has a lot of questions for Charlie about the finishing and coating options she uses on her statues. Charlie shares his recommendations for her material based on his experience with coatings at our company, when the final and fourth sister, Ruby, walks in and interrupts us. She is the youngest of them all and trumps everyone in beauty.

As the wine continues to flow, the night starts closing in and boxes of old photographs are pulled out and placed in the middle of the large dining room table. There are at least three leaves in the table. It is long enough for us all to stand around. Everyone reaches in to grab a box, lifting lids and pulling out a set of old, black and white photographs to look at and pass. The first handful is passed to me. Most of them are Great Grandpa as a young boy with his family. Then one is him as a handsome young man. He is dressed in a suit standing in front of a large colonial home. There is a dog at his side, whom I'm told is called Sparky. Then a photograph of a different man in military uniform is passed. Great Aunt Maura, seated to my right, leans over to see.

"That's Ed," she says. "That's my brother."

"You mean that's my grandpa?" I ask pointing at the man standing alone in the photo.

"Yes," she says looking down again at the cold and lifeless image. "That's right. That is your grandpa."

And that was that. There is no further discussion on him or the photograph. I set the photo down and take a step away from the table. Everyone continues to get deeper in conversation about the photos being passed and sharing family memories that I'm obviously not familiar with. I duck out from the crowded room and sneak away unnoticed, even from Charlie, to the kitchen, which is thankfully free of anyone. I lean my backside against the kitchen island and take a long sip from my wine glass, enjoying the solitude and silence, taking a moment to look around the room and at the lake outside.

The kitchen is very large and spacious. On the east side wall is a row of tall windows that stretch nearly floor to ceiling and frame a picturesque view of the lake. A wooded landscape fills the land between the house and lake outside and gives privacy from nearby neighbors. Inside, an old style, posh décor is tastefully classy, warm, and comforting.

I take another sip of my wine and turn to walk around the other side of the island. I admire the kitchen. It's built of the finest quality, including glass cabinet doors, marble countertops, and immaculate detailed tiling. Without knowing it, you'd never guess this home sits just a few miles outside the busy metropolitan streets of our nation's capital.

Decadent savory appetizers and food cover nearly every available space on the countertop. I find a tray of strawberries and dip one in a bowl of powdered sugar. As I bring the perfectly glistening, bright red treat to my mouth, someone taps me on the shoulder from behind. I am startled and choke. I whip around, trying hard to gain control of my gagging, and see who it is.

"Oh, hi, Ruby!" I gasp.

We both laugh, but are suddenly distracted by a loud commotion at the front door. We see Sarah quickly walk to open the door and in wheels an older woman with no legs. She's in a wheelchair and is murmuring loud words, waving her arms with limp hands. This must be Judith, I realize. Indeed this woman, or girl, is severely handicapped. She wheels closer to us in the kitchen, and her legs, that I had thought were stumps of an amputee, I see now end in little feet. Her opportunity to live any kind of a normal life is clearly only possible through the care of this family. Ruby tells me Judith is nearly fifty years old, but her mind is that of an infant. Interesting enough, I quickly find out that she really likes boys. None of us are able to get a clear understanding of what she is saying, but it is clear who she is directing all of her attention to—Judith is screaming, pointing, and blushing at Charlie.

Ruby tells me the rest of the family history. There are six grandchildren, in total. One has recently passed. And when the grandparents passed, they left this home to Judith. They believed everyone would want to come around and visit her at the big, beautiful family home set on one of D.C.'s most beautiful lakes. And they were right.

Getting ready to leave, Charlie and I are invited back to enjoy the home in the summer months and, without hesitation, we both say we are incredibly grateful for the invite and can hardly wait.

- ◆ -

From: Nate Brunhoff

Date: Monday, January 12, 2015

To: 'Michelle'

Subject: Re: movies ...

There is a small matter I wanted to slide onto the table. I have naturally high blood sugar. Genetic, high blood sugar will tend to feed those nasty little cancer cells. Thus, I must eat low carb foods, i.e. no sugar, no grains (breads, pastas, etc.) I tend to cheat. Genetic. Alice is my travel guardian. She guards me against the attack of the grains and all the tasty foods.

Thus, when I tend to snag a bit of the real food, Alice says, "bad dog" and Charlie gets this puzzled look across his brow. I ALLOW this because ultimately I know it is important.

What Charlie doesn't know is that Alice has saved the life of every member of the family. Seriously. She is super smart but doesn't tout it. She has told ER rooms and hospitals that they are flat wrong on medications and procedures for patients or they failed to understand Lab results (PISSED them offff) but in the end, got humble calls back saying she was right. I must confess, she has saved my life more than once so, even though it is a bit chaffing to my ego, I go with it.

I hope Aunt Maura was cool as ever.

Nathan B

⋅ ◆ ⋅

On January 12, 2015, at 10:52 AM, Michelle wrote:

... I remember busting you trying to snag treats. No cheating, Mr.!! :)

How is your health by the way? When is the next time you get screened to see progress? I hope to hear that you are kicking that stupid cancer's ＊＊＊. Really would love to hear how you are doing ... I'm proud of you and all that you are doing to try to beat it. I can only imagine how difficult it must be. And I am SO THANKFUL for sweet Alice. She is an Angel. Her wings are somewhere, I just know it ...

It's been about a year since my last physical exam, but it has always been A+. I've never had any health problems, and I have never had an issue with cholesterol or blood sugar. My whole life the doctors have always commented on my levels being very good. I used to always joke and say that must be all the cigarettes and wine! LOL Now, I will just say ... must be the wine. ;)

Going on day 9 ... WOOT WOOT! Can't wait until it's day 109 ... I should have done this such a long time ago. Silly me.

I was a little nervous to meet the family yesterday, but it went really well. Charlie and I had a wonderful time! They are all very nice people. We hope to visit them again soon in the summer when it will be warm and fun to hang out at the lake. Attached are a few photographs they shared with us. One is of Great Grandpa B, his house and his dog Sparky. There is also an old, discolored photo of a young blonde-haired soldier. The photo of the soldier I was told is your dad.

I miss you already. Hope you put my moose slippers somewhere safe. ;)

⋅ ◆ ⋅

On January 13, 2015, at 11:31 AM, Nate wrote:

Put the Moose Slippers Away ? ? ?

I am dashed. Heartbroken. Crest fallen.

Imagine the lost opportunities. A Moose dance in the hallway. Moose sounds as you walk. Peering out over the tips of floppy antlers when you kick back with a cup of moose coffee. Imagine the smile on a guest when you answer the door in moose protective slipper gear.

You. Are. Missing a Great Opportunity. Do not mistake the mirth for derision ;)

Chapter 24

I pull up in front of a brick apartment building in Old Town, Alexandria, flip on the hazard lights in my white VW R32 and put the car in park. I open the car door to a gust of crisp winter air that nearly blows off my hat and look to the double glass door's at the building entrance to see Great Aunt Maura already making her way to me. She's wearing a bright fuchsia jacket that "pops" in all the fresh, white snow. It complements her strikingly white hair. I walk around to the other side of the car to open her door and help her in to what she says is my "little whip."

Zipping through the old, romantic streets of Alexandria, we turn right on King Street. At its end, tucked nicely into the shore side of the Potomac River, is the Chart House restaurant. I had made reservations for two and we're quickly seated. Our booth overlooks the Potomac. We both pull off our jackets and enjoy the exceptional view of the Capitol building just downstream. It's a cloudy gray day, but the view and company couldn't be better. She looks mighty fabulous, in her sunglasses, which she never takes off, even all through lunch.

We're so engrossed in conversation that the waiter returns five times before we finally apologize for the last time and commit to looking at the menu to make our choices. What I struggle with most, however, is how to turn our conversation into an opportunity to ask what I really want to know.

"Aunt Maura," I say, giving up. "I hope you don't mind, but I really need to ask you something."

She sets down her hot tea and looks at me through the dark lens of her sunglasses (or at least I think she is looking at me).

"Yes dear," she says. "What would you like to know?"

With a hesitated voice, "Do you think Dad's father killed his wife?" I ask.

Clearly startled, adjusting her seating, she smiles sweetly and says, "I'm glad you asked."

She begins with a story about growing up with her brother, who is my grandfather (my dad's father), and persistently (and blatantly) disclaims is her non-accusatory observations.

"Your grandpa was always a bit of an odd duck," she nervously laughs and continues. "Even when we were younger."

"A bit chauvinistic," she says. "He always had a sense of entitlement. He was the only boy and was set to take over our grandfather's company."

She lifts her tea to take another sip but then never does. Instead, she sets her cup back down to the table and adjusts a few pieces of hair behind her ear.

"I will tell you," she confesses. "There's still one time I will never forgive your grandfather."

She pauses, once again, and I ask to please continue.

"It was one day in high school," she recalls grabbing her chin as though digging into her past to unhide the memory.

"I had returned home after class and was walked up to the stoop of our front porch by my boyfriend," she pauses again before continuing, "as he did every day."

She readjusts her seating.

"On this particular day," she starts to strengthen her tone, "I gave my boyfriend a kiss and when I opened the door, there stood my brother who'd been watching the entire time. He looked at me so disgustingly, as if I was a *****, and called me a 'SLUT' loudly, right in my face."

"It was my boyfriend!" she yells at me across the table as if she's still yelling back at him after all these years.

Her stories continue, and as a young lady between school and travels, she stayed with her older brother Ed a few times after high school. She remembers the way he treated his wife (my grandmother). Grandma was constantly belittled, rarely right about anything (even if it was a fair argument), and could never have an opportunity to stand her own. She was not a wife. She was a servant.

"I remember thinking, if that's what marriage is like," she says, "I want nothing to do with it."

We naturally start talking about Betty, the girl who lived next door and is accused of the reason for Grandma and Grandpa's separation. It is clear that Great Aunt Maura has much disdain for Betty. It comes through in more than just her words, in her voice, but in her body communication. It's obvious that Betty lacked morals and values. Even after both marriages were broken, between Grandpa and Grandma and Betty and her husband, I guess Betty was cold to the kids and kept her distance from the family. I also learn more about when Grandma moved back to her hometown in Sterling, Colorado, and how the fight for alimony and child support was a never-ending battle. Great Aunt Maura says Grandpa didn't think Grandma deserved a single penny, not from their estate nor in the support of the children. Then, the shooting happened....

"It's the strangest thing," she says. "Your grandmother was killed sitting in her chair in the living room. She was shot through a window, in the head."

"Do you think my father thinks he did it?" I ask.

"You know," she quickly responds. "Your dad told me he and the boys [the brothers] got together to discuss it and decided as a family, if their father says he didn't do it they would believe him."

Looking at my obviously shocked face, she tries to reassure me that my grandfather's alibi the evening of the shooting stood him clear. I look for room in my stomach to eat anything more and also in my heart to respect the decision made by my dad and his brothers. But as for the alibi, I'm at a loss. My grandfather's alibi was that he was in Grand Rapids on the night of the shooting, hanging out with a good friend who not only confirmed his alibi, but was also, conveniently, a cop.

"But," she adds not knowing what I'm already thinking, "that doesn't mean that he wasn't capable of ordering a hit."

She goes on to finish the story.... Just a few years later her brother died of a heart attack, and she was the *only* family member to attend his funeral in Florida besides a distant cousin (who she believes only attended because they lived in the area).

No one went to his funeral? Not even his sons?

We finish lunch and pull my "little whip" back in front of the old brick building when she adds one more piece to the story....

"Following the funeral," she says, while scavenging to find her keys, "there was a small gathering at the home and I remember feeling uncomfortable. Betty was one of only a few women in attendance and she was dressed very provocatively with all the 'mourning men' showering her with attention."

I hear the jingle of her keys and quickly open my door to walk around to open hers and help her out. Once she's standing, we give each other a big hug.

"Thank you so much," I say and lean in to plant a kiss on her cheek. "I'm so appreciative of every piece I get of this thousand-piece jigsaw puzzle."

We both laugh and hug each other once again but more tightly. She reaches into her purse and pulls out a small tin.

"I almost forgot," she says with her big sunglasses still sitting on her smiling face. "These are peppermint pecans. It took me a few tries this year, but I finally got the coating right."

I thank her again and slip her hand in mine and we walk together to the apartment building's main entrance door. The snow is starting to fall and we debate whether it will be as bad as forecasters predicted.

· ◆ ·

From: Nate Brunhoff

Date: Monday, January 19, 2015

To: 'Michelle'

Subject: Re: a new house?

Six months or so?? Very cool.

· ◆ ·

On January 20, 2015, at 11:23 AM, Michelle wrote:

We're hoping so! I'm not going to get my hopes up until everything feels a little more concrete. It's a little terrifying trying to figure out how we can afford this city's crazy expensive real estate based on my income alone but also make sure the company can survive if it hits hard times.

I did set up my first real estate alerts!

It looks like there's a snowstorm heading our way ... Clipper.

· ◆ ·

A few days ago, Marie and Martin returned home from their vacation when she pulled me aside.

"I have really good news," she said with one of her infamously large and cheerful smiles.

Did they buy another vacation home? Are they going to move to another country again? Do they want to do another adventure with us like Africa again?

"Martin and I talked a lot about the business," she said, "and how proud we are of you and how well you're doing in your career."

"The business does seem to be doing really well lately," I had quickly confirmed. "And you were right; the move to D.C. has also been really great for my career."

"Well, we talked about your financials and we want to help you with the money to put down on a house," she continued.

"Marie!" I exclaimed.

"Michelle, you can't do this on your own," she said, squashing my stubborn disregard for charity. "We want to help you."

"Do you really think we're ready to do this on our own?" I questioned nervously. "You think we can handle it? Even if the company hits a rough patch?"

"We worked it out," she said. "And, based on your income and all of us working together to put the money down, you won't have to worry about the company. You should be able to support yourselves."

I remember fighting with Marie when we first moved to D.C., telling her there's no way we'd still be living with them past six months, but she believed it would be a few years. It turns out she was right.

◆

From: Michelle

Date: Thursday, January 22, 2015

To: Nate Brunhoff

Subject: Orange you glad

19 days!

◆

On January 23, 2015, at 11:57 AM, Nate wrote:

Whew ... killer dude. Killer. 19 days is awesome as you leave the others before you in the dust.

◆

On January 23 at 3:50 PM, Michelle wrote:

HIGH FIVE

No prisoners. ;)

Here's a really random thought ...

Would've you named me Michelle?

I was just thinking about it the other day. I know you don't (ever) answer any of my serious questions in email, but you know I am still going to try.

XO

. ♦ .

On January 23 at 7:46 PM, Nate wrote:

Nope, I would have named you Scout.

Chapter 25

I't's closing in on 3 o'clock, and I've been checking the time all day. It's gorgeous outside and I'm taking off early to head south and spend the weekend at Lake Anna again. On the center dashboard I turn up the radio and open the sunroof. The old country tunes flow into the open wind. It's true what they say: you can take the girl out of the country, but you can't take the country out of the girl. I pull off my heels and toss them to the passenger seat to drive the two hours out of town with bare feet.

Following a sunset cruise on the water and grilled dinner on the patio, Charlie, Marie, and I take up our usual seats and break out the tablecloth for games. We light the colorful citronella candles at our feet and tiki torches around the porch railing. "Yahtzee!" you can hear us yelling and laughing into the remaining hours of the evening.

When the boys head in, it's just Marie and me outside. We usually always stay up for one last drink and talk before bed. I tell her about the weird name, Scout, that Dad said he would've given me.

"That's awesome!" she quickly says, to my surprise.

Her voice is an exaggerated, high tone. She has a knack for being theatrical and is good at enunciating emphatically, especially when she wants to persuade you. But I'm perplexed. All I can think of is the "Boy Scouts." Cool, I guess, but it's for boys.

"Scout, really?" I ask again scrunching my nose.

"Have you never seen the movie?" she asks in disbelief and gets up from her chair.

"What movie?" I wonder.

"*To Kill a Mockingbird!*" she exclaims, opening the slider and grabbing a throw to wrap herself in the cooling night.

"Oh, I haven't … " I admit and follow her lead, grabbing another throw before she closes the door.

I've heard of the story but never watched the film. She encourages me to look it up and find it to watch. I know it's an old classic, so I likely will find it enjoyable.

Back inside with our final cocktails empty, I find Charlie in the bedroom already asleep. I whisper "goodnight" to Marie as she walks by and I close the door. I climb in bed and turn on the TV, select OnDemand, and enter the title into Search. It populates before I finish: *To Kill a Mockingbird.*

I sit in silence for a few minutes looking at the title on the screen and wonder what answers it may hold. Could it really have significance to the meaning of the name he would have given me? My curiosity will have it no other way; I must watch it now.

By the closing scene, I'm trapped in tears. Charlie is still sound asleep beside me. I push away a bowl of white cheddar popcorn on my lap and grab a box of tissues from the bathroom. "Oh my," I gasp alone in the darkness.

The young girl Scout had run all the way home to jump on her father's lap. Justice, as she knew it, had been served. Her father taught her some hard lessons and now she understood. She could see the importance of looking at things from someone else's perspective, not one's own and most definitely not others'. The closing scene ends with them both sitting together on the porch, and him holding her so lovingly, as any proud father would.

I would be honored to have the name Scout.

- ◆ -

JOURNAL ENTRY

January 25, 2015

I am speechless. Could this movie be any more perfect?

Scout is fearless. She's curious. She's always asking questions, and she says it how it is. Plus, Atticus, who is Scout's father in the story, is a lawyer!

How have I not seen *To Kill a Mockingbird* before?

One of my favorite scenes is when Scout gets tucked into bed and reads the back of her father's pocket watch. It read: To Atticus, My Beloved Husband. She looked at her father, upset and asked why her brother,

Jem, says he gets to have the watch someday. Atticus tells Scout that it is customary for the boy to have his father's watch. So, she asked, "What are you going to give me?"

. ♦ .

From: 'Michelle'

Date: Monday, January 26, 2015

To: Nate Brunhoff

Subject: Scout

I watched *To Kill a Mockingbird* yesterday.

I have decided that Scout is totally appropriate.

I accept.

Scout is fearless, curious, and says what's on her mind, regardless of any repercussion that may follow. She is smart, mindful and respectful of boundaries, only pushing the limits with inquisitive grace.

And Atticus, her Dad, is a lawyer. He wears round glasses just like yours.

Why would you name me Scout? Does it have anything to do with the movie? I must know more ...

XO

. ♦ .

On January 27, 2015, at 11:33 AM, Nate wrote:

That's a much harder question. You asked the question and "Scout" instantly came to mind. If the answer comes that quick and effortlessly, it must be the right answer ...

. ♦ .

On January 27 at 8:19 PM, Michelle wrote:

Well, I find it fitting that I can relate so well to the character of Scout. I wonder ... In the movie, Atticus is a defense lawyer. Is that the same kind you had desired to be?

XO,

Scout (ha!)

· ◆ ·

On January 27, 2015, at 11:33 AM, Nate wrote:

The name was picked intentionally. Consider the first two entries:

http://en.wikipedia.org/wiki/Atticus

· ◆ ·

Right now, I feel child-like.

Like a modern-day Charlie in a Willy Wonka Factory, only I'm nearly twenty years older feeling giddy in a completely normal house. I see now one small but important truth. While it may be a simple revelation, it is not one that is short-lived and will last a lifetime. The joy of a meaningful moment like this makes you want to share it with everyone, as if you can pass it along as easily as an infectious yawn.

Happiness is obtainable by every person in this world, regardless of their situation, culture, ethnicity, monetary status, or any other thing you may think to list. It's a mindset. Similar to the lesson learned by Scout, you can't always rely on your own beliefs or on others. We need to be open to the world around us and new ideas that are righteous. If you don't have happiness now, rethink your world and get it. Everyone has the opportunity to have it. It's as simple as a decision: either change your life or change your view on it. It's important to remember that everyone has trials in life. And let me emphasize: *everyone*. While your trials may seem hard, there are always others who have it harder. Eliminate those worldly stereotypes, push out the negativity, and open your mind to everything around you that can and should be appreciated.

For how many times are we told when we're younger, "You can be anything you want"? It frustrates me incredibly that I, too, once just brushed off the idea as a fairytale. As if it were a fantasy only told by ignorant adults who want to see you accomplish what they couldn't. But what unveils every time is a truth across every generation, that your mind, persistence, and determination are what make anything possible, regardless of how many times you may fall or fail.

·　◆　·

From: Nate Brunhoff

Date: Sunday, February 1, 2015

To: 'Michelle'

Subject: I have decided upon something fun

That will illustrate the evolution of literature and its cousin, film in a beautiful niche genre.

First manifestation thereof will appear in your snail mail box in a few days.

Dad

·　◆　·

On February 2, 2015, at 9:08 AM, Michelle wrote:

Oh, I'm excited! This will be fun.

I was hoping we may find something you can teach/share with me. You are obviously very knowledgeable and I want to take advantage of it.

Day 29!

·　◆　·

On February 3, 2015, at 6:37 PM, Nate wrote:

Day 30? Just awesome.

Chapter 26

"We remind you that this is a non-smoking flight," says the attendant holding a dated microphone device.

Her appearance is about as bland as her record-like voice. Dressed in a cheap cotton navy blue suit with red accent trim, she makes motions in robotic form with a sterile face as she tries to illustrate the instructions she reads from a card. When she finishes, she clips the mic back into its holder on the wall and then *throws* the instruction card into a cabin door above. I think she may not like what she does.

She starts making final rounds before take-off. I grab my headphones and a magazine before shoving my bag under the seat at my feet. I've never been a huge fan of Las Vegas, but I am looking forward to this trip. After the marketing conference, Charlie and Marie are flying in for the weekend and birthday celebrations—it's Charlie's big 3-0!

* ◆ *

From: Nate Brunhoff

Date: Saturday, February 14, 2015

To: 'Michelle'

Subject: Congrats

Alice has relayed to me that this year (perhaps your first with this company) that your presentation materials garnered 3rd place at the conference. Considering your competition in experience and their resources – this is a serious garland.

Very cool. Go purchase at least one shoe store.

= ◆ =

"Are you nervous?" I ask Charlie.

The conference is over and Charlie and Marie just flew in earlier this morning. It feels as though things are changing in both our personal and professional lives—and while it feels for the good, it is a struggle and stressful to deal with all at the same time. I have more than a month of quitting smoking under my belt and multiple blisters on my heels from walking back and forth in the miles of hallways between the Encore and the Wynn for the conference. A lover's quarrel is due, but not tonight. Growing pains is what I keep calling them. We are going through a phase that will hopefully bring us to the next bigger and better stage in life.

So, what better way to welcome it than to embrace today's Valentine's Day excursion! Charlie grips the wheel and I hear a loud, deep rumble from the engine behind us. He glances over to me and with a big smile becomes a boy again as he lets go of the brake pedal.

He precariously pulls the car out of the garage. He's living a dream, like a Make-A-Wish kid who only gets to experience something this grand if he is dying. I look around at the interior of the vehicle and admire the thick red stitching detail in soft black leather. A 458 Italia silver emblem shines in the sun on the dash. In the back, there are no seats; it's all motor covered with glass.

"How much do you think this car is worth?" I ask Charlie.

"To buy brand new?" he says while shifting into gear using the paddle shifters on the steering wheel.

"Yeah."

"About $350,000," he says looking over to me with another big, boy-like smile.

We come to the first intersection on the main road. Charlie brings the car to a stop and he gets resituated, moving his butt and back getting comfortable in the driver's seat. He catches me mid-snap of a selfie in the reflection of the side mirror.

"Do you remember what button is for the lift?" he asks.

I look up from my phone, and the mirror, and notice the huge divot in the road in front of us. This may be the one time I actually fully listened to instructions because I was so terrified to be responsible for possibly the most expensive thing I have ever touched. In the center counsel between us I point to the button next to the window controls, "It's there." He pushes the button and we sit in an awe of silence as we feel the car slowly lift up to four inches from the ground.

"That's crazy," I say, laughing in disbelief.

Charlie throws it in gear and gives it muscle, and we "take off." Riding in the beautiful, sparkling red Ferrari, we cruise the highways of Las Vegas and head out of town to Red Rock Canyon. It's a beautiful day and a comfortable eighty degrees in the desert. We cruise with the windows down and our hair blowing in the wind. At a scenic pullover at Hoover Dam, two young boys standing on the side of the parking lot start whaling their hands up in the air to get our attention. The look on their faces is returned by our own; we are looking at them looking at us in disbelief. Charlie pulls up by them. One of the boys quickly runs to his mom and snatches her camera and starts snapping photographs. Soon others join, and the other boy just stood there amazed. I was glued to my seat. I have had moments living like a (false) star and parading through some of America's biggest cities and finest homes and boats, but this tops the list. Constantly being mistaken for Paris Hilton while living in Los Angeles was considerably the bottom. Not because I have any particular opinion of her, but I would rather not be yelled at with someone else's name.

Charlie keeps moving the car slowly through the growing audience and we find a somewhat private spot in the lot to park. On top of the bridge walkway of Hoover Dam, looking down, I feel my stomach drop nearly as much as it did when Charlie opened up the Ferrari for the first time on the main road.

This place is a true wonder. The dam is incredibly expansive, but just as breathtaking as its size is the thought that it was created by man. Built in the 1930s during the Great Depression, it is said to have taken more than a hundred lives. Today, the reservoir water level sits well below the canyon trenches and you can see a distinct line in the rock where the water level used to exist for many years, hundreds of meters above. Between the marvel of engineering and the shocking effects of epic droughts in the West, Charlie and I sit for a long moment in silence. Then Charlie walks to the lookout point and peers over the side of the Reservoir.

"Oh, wow, look!" he yells back to me.

I quickly join him in peering over the edge. The rock cliff glistens in the sun, covered with silver coins and copper pennies.

"Let's make a wish!" I tell him, pulling out a quarter from my purse.

We hold onto the quarter together. With our hands intertwined and eyes closed, we both make a wish in silence. We open our eyes at nearly the same time and throw the quarter, then watch it jump and hear it ting until it eventually lands far down the cliff's edge. I wonder, what did he wish for? My wish is always simple and always the same, over and over, since a young girl.

On our way back to the car, we find a souped-up Audi has parked next to us. I know what's going to happen.

"You're not going to race him, are you?" I look over to Charlie.

"No, babe," he promises.

Not even five minutes later, we're back on the road and I'm screaming and clenching the handle, holding on for dear life. When we finally slow down, I gather my breath and my heart.

"How fast were we going?" I ask.

"133," he says.

• ◆ •

On February 17, 2015, at 9:45 AM, Michelle wrote:

Thank you! I honestly couldn't believe that I received recognition. My materials were in four of the eight categories! I received two, third places and two honorable mentions, but I know I can grab higher ranks next year. Now that I am in a position where I can focus 75 percent of my work on design, I can see the improvement. A secret between you and me, I am what could be considered a self-taught graphic designer.

Since grad school, I have been pinged for creative design in nearly every office I've worked. I was always the only one who knew the programs and have an eye for design. But I really love doing it. When I moved home from LA, I looked into going back to school for graphic design. I learned that I would have to do another four years and it would not include a master's degree. I said PASS.

Since, I have taken every opportunity to continue to use and improve my skills. Now I am teaching seven girls on my team (that did go to school for design) how to use the programs and how to fix their errors.

Sssshhh. This is top secret. ;)

XO

• ◆ •

On February 17, 2015, at 1:09 PM, Nate wrote:

I suggest you go back to school. Seriously. If you think that what you're doing is fun now, wait until you get in class with a bunch of kids that LOVE what they are doing. It's electric. I did it with Photoshop and was blown away. I couldn't wait for the classes each week. Try it. Just one class at a time. It will pay off in Entertainment and in productivity and expression.

· ♦ ·

Everything was going great, and then I'm not sure I understand what happened or how I got here. I'm hunched over my knees sitting on the bathroom floor with my hands covering my eyes. My mascara is dripping black spots onto my silk dress and I can't catch a breath for the life of me.

When Marie and Charlie arrived in Vegas a few days ago, they phoned the room and I was so excited that I sprinted down to meet them with my cover up still on and flip flops smacking the floor beneath me. We've been going on a lot of trips lately but this was going to be the most fun.

Charlie had mentioned that his friend from school was a DJ out here and might be able to get us some perks, so when they showed up in a limo at the front of the hotel, I have to admit I was speechless. We've laughed about the star treatment we've been enjoying on this trip, but now it's not feeling worth much.

Dinner reservations earlier tonight were at 6:30 p.m. It was the only spot we could get at Giada De Laurentiis' restaurant, and we had a $400 voucher from Charlie's DJ friend, again.

We ordered oysters and shrimp and a bottle of champagne. We had a lot of money to spend with the voucher and we knew how to spend it. We ordered two fine reds with dinner, a rack of lamb with filet and salmon, and a side of butternut squash soup. It was all delectable, the service was great, and the ambience was perfect.

A limo picked us up to bring us to our next destination, but Marie and I were both tired. We had full bellies and going back to the hotel room sounded really nice. We dropped Marie at her hotel first. Charlie ended up talking me into another drink. I had a glass of wine with him and a good hour playing the games right in front of us at the bar. When the bartender walked over to give me another one, I was ready to close out and resign to our room, but Charlie wanted to play a few more games, so we decided I would just go up and he'd come up in a bit.

When he didn't come after a bit, I grew restless. When he started to not answer his phone, I really started to worry.

When he finally came walking in during the wee hours of the night, I was still wide awake and at my wits end. Where was he? Why couldn't he answer his phone? But very little of these words were shared once I saw his eyes. Those are the eyes that you don't mess with. They don't happen often, but when they do, you know you are looking at someone else. They are dark and they are distant, and it is scary.

The rest of it is a blur, except for being pushed on my back side against the window of glass in our room that stretches from floor to ceiling and with the strip many floors below. His fist held high and threatening in my face, Charlie yelling in rage, "I will kill you."

What did I do? I'm so upset. I feel broken, defeated, and confused. He never hit me. He left the room, leaving me sitting here hyperventilating on the floor in a pool of black mascara tears trying to understand what just happened. The pain I feel is so deep and real, it hurts more than if he would have actually hit me. If I really did something to cause all of this, I am seeking God to please help me understand. I know Charlie's upset and I'm annoyed. He has a lot of stress with the business, but I am feeling like I no longer know how to understand (or even deal with) him.

I cry myself to sleep and when I wake, I am just so thankful he is there. We fly out later today.

Much of the trip home is shared in silence. I'm busy racking my brain trying to understand what happened. When we get home, I am surprised to find a package from my father. Excitedly, I open the Express envelope and find inside a book with instructions to flip to the pages of the Maltese Falcon:

> *The creatures of the forest tell me you would like an author of note.*
>
> *To that end, I would like to introduce you to two authors whose style is astounding for its comprehension. I call it the poetry of prose or the prose of poetry, depending on my caffeine level.*
>
> *As you read you will discover – and I promise you will love the art of language. Sometimes you will laugh. Sometimes you will go "wow." Breakfast may never be the same.*
>
> *Your mission, should you accept is to read the immortal "Maltese Falcon." Let me know when the covers of that short story close and we will forge ahead into film and go where I*

*assure you few people have gone. If you read other classic short
stories of this author (since it is on your night table) let me know
which ones ... The Thin Man?*
Pops

I pull the book out from its hard cover sleeve (I always prefer the read
without it). On the front side, debossed in gold foil is the title, *The Library of America*. Its cover is made of brown twill and has a rich maroon embossing on its side with gold trimming and lettering that reads
"HAMMET." Underneath, and in italics, *Crime Stories and Other Writings*. I open to the Contents page but am confused. I read the note again
and search up and down the indexed lines of content to be sure I didn't
miss it. Maybe Maltese Falcon is part of one of the short stories under a
different name? I snap a pic of the contents page with my phone and text
him the screen shot.

◦ ◆ ▪

> Did you send me the wrong book?

DAD

> How embarrassing. Let me check ...

> Akkk it's pres day! I sent you the companion text
> intended for another day and can't ship. You
> may want to keep your powder dry. I will send
> the intended book and you should have it by
> Wed. Mea Culpa.

> I will read this book in the meantime. Means so
> much to me. It really does. Thank you! Xoxo.

Chapter 27

Things between Charlie and me really haven't been the same since we got home from Vegas. We made amends the next morning after the terrible fight, but something is off, and that fight has left a thick ick in the air that will not be dissipating any time soon. I simply can't explain or justify any of it and it was scary. We've had a few bad fights in our many years together, but none like that, when I fear for my life—well, except for the one time, very long ago, when we were first dating.

It was before our breakup in 2009. Our fights would always escalate out of control quickly then, and I've always believed that's because I didn't know how to handle him. I was stubborn in my younger years and would spitfire words right back; the same nasty stuff that came out of his mouth, I would feed right back to him. I could play hard. It never got me anywhere with him though, as it shouldn't in any situation, but with him it would only escalate our fights into chaos, or what I would call "the scaries."

His words could be very threatening; hard liquor was most always involved, and he flung his fist in front of my face a few times but only to scare me. And stubborn me—I wasn't "scared." What I hated the most though was when he would restrain me. Ugh. I absolutely HATED being restrained. I'm not claustrophobic, but it would absolutely terrify me that no matter how hard I would plead and try to escape, I could not move or get out of his tight grasp.

One time, after dating for nearly a year, we went out for drinks with his friends and mine. We had moved in together at this point and were living together for just a few months. That night, the drinking got out of control, and so did he. Lo left as soon as Charlie swore at her and threatened to throw her off our third story balcony. Then, when we were alone and still fighting over the incident, he told me he had a gun and would kill me. I had never had anyone close to me scare me like that, ever. For it to come from someone whom you love and who loves you, is so confusing. I remember trying to be sweet and convincing him to calm down, and then quickly grabbing my phone, running out of the apartment to call the police. By the time the cops showed up, Charlie had already come downstairs and found me. He had started crying hysterically. That's when I first learned that his father could have a terrible temper when he got drunk, and it was his biggest fear.

I remember thinking even then, how can a boy with so much heart have something so dark inside him. It was a big learning moment for us, and we continued to grow from there, working to try and understand how to deal with our differences, feelings, and reactions. It wasn't perfect—no relationship is—but our adolescence did get the best of us at times.

After we bought our first house together, I thought it would save us, but instead it broke us. Everything we had learned to respect about one another went out the door. Those dark drunk eyes came back, and they returned time and time again. One night, I was doing laundry and found an empty pill bottle with his father's name on it in his jeans. When I questioned him about it, he became quickly infuriated and locked me in the basement. Things continued to spiral out of control and it was only a matter of months of us moving in to our new home together that I moved out.

Our separation lasted for almost a year. In my head, I was done. I could never go back to that kind of a life. But yet, no matter how hard I tried to move on, my heart still yearned for him. I was still madly in love with him. Our love then, as it is now, is the most passionate love I have ever experienced.

I eventually gave in to my heart after receiving a package in the mail from Charlie. It was a long, heartfelt love letter and a confession. Taped to the last page was a necklace engraved with "One Love." He messaged me a few days later and asked to meet at the park. I agreed, and when I pulled up, he was there waiting with our dog Bernie—who was tugging at him to run over as soon as I opened the car door. After the hugs and hellos, we walked to a wooden picnic table in front of the city water department building with a view of the lake. I popped a seat on top of the table with my feet on the bench. As soon as Charlie did the same, the wood broke under him and sent us both flying. We both broke out in hysterical laughter. Talk about an icebreaker.

That evening, with the falling sunset, broken picnic table, and Bernie at our side, he confessed everything I already knew but had felt crazy for thinking because he was always denying everything. He finally told me everything. When we bought the house, he had started to dabble in medication that was not prescribed to him. Some of the guys at work introduced him to pain killers and he was mixing them with drinking when he went out. It broke my heart to hear that it only got worse after I moved out. It got so bad, to the point that he would wake in the morning and feel sick with sweats and shakes, and the only way it would go away was to pop more pills. That's when it really started to scare him and he finally opened up to his parents and got help.

I remember feeling so overwhelmed with emotion. To not only hear that after all we went through I was justified in my questioning—but it also hurt to hear about all his pain and suffering. After opening up to his parents, he admitted himself to rehab. He was clean a few months, seeing a therapist, and expressed his desire to take his life back, promising he would never treat me wrong or let me down again. His doctor prescribed him Suboxone (a dissolvent film) that sounded promising. He was told it would help him break the opioid addiction at a slow and healthy pace that the human body needs to fully recover without any remission. He could be completely recovered in two years or less, from what his doctor had seen, or up to five years for anyone who struggles. We had no doubt that he was strong enough to recover quickly.

It was in that moment, sitting on the broken picnic table, that I decided. He's not perfect. We all have our faults and someone is going to love us regardless. Someone is going to love him, and I want to be that someone. It's going to be me.

But, of course, it was never that easy. There was a marquee night soon after getting back together that dropped the weighted rope and opened the curtains to the theatre again. It took a lot of counseling, family, and sobriety for me to be convinced that we could have another chance, and it was all based on hope and the belief in faith and love. After many tears and hard conversations, we realized together what was most important in our lives—what we had, have, and what we missed—each other. We committed ourselves to being a better "me" and a better "us." Charlie also stayed committed to the Suboxone as the doctor prescribed. I can't count on my hand how many times I have seen Charlie drink more than two drinks since. Looking back, it felt as though we went through war. We were on the front lines of a battlefield, and when we came out together, we came out stronger.

But now things are stressful again. I feel the war but we're not in it together. I don't feel him at the front lines alongside me. And what's really bothering me is he's not letting me in on what is going on. I can't help but feel that same feeling as that terrible day when I found the first empty pill bottle in the laundry and lost my stomach. You know something is not right; you feel it in your gut and you know it in your heart, but you are in the dark and can't pin it down or make any sense of what you try to understand is really going on.

The next week after we returned from Vegas, police visited our company office. Before the holidays, we had three employees; now we have none. Charlie fired one the night before Christmas for not being trustworthy and stealing, and now we had to let the other two go because of a crime conviction. It turns out that while we were away on holiday travel, the ex-employee who was fired hooked up with the other two employees (who are cousins) and used our company van to break into a local junk yard down the road. They stole car parts and then sold the metal to another company in the neighborhood.

So, with the scare of the cops and the diminished employee support, I know Charlie has a lot on his plate and is stressed out. It's honestly hard for me to empathize though because I have a lot of things *overfilling* my plate. I'm working hard to help support him in building our company together, all while maintaining my own full-time career. I'm carrying alone a lot of the weight of the cash flow and trying to save for a down payment on a house. We went from having our own beautiful home in Michigan to living with his parents, whom I love and adore, in D.C., and it's going on three years and I just really, really need to do me. I'd rather focus on what we're going to do next. I need plans. I need to know the light is at the end of the tunnel. I don't put my stress on him, so why does he put his on me? I need him to be a part of our team again.

I head to bed early and grab the book Dad sent me by mistake. I pull it out from its cover again and flip open to the contents page. Running my finger down the list, "Red Harvest ... The Dain Curse ... The Glass Key ... The Thin Man...." I stop at "The Thin Man: An Early Transcript," follow my finger to the right, and flip to page 847. I turn through the rest of the pages quickly. To my surprise, it's an incredible read. I enjoy the unique style of storytelling, most especially the introduction of the characters identified only by their human characteristics, their names left to be a mystery until he has time to build their characters. Hammett has a unique writing flair. Before long, Miles is dead. Thursby is dead. Ms. Wonderly is now Brigid O'Shaughnessy and is hidden in a new hotel under another name I have already forgotten. She gave a lot of cash to protect her from something we still have no clue about, and a man just visited Spade in his office and held him at gunpoint.

"BANG!"

The loud noise startles me and I catch the book just before it hits the ground. For the past hour, Roger had been playing with the balloons on the floor, leftover from Charlie's birthday celebration. This time he got one, scaring the daylights out of me!

My heart slows to a steady pace again and instead of reopening the book I drift off in my thoughts, replaying many of things that have happened most recently.

I've never lost my faith, or have I, I wonder? I've convinced Charlie to pray with me maybe a handful of times, but nowadays I pray in the secrecy of a bathroom and rarely have an opportunity to talk about it with family or friends. Having faith is a bit taboo in this household and is normally only mentioned to poke fun. My conversations with faithful friends back home are then also so quickly overshadowed with trying to catch up on life, being separated by so much time and so many states. Rarely do I get a chance to talk about it or even time to devote or dream. I need a renewal or reminder. I know the magic of faith always exists and is around us every day, even if we may forget or fail to see it.

◦ ◆ ◦

From: 'Michelle'

Date: Thursday, February 19, 2015

To: Nate Brunhoff

Subject: Curious

I'm almost done with the Thin Man short story. It's exceptionally good and has me turning the pages every time I open it before bed. If I do not finish it tonight, it will be done by tomorrow night and I can start the new book this weekend. I will let you know my thoughts on Thin Man once finished. I can't wait to start the real lesson!

I am curious – *what do you believe in?*

:)

◦ ◆ ◦

On February 19, 2015, at 7:51 PM, Nate wrote:

The closest direct evidence we have, the writings of the Saints, the manuscripts, is 400 years after the death of Christ. What many people do not know is the recounting of Christ's healings in which the Greek and early Latin state very clearly that Christ was exhausted and needed to rest. He was human. Not a God. You will recall the rumor test in school. The teacher would impart to a student a simple factual statement. At the end of the school day the last person in the class recites aloud the factual statement he or she received.

Reallllly??? Add four hundred years of the oral tradition.

What of Edgar Cayce?

There are a lot of things that are Marvelous. Alice is one of those. Take six vials. One vial will have a medicine or homeopathic remedy. The remaining five vials are empty. Put each under a piece of paper all side by side. She can tell you instantly and without error which is which. We don't talk about it because if you don't understand energy, then an observer will think it's all Penn and Teller.

Then we need to talk about the presence of my mother at the dinette table while playing Yahtzee in November with you. With regard to that "presence", all three women, separately in time and space, Alice, Maura, and you, stated without hesitation that it was my mom.

At another time, I had become very, very, very sick and I could see without doubt my grandfather (a physician) watching over me and nodding approvingly. He passed away many decades ago, but there he was ...

· ◆ ·

On February 20, 2015, at 6:38 PM, Michelle wrote:

Growing up, I did not have much faith in God per se. Without being told or educated on faith, however, I always had a sense of a higher power—something else. And I have always felt someone with me. When I met Lo in 6ᵗʰ grade, she and her parents introduced me to church. Her mom would read us passages from the Bible on the weekends and explain them to us in modern day language that we could understand. I was always very fascinated. Then, when I had to move in with a friend and her family in high school in order to stay in town and not move away with my mom, I was introduced to a very strict religion. They were Baptist. I'll never forget the first sermon I attended with them. I had been attending church for a few years now and felt like I was a good person, but yet this pastor had me running through the pews to the bathroom where I found an empty stall and hid myself to cry.

Religion is supposed to be for the greater good, to teach love and understanding. But yet, every war is over religion. And I have always wondered ... if Christ did all those amazing things in front of me, like parting the Red Sea and healing the sick, well * * * *, I would have believed in him too! Why did he show all those people so many years ago all the many miracles, but cannot show us today? We are supposed to just believe. As a girl with lots of pride, I want to say show me!

Yet, most everyone believes in a higher power. Whether it's God, Buddha, the stars, nearly every one of us across all countries, all continents, all races and all cultures, all believe in something more than just us.

The stars and ghosts do interest me most. And interestingly enough, those are both existent based on the belief of energy.

As I said before, it is true, I don't know why but I do think it was your mother who was with us that first weekend we met. I will also say I don't know why but I think the angel I have felt with me my whole life has also been your mother. I can very confidently say that without an angel, I would not be where I am today.

There is something out there, I just know it. If you find out first, let me know— and I'll do the same for you.

XO

*　◆　*

I type D-a-s-h-i-e-l-l H-a-m-m-e-t-t into Google search and hit enter. Scrolling down the page, I click on an article by the Francisco Gate, "Dashiell Hammett's legacy lives not only in his writing, but in his living—rough, wild and on the edge."

In the first paragraph, I learn he is one of the most brilliant and most recognized writers of the 1930s yet sadly he drank himself broke and eventually to death at sixty-six, the same age as Dad.

The article reads on that thirty-three years earlier he began writing the book that would fully proclaim him as one of the best detective novelists of his time, *The Maltese Falcon*. I continue to scan the paragraphs in disbelief of the irony of his noted ages and catch his time writing and living in San Francisco. I hit ctrl + P on the keyboard and click print. With the pages warm in hand, I read each more closely, as I had "The Thin Man." At the end of the article, I snap off the cap of an orange highlighter and touch the felt tip to highlight a quote he had told the reporter: "I stopped writing because I found I was repeating myself. It is the beginning of the end when you discover you have style."

What's interesting is that many times we can't see our own style. We are often shadowed by conformity, in education, culture, and family. At a young age we are pushed to decide what we want to be and then are defined to live within a set parameter of respectable means. But is that truly who we are or what we want to be, and who can recognize that truth but us?

Chapter 28

Over think things? Who me? Ha. (Insert knowingly nodding head.) Second-guess a decision? Ack. Multiple choice tests are my greatest enemy!

A few months ago, I was home, and Lo and I were out to lunch with a former high school teacher. It had been more than fifteen years since we both sat in her class, but less than three since we had our last drink together. She's elderly now, but that has only made her wiser and more beautiful. Her vibrant, spunky age can be counted in the number of times we all laughed at the table. She made jokes about her (barely) thinning hair and made sure we knew her excitement for all the fabulous wigs she was ready to start buying. While debating over accepting a head of thinning hair or buying a wig, we somehow got on the subject of multiple-choice tests.

"They don't bother me," she said confidently, setting her wine glass down. "I always just pick one, and if it says 'All of the Above,' then I always pick that instead."

We went on to argue how valid this thesis is, and I remember thinking: (a) she's got the inside scoop and (b) I could seriously benefit from this strategy.

It's said that part of your brain is responsible for analyzing problems of hundreds of variables; it is your prefrontal cortex. The part of your brain responsible for overthinking is your stupid.

◦ ◆ ◦

JOURNAL ENTRY

February 28, 2015

Ever since he gave me this book, Dad and my conversations are more frequent and filled with purpose.

He recently put me to task and instructed me to go back to chapter one and re-read the introduction and description of Ms. Wonderly and compare it to a later reading in the chapter when she describes her sister's kidnapper, Mr. Thursby. He sent me his analysis. I, in turn, sent him mine. While our interpretations differ, I do think they have potential to go hand in hand. Possibly a clever combination of two deeper meanings by two smarty pants?

I'm just hoping I did not fail the task and am in anticipation to hear what he says back ...

* ◆ *

From: Nate Brunhoff

Date: Sunday, February 29, 2015

To: 'Michelle'

Subject: I think you may be over thinking the casual query

The issue is whether or not you agree with the following perception.

Ms. Wonderly at the outset deports herself as a fluttery, slightly historic [sic] woman, who is reluctant to give detail except for the facts that Thursby is dangerous, her sister is missing, and her parents are out of town, etc. Then, when asked to describe Thursby, she suddenly catalogues him with minute detail.

My perception was that such a machine gun recitation would have been better served up if she had handed a picture to Sam, or even Miles, for their recounting of features. In the alternative, the recitation could have been a bit staggered and hesitant to be in keeping with her previous monologues.

Do you agree or disagree? Not to put too fine of a point on this, the lives of your dogs hang in balance.

Mr. Smarty Pants

* ◆ *

Logging into work email this morning, Dad's message is the first to pop up as the messages load. A colleague walking by my office at the same time catches me laughing and pauses to do a double take. I reassure him it's just a message I received and greet him with, "Happy Monday!"

The messages come in like clockwork now and nearly every day. It's as if he is reading with me. Every page I turn, I wonder, so does he? You can only imagine how much I love that idea. It's not "moments like this" but it is this moment that I could care less about all the years without him.

. ♦ .

JOURNAL ENTRY

March 2, 2015

It's already March and today was one of those days you look out the window and are so sad to see the world outside still frozen. The sky is yet again one big, gray cloud and the ground is covered in graying, dirty snow. If we're lucky enough to see a peek of sunlight, it's usually blinding and the highlight of conversation that day.

It's Sunday, and I'm staying in bed. I'm perfectly content with letting this day slip away just as all the last months but only because I want to get lost in this book.

. ♦ .

From: Nate Brunhoff

Date: Tuesday, March 3, 2015

To: 'Michelle'

Subject: Note in passing ...

It occurred to me that I should clarify ...

In our adventure into lit and film, I am not merely directing traffic. If I suggest that you read the Maltese Falcon, then I, too, read (re-read) the Maltese Falcon and the same is true of the films that accompany the suggested texts (which will be sent to you).

I read more slowly than you do because I have a reading disability and because I tend to savor the language. Hence you will be subjected to quoted passages that astound my sensibilities or make me laugh at the cleverness.

e.g.

"That, that story I told you yesterday was all, a story," she stammered and looked up at him now with miserable frightened eyes.

"Oh that," Spade said lightly, "We didn't believe your story."

"Then?" Perplexity was added to the misery and fright in her eyes.

"We believed your two hundred dollars."

"You mean?" She seemed to not know what he meant.

"I mean that you paid us more than if you'd been telling the truth," he explained blandly, "and enough more to make it all right."

Spade put the cigarette in his mouth, set fire to it, and laughed smoke out.

Because you have said you want to write the great American novel, I have chosen for you two authors that will change your writing style forever. Hammett and Chandler. The two authors, one slightly better than the other especially at similes and metaphors, exemplify compression. Recall that Hemingway considered it a good day if he wrote one hundred words.

I am on Falcon's chapter VII but I will catch up soon while you wander off into the unanticipated but now incorporated land of The Thin Man. I hope to be able to send you the film materials on the Maltese Falcon on Monday.

◦ ◆ ◦

On March 3, 2015, at 8:53 PM, Michelle wrote:

My goodness!

Now I'm inspired to find a few of my favorite parts from Maltese Falcon. There is one in particular that sticks out. It actually had me belt out in laughter when reading it. I will find my passages and write you in greater length tomorrow.

I have already wandered off, but take your time, please. And I am not sure if it is possible, but I may be enjoying The Thin Man slightly more than the Maltese Falcon. Maybe it was the early writings that hooked me.

Please give hugs to Alice and Oreo. I miss you all.

More tomorrow,

XO

. ♦ .

On March 3, 2015, at 9:04 PM, Nate wrote:

I am most pleased to hear this. Since you find a better plot and characters in The Thin Man, let's do Maltese Falcon followed by the films, then The Thin Man and the films that follow the same before tasting Raymond Chandler.

Quite exciting this is ...

. ♦ .

On March 4, 2015, at 6:16 PM, Michelle wrote:

Yes!

And I do apologize for the delay today. One of the girls at my office (not the shop) quit today. It's not anything I can't work through, but it does come with some unique challenges. Change is always good though and change is in the air – in more ways than we know!

So, with Hammett, my Pinkerton Pal ...

One thing that continues to bother me in his writing is his descriptive of lighting a cigarette. He uses the action word "lighted" as opposed to "lit". A great example is in this fabulous sentence: Spade lighted his cigarette, leaned back comfortably on the divan, and spoke with goodhearted carelessness.

I love this sentence and the thought of him leaning back, throwing up his feet on his desk and talking in poetic, lighthearted fun, but my mind stumbles and gets stuck on "lighted." He lit it. He didn't lighted it, right?

. ♦ .

On March 5, 2015, at 11:18 AM, Nate wrote:

Good question! Lighted and lit each work as the past tense and past particle of the verb light. Both have long histories in English and are used throughout the English-speaking world, so you are generally safe using the one that sounds best to you. Neither form is inherently more American or more British. Both forms are hundreds of years old, and each has had periods of prevalence throughout history. It just happens at this stage in history, lighted is more common in American English than elsewhere.

To us, in this period, lighted appears awkward.

Hammett, your Pinkerton Pal? THAT is funny!

Chapter 29

I stretch my arms and roll to the side. I love waking up here. I smile as though I'm pleased with myself and look around my surroundings. The walls are painted a bright baby blue and colorful fish décor catches a glimmer of the morning light. I put my arm around Charlie and grab him closer, while touching my toes on our snoring dog lying at my feet.

The past few weeks have been filled with stress. I lost a graphic designer and am covering her work. I've been at the office most nights until ten o'clock, and even midnight a few times. I know I push myself too hard at times, and it's exactly what I'm doing now. Everything was okay until Thursday, at one o'clock in the morning. I broke down. My nights at the office are late, but Charlie's have been even later. Our dinners are eaten apart and we're feeling more and more distanced. Dinner has always been my favorite "us" time. To sit and relax, enjoy each other and good conversation over a warm plate of food. Every night I still cook, but now only to package it up neatly, and put it in the microwave ready to reheat with a love note left on the counter. All I can hope for is that I'm still awake when he finally comes crawling into bed.

The stress is piled high, but we're at the cottage this weekend to relax, just he and I. I take a deep breath and curl up my toes, giving Charlie a gentle squeeze and I feel him squeeze back. I catch my phone lighting up on the night stand and pull my arm from Charlie to check it. It's Dad. I haven't heard from him all week, which was no longer normal.

. ◆ .

DAD

> **Books n' films**
> Yes. Really liked Most Violent Year which was studiously not violent. Will put in tomorrow's mail, next adventure.

Hey there! Been wondering where you've
been wandering ... I loved Most Violent Year:
"Leading a life that is 'most' right."

• ◆ •

Uncle Ed was visiting Dad last weekend, so I bet they watched it togeth-er. It's definitely Dad's favorite thing to do when company is in town, to treat them to a movie and then dinner to discuss it afterwards. Alice had messaged me a few cute pics of them together during his stay. I wonder if they talked about what I told Dad during our last visit?

I can't help but admire my freshly painted pink toes and how cute they look comfortably propped up on the striped ocean blue ottoman in front of me. Charlie and I have the weekend to ourselves and I'm enjoying some "me time" painting my toes and enjoying the view of the lake. I grab another quick peek of approval before lowering my gaze back to the open magazine on my lap. I flip a few pages, snap it shut, and throw it back in the stack of *Southern Living* magazines at my side. I grab another to thumb through. I'm looking for inspiration and a recipe to cook something new and delicious for dinner tonight.

Tonight's meal is what I've named "The Last Supper." Tomorrow, I'm getting a tooth pulled—the very first step in the long process of getting braces. I'll be a thirty-three-year-old with a metal mouth. And it won't be until I'm thirty-five that they'll come off! I am a little nervous but mostly excited to have straight teeth. I can only begin to imagine how it will feel, the day when I can shine a glowingly confident and nearly perfect, pretty smile. I have always been incredibly self-conscious of my teeth. Having a smile with straight pearly whites is something I've dreamed of my entire life. My top line is slightly crooked in the front and the bottom is totally jacked. The crowding is so terrible that they have to extract a tooth to make room to straighten out the others. The one they are pulling is completely sideways and smack dab in the middle of my bottom line.

Charlie once nicknamed me "CT;" it was his loving (or not) acronym for crooked teeth. Thankfully it didn't stick for long, not like "bird" or "moose," which is the latest and most popular. I don't know if he ever knew how much "CT" bothered me, but he did stop using it when I made it a point that it was enough.

I close the last magazine and pick up a stack of torn-out pages. I thumb through those next and narrow down my choice. Tonight we'll enjoy lamb with sautéed apples, flatbread with ricotta and parsley, a fall harvest hash made with bacon, Brussels sprouts, and sweet potato, and for dessert, caramel apple fantans.

*   *

From: Nate Brunhoff

Date: Friday, March 20, 2015

To: 'Michelle'

Subject: Home entertainment

Michelle:

I am sending today the last, and most renowned, Maltese Falcon with Humphrey Bogart. I take serious issue with the casting of Effie and Bridget, but we can chat about that soon enough.

From here, the transition was to go to Raymond Chandler's "The Big Sleep" with Humphrey Bogart (clever transition eh?) ... but excitement got in the way of those best laid plans and all things detoured over to "The Thin Man."

In the early movies, they did not have special effects. They had plot. The only way to move the plot forward was dialogue. Thus, you will find in "The Thin Man" snappier, witty repartees that rarely exist.

The Thin Man so captured the public's attention that 6 short movies were made. I will send the boxed set next week. It will give me a slight chance to catch up. Sighhhhhh

In the meantime, you may want to invite your in-laws to watch the Bogart version. It still holds water very well. (no pun intended)

Pops

*   *

"I know these tools look ancient," the nurse says with her back turned towards.

She slides two large, bulky, metal mouth objects onto a blue cloth covered tray at her side. I wiggle in my seat and whisper under my breath ... get me out of here! They look like something you'd see in a historic documentary about chipping into stone to find artifacts. I take a deep breath and slide down in the dentist chair. I keep thinking about my terrifying nightmares of losing teeth. And yet here I am volunteering to have one of them pulled out—and we're going to do it caveman style? I'm not scared; I'm petrified! What did I sign up for? Do I really want to do this? Maybe I am okay with my smile?

She starts numbing me up with a needle poking inside my mouth and into my gums. My hands are tightly clenched and getting sweaty. By the fourth poke, I can no longer feel anything. She says it'll be a quick, easy pull.

When the dentist comes in, I grab the chair arms. He grabs a caveman tool. I have no feeling—thank God!—but I can *hear* the muscle tear and bone start to crack as he yanks at it. He yanks again and again, and *again*. My eyes are as wide as my mouth now and he can see it. What is going on? I thought it was going to be a quick, easy pull?

"It should have come out quick," he says looking over to the nurse with a slight look of perplexity, "a small tooth like that."

Please, just come out, I start praying over and over again. Finally, the "little" tooth breaks free from my jaw.

"I'm never doing that again," I hear him say to the nurse, this time quietly under his breath.

"Me neither!" I laughingly express loudly.

· ◆ ·

> Got my tooth pulled! Ahhhhhhhhhh
> Spacers go on next Friday and then braces April 3!

ALICE

> On dad's b-day :)

> Just what he always wanted. LOL

ALICE

> He had braces when he was young but pulled them out one night because they hurt. Are you surprised? LOL

> Ouch!!! What a rebel.

· ◆ ·

From: Nate Brunhoff

Date: Sunday, March 22, 2015

To: 'Michelle'

Subject: Home entertainment

Dear In-Depth:

Please note that the materials I send are for joint entertainment.

There is no obligation and no timeline. **** happens. Thus, for the last 6 Thin Man movies that will land on your doorstep, this coming week I would suggest after Maltese Falcon, sampling #1 and #6. If the presentation holds your interest, fine. Spin away ... if not, then skip it. Older movies are often a little difficult to savor.

I noticed that you're having more east coast weather fun. Cool. I assure you Spring is in fact coming.

I hope Charlie found a replacement for his employee. The less time he spends in the paint booth, the better.

Soon Baboon.

· ◆ ·

On March 22, 2015, at 5:29 PM, Michelle wrote:

Pops,

We're driving back from the cottage tonight. I was a little nervous to leave town again, because we were just there last weekend, but with everything going on between the shop and the office ... I'm so glad we did. We're both running hard, long hours but conquering * * * * and getting it done!

Getting my tooth pulled on Friday was terrifying; I'm not going to lie. The utensils they used were the same ancient tools used by the Mayans to carve in stone. I had thought I'd be more scared to walk around toothless than to actually get it pulled. That is in hindsight. But what is exciting is my braces go on April 3—your birthday! Haha. Just what you always wanted: a thirty-three-year-old with a mouth full of metal.

Have you finished reading the Maltese Falcon yet? I'm so curious to hear your thoughts about the end and why Effie is so upset.

Later Gator.

. ♦ .

On March 22, 2015, at 7:07 PM, Michelle wrote:

Overall rating: Good

Maltese film is dated and held prisoner to the technology of its day but tastefully done. They did a great job selecting which major key plots to pull from the story, and it was not too far-stretched from the pages of the book.

The affair between Wonderly and Spade was most prevalent but felt a bit exaggerated. And Effie had such a small part in the film. If it were me directing, Effie would have had a lead role in the film, as I think she is an important character with many layers in the storyline.

I, of course, was disappointed to still not know why Effie is upset at the end of the story because the film ends differently. Instead, Spade visits Wonderly's jail cell and feels regret. An interesting twist separated from the book that I was not expecting.

I will put in Bogart's film tomorrow night. I am hoping to see more Effie as she is my favorite character.

You know what may have been most interesting ... to watch the film first, read the book, and then watch the film again. I am just wondering if some of the pieces I picked up on naturally from reading the book may have been more confusing when watching the film. Hmmm.

Oh how it leaves you wondering, that Wonderly.

Night!

A Toothless Moose

◦ ◆ ◦

On March 23, 2015, at 12:12 PM, Nate wrote:

Yep. I think you are in for a surprise in the Bogart treatment.

◦ ◆ ◦

From: 'Michelle'

Date: Thursday, March 26, 2015

To: Nate Brunhoff

Subject: Life in the fast lane!

Today is a replica of all other days this week; I have failed in getting anything done to benefit my personal happiness, and that includes hanging out with the Thin Man.

Tonight, I will be enjoying a big glass of wine. Good news to share soon with regards to both work and our business. Full updates to come this weekend.

Set on cruise control ...

81 days,

XO

◦ ◆ ◦

On March 27, 2015, at 11:22 AM, Nate wrote:

Dear Racey Chic:

I am most curious about your home "life style." That is, are your in-laws in VA fascinated by music? Do they constantly play music and collect rock star posters? Are there musical instruments strewn about? Are you short on space for the time-being? Do you have a reading room? Is your Home Theater still in boxes? Does your father-in-law go to the shooting range every weekend? Does your mom-in-law have an autographed M. Stewart apron and go nutz over the latest salad recipe, or does she go hunting with Missy Palin?

Mr. Nosey

· ◆ ·

On March 28, 2015, at 11:18 AM, Michelle wrote:

You have a good nose. Our "life style" has no style haha. We are blended for the time being. Our personal space is a guest bedroom. Besides the extra closets in the house, it is the only space we can call our own. The rest of our life is in boxes in a storage unit.

We are living in a three-level townhome. It is very nice and more spacious than you would think. We are not on top of each other, and the different levels offer a nice array of privacy and space. Charlie and I split our bedroom closet for our everyday gear. He then has the office closet for work clothes and coats and I have the basement closet (two floors down) for all my work clothes. We also have a number of totes in the garage that we switch out for seasonal.

Martin is currently at work and is always working. He is traveling the world most days and speaks fluent Swahili. He sends us pictures of skinned goats and flying in helicopters with princes. His tales are my favorite. Last weekend I smoked a cigar with him at the bonfire while he shared stories and I asked a million questions.

We call Charlie's mom, Schwiggly. She schwigs and she jigs LOL. She's a lot of fun. Her style is very exciting and vibrant. Bejeweled artwork and large refurbished antique pieces of furniture are spread throughout the home. We like to go antiquing together and both love to collect green depression glass.

Our three dogs keep it very lively and interesting in the house. They are currently strewn about the floor at my feet, each with a bone. The Eagles are playing from the stereo.

Spacers were put in my teeth yesterday at lunch. There are small rubber bands stuck in between my teeth that are quite painful and very annoying. One more week until I'm a real brace face!

XO,

Moose

· ◆ ·

It's another late night at work. I'm a broken record at this point. Walking down the dark, barely lit halls of our closed office building, it's depressing and tiring, and yet I know Charlie won't be home either, so I'm in no rush. Both of our jobs are so demanding right now. All I have to look forward to anymore are the last few minutes before we fall asleep, hoping we'll actually spend it together.

I pull up to the mailbox and cuss out loud. I can never find the key. Why do I not put it on my keychain? I grab the stack of mail piled so high that I can barely squeeze it out from the corners of the box and end up tearing a few pieces. I throw it all on the seat and turn the car around to park on the street. Without fail, as soon as the car door opens, the terrible screeches of Bernie begin.

I try to carefully set the huge pile of mail on the small console table set against the stair wall in the entryway but a large FedEx envelope slides out from underneath and brings the full stack crashing down to the floor behind me. I notice the big envelope is addressed to me. I rip open the package and pull out a letter.

> *Greetings and Felicitations –*
> *99% of real people have no clue there are two Maltese Falcon movies before the famous Humphrey Bogart version of 1941. I will be the first to concede this is an indulgence of academia.*
> *Enclosed you will find two disks. Why #2 and #3, I don't know. They are the first two versions. I will send the Bogart version later this week. This will bring us to The Thin Man films which I will send you soon. There are six disks. This will keep you occupied on those long, lonely late winter evenings in which*

you have only one lump of coal to heat your warehouse size home while you wait for Charlie to come back from the mines.

    … then we can move on to my absolute favorite; Raymond Chandler.

    I know that you are worried about whether or not you will be able to write the great American novel now that you are the same age as Christ. However, take note if you would that Chandler did not write his first novel until the age of 44. That means you have a few weeks left.
NB

                                    • ♦ •

From: 'Michelle'

Date: Saturday, April 4, 2015

To: Nate Brunhoff

Subject: Here's something to bite into

Did you have a good birthday? Your present will arrive soon! :)

I need to catch up on reading. I did watch the Bogart movie on Sunday. I really liked it. I still don't know what the * * * * Effie is so mad about at the end?

XO,

Brace Face

                                    • ♦ •

After all the pre-preparation, along with being toothless and having an empty hole in my bottom teeth line, I can honestly say I woke up very excited. Today is the day. I finally get my braces on. The entire process has been long, painful, and super annoying, including the first consultation, two follow-up appointments, a casting, a tooth pulled, and then spacers for another week—but worth it.

    Our office closed early today for Good Friday and I left around one o'clock. I'm a little nervous whether I'll make the 2:30 appointment. The drive normally takes around an hour, but it's raining in D.C., which means traffic is as bad as if it were a snowstorm. People do not know how to drive here. My orthodontist's office is in Damascus, Maryland—a quaint town in the country about forty minutes north of D.C. The doc shares a space with my dentist in town, but only on Fridays. For this procedure, I have to go to his main office.

I finally arrive, but I am very late and blame it on the rain. Ironically, the excuse is knowingly accepted. The doctor meets me in the lobby and escorts me to the middle of a room that feels incredibly short, possibly because I am the tallest person standing in it. All of the chairs have small children in them. He stops and waves his hand to gesture to one of the chairs next to them. I laugh a little and then squeeze my giant body into the small chair.

To my right, a kid who fell from his bike and hit a big rock knocked off a bracket and was getting it repaired. To my left, an adorable little chunk. His wires are bent because he was eating candy. He admits to the hygienist that he also hasn't been brushing or flossing. The sweet boy just keeps answering all of her questions fully admitting to all his failures. I appreciate his honesty and innocence. He's absolutely adorable. My ortho motions again to lay my head back in the chair. He places an incredibly uncomfortable, large, plastic piece in my mouth to keep it open and then quickly begins the process.

It's painful. Swallowing is a task and the taste in my mouth is terrible. I'm not aware of the time but it feels as though I've been lying here with my mouth held open for an hour. My fingers have been piercingly clenching my crossed arms above the elbows. I'm starting to think I may not be able to go any longer when he leans over so I can see his face.

"Okay, we're done!" he says with cheesy excitement. "You can have your mouth back now."

And with that, he motions to the assistant who hands over a mirror and removes the oversized plastic bites from my mouth.

Staring at myself in the mirror and seeing my brace-filled mouth, I look weird. I slide my tongue over the metal brackets. Gross. It feels even stranger swiping my tongue across my teeth. I can't help but laugh at my own distaste and discomfort. I can barely close my lips over the brackets. I laugh again trying.

"We got almost everything on," he says, "but I'm going to need to see you again in thirty days to finish."

"I think I owe that to you after being so late," I say. "I'm so sorry again. Fit me in whenever you can and I'll make it happen."

Walking back up to the front lobby, I set my purse on the counter and pull out my checkbook, greeting the receptionist awkwardly with my new mouth full of metal, trying to smile.

"What's the total I need to pay today?" I ask.

It should be around $1,400 because I owe a twenty percent deposit. I have proudly saved up all the money myself. After all these years, I finally have the means. She stands up from her seat and meets me eye level through the glass window.

"You don't owe anything for this visit," she says sweetly.

"Oh," I start to question my memory of the payment plan. "Do I pay you when I come back then?"

"Not at all," she says. "Someone called and made a deposit for you of $3,000. She put fifty percent down.... "

She didn't even finish her sentence and I was choked up with tears.

"Oh my gosh," I whisper, trying to gather my composure, "I know who she is.... "

I can't believe it. This is the best surprise I have ever had. No one has ever done something so thoughtful and so giving. I thank the receptionist again and swipe to favorites on my phone walking out the door. I tap on Marie's name. She answers and I choke up with tears, gargle in thank yous.

I can't wait to get home to hug Marie. I also need to make it to the post office before it closes. I need to mail the package to Dad for his birthday, another used bookstore treasure. This one didn't take as long as the first to find, but I did go back to the same bookstore. I somewhat had my bearings this time, walking around the towering bookshelves. And knew exactly what I wanted to find, an old book on the origin of film, or some kind of historical documentation on the transit of text to film. It only took an hour before I found it in a stack of towering books. It had a fragile and well-worn cover and was published overseas. The price tag was still on the inside cover. What's unique is that it's not a story about the development of film, but instead its acceptance into society. Interestingly, the pages contain several countries with similar laws written to try and control or suppress the new medium.

I am feeling a little nervous about my braces being on and how Charlie will respond. I imagine kissing will be a bit different.

◦ ◆ ◦

From: Nate Brunhoff

Date: Monday, April 6, 2015

To: 'Michelle'

Subject: This book is

Most curious. It appears to be published in Britain for an initial cost of one shilling net.

The text looks like it is a cross among a procedure manual, a business plan's State of Purpose, and a moral compass! India will not use film for evil. (Recall India was still a colony of Britain in the 1930s when this was published.)

NB

Chapter 30

Where did April go? I wonder, flipping the calendar on my office wall. It's Monday, May 4, and out the window, stormy dark clouds are casting out the morning sun. I feel underwhelmed and overwhelmed. Charlie and I are still at odds. We just got back from a weekend getaway to Florida, but it was more of a tease than it was relaxing.

My computer is streaming the sounds of riots in Baltimore. It is day three of rioting there and it feels surreal. Did I miss something? Have we traveled back in time and are reliving the ignorant days of colors versus whites? I thought we were well over this these days, but I guess not. I watch a news clip of the terror and destruction in the streets, when a determined mother marches into the crowd or rioters, finds her grown boy and slaps him. Wow, that was a bold move. You can tell she could not care less about what anyone thinks. That is her boy, and it is apparent that he is not acting in accordance of the principles and values she has taught.

* ◆ *

From: 'Michelle'

Date: Thursday, May 7, 2015

To: Nate Brunhoff

Subject: Hi stranger.

New marketing coordinator trained and on-staff!

On another subject, last year I took a few training sessions with a golf pro and accumulated all the gear I need to play the sport: shoes, clubs, bag, cute outfits ... now this year, I am going in all the way. I joined a women's golf league. Beginning next Wednesday, I will spend this summer leaving the office early for a stress-free evening playing golf.

How you doing? Feeling? Whattaya been up to?

XO,

Recovering Moose

. ♦ .

An article came out in the *New York Times* this week. The number of Baltimore businesses known to have been damaged by riots and looting last week has reached 300. This damage has all been done by their own community. The very same people that live next door, that you see day after day, month after month, and, for some, years after years. The very thing they are fighting for, a way of living out of disparity, is in turn destroying their own community. It feels like a senseless reaction.

We share conversation and exchange different stories and thoughts on the riots during our drive to the golf course. It's Mother's Day and Charlie, Marie, and I have been on the road for about an hour now. The sun just rose and we're heading to Winchester's Rock Harbor Golf Course in the Shenandoah Valley, home to Patsy Cline, and treating Marie to eighteen holes. This will be my first official full game of golf before I join the league this summer.

I don't even remember when or how it happened, but I must have at one point said something in passing to either Charlie or Marie. I could tell when they played that they really enjoyed the game and I was always curious and wanting to know what it's like to play golf. They both started gifting me golf items for birthdays and holidays. When Charlie took me to a golf club down the street, I won a free lesson and a pair of Nike golf shoes. That was everything I needed. Now, I have everything I need to play. Marie invited me to join her ladies golf league and says there are some serious golfers but also some really poor players. She promises everyone is just there to have fun and to encourage one another to get better at the game.

"Michelle," she had said in her staple I-know-what-I'm-talking-about-so-listen-to-me, "the only way you'll learn is by getting out on the course and playing."

Charlie took me to his favorite driving range last week and showed me how to practice my swing, reminding me of all the things I had learned in my golf lesson—there's so much to remember! It was also Charlie's idea to treat his mom to a game of golf today. He knew she'd love it and he wanted me to get more practice in before my first game with the league. I had found Rock Harbor in a search online. The rates are great and the course has good reviews, too, but more importantly (for me), the historic downtown looks adorable. Plus, the 17ᵗʰ hole sits on top of the valley looking over the 18ᵗʰ hole with a green in the shape of a heart. None of us have ever been here before and we're not disappointed driving in. The course is stunningly gorgeous. The rolling hills of the Shenandoah Valley make for a beautiful backdrop.

After eighteen holes, we're walking through the historic downtown of Winchester, when Marie throws her arm around me.

"Look," she says. "Look at all you have accomplished lately."

"Yeah?" I say, even questioning myself. "It is kind of crazy, right?"

I think about everything that has happened recently. I found my father, I have braces on my teeth, I quit smoking after more than fifteen years, and now I'm playing golf. I can really feel for the first time a sense of accomplishment and appreciation for myself, a great sense of pride. I also recognize that Marie's been very impactful and helpful with everything. I reach up and grab her hand that's still wrapped around my shoulder, and I squeeze it tight.

· ·

On May 16, 2015, at 4:48 AM, Nate wrote:

Disc 4, 5, 6 are written by someone else entirely- says so on the credits. The disk has "The Thin Man" on it because the title sells, especially in series – and Nick and Nora and Asta are Primal names. Probably copyright at the time of production.

If The Thin Man were a board game, you only need a few pieces ...

1. Two Murders and an adoring crowd.
2. Nick, Nora and Asta. Asta is useless. Gets replaced in disc 6.
3. One Doctor with thick lenses that attends to one woman only and contributes nothing.
4. A dinner or a restaurant for a dinner.
5. One cop that looks like a thug.
6. One creepy guy with a thin mustache to make you think HE did it.
7. One maid.
8. One shorter than usual thug that loves Nick for sending him "up."
9. One dubious marriage or "relationship."

Disc 4 was boring because it was probably written with a bazillion loose ends. You couldn't guess who dun it because the writer hid the clues from behind his back.

· ♦ ·

On May 16, 2015, at 10:14 AM, Michelle wrote:

10. A good looking gal up to no good!

☺

· ♦ ·

JOURNAL ENTRY

May 29, 2015

The rioting has quieted and so has my father. It's been a few weeks since I last heard from him. I finished the Thin Man collection set, skipping 4, 5, 6 discs as he suggested. I really like the Thin Man and can say I love it even more transferred to film.

Nick and Nora (true names are William Powell and Myrna Loy), have such great wit, sophistication, and class mixed with an approachable personality and are charmingly irresponsible. I also learned that these actors succeeded from silent films to the talkies—with the Thin Man as their star breakout talkie debut. Pretty cool.

People, then, did not think that talkies would succeed, that it was just a fad. It just goes to show the resistance to change is as old as time—even for those things that are more obvious. New is scary because it's unknown. Just like my father.

What I can't figure out is **why** I am still fearful from time to time that I will lose him again. I guess I would be a fool not to, and I want to be prepared if it happens.

I've asked him multiple times about his health lately with no reply. What secrets does he hide? What's the truth about him? Only with time can you learn all their bits and pieces. Unfortunately, I don't have that on my side.

· ◆ ·

The next month falls silent. I didn't reach out nor did he. My worries are no longer anything to do with me, but instead a concern for his health. But the weeks go by just as quickly as the weekends and now it's nearly Father's Day. I open the closet and grab a bright green raincoat. It's a bit child-like with pink lining, large pink buttons, and a matching pink zipper, but it's one of my favorites. Since writing a Father's Day message for an e-newsletter at the office, I have been celebrating the thought of it for the very first time—this Father's Day I have a father to celebrate.

I close the house door behind me and am drenched in the mere seconds it takes me to turn the key and lock the door. I sprint and splash to the car, jumping in the front seat and slamming the door quickly to stop the blowing rain from following me in. Puddles of water gather from a stream down my coat to my lap. I swipe them off and turn the key. I'm not sure where I'm heading, but I intend to find another gift for Dad.

Frank Sinatra begins playing in the distant sound of the speakers. I turn it up. As I drive aimlessly towards the city, I rack my thoughts with questions. What should I get him? Is a gift for Father's Day cheesy? Maybe just a simple, small gift? Or maybe, instead of a gift I think he'll like, I'll get him something I like and can share it with him? I've really enjoyed him sharing his world with me lately, his passion for literature and film, so maybe now I should share back? I know he really likes music, too, so maybe a favorite disc like Frank Sinatra, and oh, a movie … Footloose! Hmmm.

· ◆ ·

From: Nate Brunhoff

Date: Thursday, June 17, 2015

To: Michelle

Subject: Cheesy?

Yes. Ugly arrived by stage coach today. Dusty but fully intact. The box is so well sealed (are you shipping drugs?) that I had to send it over to the machine shop for opening. I will be in touch as soon as I figure out the import of this generosity—the inner deeper meaning ... be well and pat a dog.

. ◆ .

On June 17, 2015, at 8:57 PM, Michelle wrote:

Hope you didn't miss the warning label. Do Not Open Until Sunday, or you may witness a burning bush. Scary stuff.

. ◆ .

On June 18, 2015, at 12:09 PM, Nate wrote:

Warning label acknowledged.

. ◆ .

JOURNAL ENTRY

June 21, 2015

I am looking at the torn pages between my last entry and this page here. The missing pages are the ones I tore out on my first trip to meet Dad in San Diego! On those are the pages I wrote the goodbye letters at the apartment to thank them for everything. I remember the tears that dropped and smudged the ink as I wrote. And I remember the fight that Charlie and I got in.

I was so fragile. I was unsure what would happen next or if I would ever see my dad again. I had put all my focus on the "here and now," so when it was over, reality quietly set in.

It's a bit of irony that I have reached this spot in my journal and on this day. Today is Father's Day.

It's been nearly nine months since I received that first message from him in my email and here we are still together and building a relationship.

As the days go by, so do the butterflies and magic. And before you know it, you reach a time when everyday is just every day. But what I need to remember is that it's always still there; sometimes I just forget to see it. And every now and then, I am blessed to be reminded. Just like these torn, ridged stubs of paper left here to remind me on this special day of that special memory meeting my father for the first time.

How cool. God is good.

◦ ◆ ◦

From: Nate Brunhoff

Date: Saturday, June 20, 2015

To: 'Michelle'

Subject: It was ...

Two days ago that my integrity was compromised. It seems my snuggle bunny opened your package and announced, "OH LOOK what your daughter sent!"

Since I had promised Not To Look Until Sunday, I have fathomed a way to fix this travesty. Since it is my FIRST father's day card. ever. I am going to frame it, hang it, and send you a pic :-)

Thank you for your kindness.

NB

◦ ◆ ◦

On June 21, 2015, at 7:27 AM, Michelle wrote:

Today is a special day.

And to me, you are one of the most special people in my life. Can I just say, I am so happy and so thankful that we are together.

Ha, I thought, oh you sneak—opening your gift early! But it also warms my heart. I'm so glad you like it. And I hope you enjoy the rest of it, too.

Happy Father's Day!

◦ ◆ ◦

On June 21, 2015, at 1:53 PM, Nate wrote:

Yes, I kept my word and did not peek until Alice raised the veil. I have listened to all of the tunes on Frank's CD and there are some amazing tunes. Footloose is up next.

* ♦ *

I wake this morning feeling blue.

"What's wrong?" Charlie asks knowingly and turns down the comforter to swing a leg over mine.

"I just feel defeated," I say, not knowing why.

Looking over to the corner of the room, I notice the ivy in the early morning light from the window. It's dried-out again and needs water.

"I really do," I continue.

As hard as I try, I can't feel positive right now and I don't understand why. My thoughts are all-consuming. The business is struggling, work is still consuming me, and we're going on three years living with his parents. And now, finally financially stable and looking for a house, it feels impossible to find anything because of the ridiculously high housing prices here. And, no matter how much I practice golf, I can't get a decent score! My communications with Dad have dwindled to nothing of substance, I really miss my girlfriends, and I'm just overall feeling a loss of sense of self. I'm just feeling, a lot.

Charlie leaves the room and I clasp my hands to pray, "Dear Lord, please give me strength. Don't let me ever give up. Help me enjoy life for its mystery and may I always see the magic of every day. I am so incredibly thankful. Amen."

* ♦ *

From: 'Cara'

Date: Thursday, July 2, 2015

To: 'Michelle'

Subject: I have something important you need to hear

I've been listening to a song on repeat, and when I was just driving I realized that this has to be your current theme song. Seriously. I listened to it again, thinking of it from your perspective ...

* ♦ *

Still lying in bed, I close the email from Cara and listen to the song. She's always the friend who has a special knack for being completely relevant and somehow knowing. It's the "Fight Song" by Rachel Platten. I pay as much attention to the words as I do the beat. It has me mesmerized.

Then a ding and text comes in from Alice. I pause the song and stare at her message blankly....

She says he's anemic, my dad. What does that mean? It's not good; it can't be good. But how "not good"? Should I be worried, scared, nervous....?

It's late morning now. I can hear what sounds like the faint sound of sticks hitting felt drums with a steady whizzing breeze that cracks on the window panes. The rain sounds different. I slide out of bed and wrap a throw around my shoulders to make my way to the kitchen and throw on some coffee. I'm staying home today.

Chapter 31

We're heading home to Michigan in a few days. It's our bi-annual summer trip home. I haven't seen every-one since the holidays, and I can't wait. I also can't wait to take my mind off of everything. Charlie said he'd be working late tonight, so I'm surprised when I see him at the house.

"I need to talk to you when you have a minute," he says, stopping me at the top of the stairs.

"Okay, we can talk now," I say sliding by him setting down my bags. "Everything okay?"

"I've just been thinking a lot about going home … " he says, and as his words trail off, his voice gets muffled by the increasing sound of my heartbeat. I can feel my body temperature rising. If we don't go home, I will be devastated.

"I think maybe you should go home without me," I hear him break back in. "I'm behind in work and could use the extra days to get caught up and bring in some more money for the business."

Wow. My thumping heart quickly changes to the beat of the song Cara had sent. I thought he was going to cancel our trip. I'm pumped! I can still go home *and* have girl time. I'm freaking out, ready to throw up my hands and dance like a white girl at a gospel choir.

"Are you sure?" I ask, reeking of insincerity. "I could always call Cara and see if I can stay with her for a few days."

"Why don't you call her now?" he hands me my phone. "I'll look for some flights."

I dial up Cara and Charlie waves me over shortly after she answers.

"Can you hold on a second? I'm sorry," I say to Cara.

Charlie shows me a flight he found and it looks good. I give him the thumbs up and let Cara know what's going on. We wrap up our phone call joyously screaming in excitement like two teenage girls at a Justin Bieber concert. After we're done, I find Charlie back in the kitchen.

"All set?" he asks.

"Yes! You think I should book the tickets tonight?"

"You're already booked, babe."

Seriously? He has never booked a-n-y-t-h-i-n-g besides a golf tee time—not a plane ticket, not a hotel or rental car, not any kind of an appointment, even if he needs to see the doctor. I push my curiosity to the side and give him a big squeeze and kiss. I'm bewildered but more ecstatic and could care less about anything else except going home and spending time with my girlfriends.

"So, you'll drive in on Wednesday then?" I ask, remembering his parents' move. "I can help your parents if they need anything before you get in town...."

He was back upstairs before I could even finish the sentence. We had just found out a few weeks ago that Charlie's childhood home in Michigan sold and his dad, better known as Big Pops, and stepmom, Katie, are planning to move the same week we're in town. It's such a beautiful home they are leaving, but an even more beautiful one they are moving into. What will be missing though is all the family memories. All the Christmas mornings, birthdays, and holidays spent together, the family pets enjoyed and lost, Sunday dinners and summer campfires, painting new walls and busting down old ones.... If we could separate the layers, thin it out, and slide it through a film projector, it would play more than any camera or memory could capture. The good and the bad, the trials and the wins, the tears and laughter, the hugs and kisses, the ring of every doorbell, and every time the front door opens to the time it closes, and now an ending ... but also a new beginning.

I hop down from the second step in the stairwell (still excited) after realizing Charlie was gone and not listening. I pour a celebratory glass of wine and take a seat in the chair next to the window that reveals how late at night it is by the dark outside. Ahhh, I can finally start to unwind from the day. I throw my legs up over the chair's arm rest and look to the clock on the wall. It's well past ten o'clock. I sip my wine and think about what all we'll do back home, swimming in the pool, golf cart adventures down the dirt roads, arts and crafts in the garage, and spend the rest of the night dreaming.

I wake before the alarm goes off. The room is already half-filled with sunlight. It's another bright, hot morning in D.C. Traffic is so terrible even my hidden shortcuts, carved out after many mornings of taking random side streets to escape the congested routes, are not even giving me a break.

Out of habit, I exit the elevator and turn left to sneak in the back entrance to the office, but then quickly remember that I'm not late and proudly turn back around and walk to the main entrance. A few guests are already seated in the main lobby waiting for the closing appointments with our realtors. I open the glass door that now features our new company logo in gold decal. It looks good. I admire my own work. I flip the light switch in my office, throw my bags down, hang my coat on a hook in the corner, and turn on the desk lamp. It's been a while now, so once the computer gets started up, I send Dad a quick note to let him know the news and that I'll be out of pocket the next few weeks traveling home.

Driving home later in the day, I message Charlie to see where he is and what time he's getting home. He calls me.

"Hey babe," I answer.

"Are you done already?" he asks.

"Yeah, what time you think you'll be home?"

"You're not going to believe what happened!" he exclaims.

He starts talking so quickly, I have a hard time keeping up. Something about the brush-and-roll paint company we've been trying to partner with to create a referral system. The owner invited him to dinner tonight to talk business, so he's on his way there now. I wish him luck before we hang up. This is perfect because I haven't packed, and I leave tomorrow.

"But wait!" he interrupts before hanging up. "I have more."

"Really?" I question, taking a finger away from the end button.

"Our paint supplier invited me to a golf outing they sponsor on Monday," he says.

"Charlie, that's awesome!" I exclaim, almost having a hard time believing it to be true. "These are both really great networking opportunities!"

"They're also giving me time to talk in front of the golfers."

"No way," I question again. "Seriously? You'll have to bring a box of business cards. And you should offer a special discount to everyone there!"

We go over all the main points of the business that he can talk about and then agree on skipping dinner tonight. I can pack, feed, myself and we'll just see each other later. Within twenty, I'm home and have clothes spread out across the bed and on the floor. Marie arrives home around thirty minutes later and peeks in the room to find me. All I hear is her laugh coming from the door behind me.

"I know," I turn around admitting. "I'm the worst packer!"

I have the hardest time making decisions and would rather have too many options than be disappointed I didn't bring something.

It's around 9:30 p.m. and I've narrowed it down as much as I can. I start zipping everything up and text Charlie to let him know I'm finished packing and check in on where he is and how dinner is going. At 10:20 p.m., I text him again with a question mark. It's not normal that it's been almost an hour and he hasn't texted back. He responds right away.

CHARLIE

> I'm glad you text! We both had no idea what time it was. It's going great and I'll be home soon! :)

It's closing in on 11:30 p.m. now, so I put on my pajamas and crawl into bed. I send him another text, and then another question mark. No response.

I turn off the lights and turn the TV down low. I scoop Bernie into my arms, put a paw in my hand and try to close my eyes. After fifteen minutes, I send him another text. No response. I call. I get his voicemail. I have every feeling in my body that something is not right. Normally, when I have this feeling, I convince myself that I am overreacting. But something is different about tonight. Something just feels very off—wrong and not right.

It's 12:30 a.m. now. There has still been no communication, and he again does not answer my call. I'm so upset my body is trembling. I'm beyond worried, and I can no longer ignore this feeling that there's something more. For those other times I may have just thought about it, tonight, I am doing it. I pull the covers off and set Bernie to the other side of the bed. I grab my phone and walk to the neighboring bedroom set up as a home office.

No one else is home tonight, which is another reason it's so strange he is not. His parents are traveling and left earlier tonight. Charlie and I could have had time alone tonight, without them, before I leave for a week without him.

I flip on the small desk light and turn on the computer. After it loads, I open the internet browser and go to Gmail. I log off my account and enter in his email. I manage everything in our life, including most all of his accounts, so chances are I know the password to his personal email.

And just as I had presumed, bingo, my first try works. What I wasn't expecting, however, is the first email I see.

Or was I.…

Chapter 32

From: 'Victor'

Date: Monday, July 27, 2015

To: 'Charlie'

Subject: Re: Horseshoe Anniversary / VIP Golf Outing

Can you attend the golf outing?

Please let me know if you have any questions.

Victor | Executive Casino Host

Horseshoe Baltimore

◦ ◆ ◦

Casino … golf outing … I'm recalling our conversation earlier about the networking opportunity from our supplier who is sponsoring a golf outing.

And wait! Victor? That is the "friend" who is supposed to be a DJ and who Charlie reconnected with before our last trip to Vegas and visit with Dad.

Ohhhhhhhhhhhhh … oh my.

I read the email again and click open the attachment. The golf outing is on Monday. You have to be kidding me.

I start recalling the restaurant we went to at Hurrah's casino with Dad and Charlie's surprise treat to thank both Dad and Alice for their hospitality. It was a four-star venue and we were treated like VIPs. We were even escorted out of line and seated by the manager. The events start flooding in as if I had just opened Pandora's box. I take a screen cap with my phone for evidence and go to his sent mail. I wonder, how long has he been going to the casino? Is this why our company's money is so tight?

. ◆ .

On July 6, 2015, at 1:37 PM, Charlie wrote:

Victor,

Sorry man been busy!! Thought I was going to be out of town but will not be. Can I still play in the golf outing? Let me know, thanks!

Sent from my iPhone

. ◆ .

On July 6, 2015, at 1:41 PM, Charlie wrote:

Hey, I also want to attend the event this Saturday night, First Anniversary Party. Let me know about that as well. Thanks again for all your help Vic.

Sent from my iPhone

. ◆ .

What is that noise? I hold my breath in the silence of the dark to listen closer. OMG, it's my own heart banging in my chest! It's thumping so hard I can audibly hear it and I am so outside my mind that I truly didn't even realize it. Breathe.

How much of what has been a lie and for how long? How is he pulling this off? Is he gambling, instead of working?

I keep digging through the emails and start obsessively taking screen caps. I send them to Marie. This has got to be what is going on with the business financials; it's so clear! I'm not reading anything anymore, just scanning and whizzing in a panic as though I would find something more, searching for the answer to *why* this is all happening.

All bets are off now; and what a terrible pun not intended. But what can I trust anymore? How hard is it to be honest? If he's lying about this, what else is he lying about?

. ◆ .

From: 'Victor'

Date: Wednesday, December 14, 2014

To: 'Charlie'

Subject: From Victor Johnson Horseshoe

Good Evening, Charlie.

It is my pleasure to introduce myself as your Executive Host at the Horseshoe Baltimore Casino. I look forward to being your personal connection to all the action and excitement we have to offer here in Baltimore and at any of our Caesars Entertainment properties across the country!

As your host, I will keep you informed of upcoming promotions and special events, as well as assist you with booking room accommodations. You'll see that having a host will make your experiences even more fun and memorable!

I have enclosed my contact information for your convenience. If you have any questions, or if I can assist you in any way, please don't hesitate to call me. Thank you in advance for your continued visits to The Horseshoe Baltimore, and to our other Caesars Entertainment Properties. I look forward to hearing from you in the near future.

Sincerely,

Victor

Executive Host

                                    · ♦ ·

And there it is. It was all a lie. I scan to another email about Charlie picking up his awarded Best Buy gift cards. I not only remember them, I remember using them! I didn't see any of this coming.

The phone rings....

I answer; it's Marie.

"I knew something was going on!" I quietly squeeze out through the choking tears.

"Unbelievable," she said in a quiet monotone and pauses.

We both sit in silence.

"I honestly don't even know what to think right now," I eventually break the silence in snot and tears. "We both knew something was up, but, how much of this is...." I couldn't continue.

"Have you talked to him?" she asks.

"No," I quickly reply. "That's why I found all this. He's still not home tonight!"

I look at the clock and it's approaching 1:30 a.m.

"Okay," she says calmly. "This is what we're going to do."

I'm listening intently. I know she has more rational thoughts than I do right now.

"When you get to work tomorrow morning," she explains, "print everything. We both know he can talk circles around us, but if we put the hard evidence in front of him, he will have to answer to it."

"Yes," I realize she is so right and I have the first positive thought I've felt all night. "Great idea!"

"But you have to pretend you don't know what's going on," she insists. "We need to deal with this as a family and when we all get home. I think we should get a counselor to help."

"Oh man, okay," I agree. "But do you realize how hard it will be for me to act like I know nothing?" I pause, knowing myself. "Marie, I honestly don't know if I can pull this off. I'm literally known for showing my emotions on my face...."

"You don't have a choice," she reminds me.

She's right. If we are going to do this right and pull it off, we have to be smart. It has to be taken seriously, planned and impactful.

We hang up just as I hear the garage door open and I glance again at the clock. It's almost 2 a.m. now. I have to work a full day tomorrow and then fly out. I know I can't hide my feelings, so I sneak into bed and pretend I'm passed out.

I hear him come up the stairs and can tell before he even turns on the light that he's drunk. He slurs his words so much that I can't even understand them in my fake sleep. He picks up a pillow off the floor and throws it at me.

He's super drunk.

He actually wants to pick a fight right now? I pretend the pillow wakes me up and then do everything in my power to keep the situation at bay. Finally, he leaves the room. Ugh, my stomach turns inside out and clenches in knots.

I wake the next morning with Bernie intertwined in my legs. I wipe the dried tears from my eyes and get ready. Charlie's still passed out and snoring on the couch downstairs when I leave for work. I text him later in the day to make sure he's still planning to drive me to the airport.

> I'm leaving here in 15–20 minutes, can you still bring me to the airport?

CHARLIE

> Of course! :) I'm already heading back to the house.

I somehow still beat him home, even though he said he was heading to the house a while ago, and am waiting for him in the driveway. When he finally pulls up, he explains how he got caught up in traffic. I'm beyond getting annoyed, plus all I can show, amidst all reluctancy, is calm and cool.

"Babe, I'm sorry about last night," he says as he grabs my water bottle and carry-on bag to help me in the truck. I believe he expects this apology will change the mood of things. However, he has no idea where I'm at right now, mentally. He's on a little boat floating at sea in the sun and I'm running the beaches scraping up my feet on rocks and shells.

"Hey, I found out I get to talk for at least twenty minutes at that golf event," he quickly follows, trying to change the conversation.

"Have you thought about what you want to say?" I ask and look straight, deep into his eyes. Can he look at me and respond knowing full well it's all a lie?

"I did!" he says, excitedly.

The next twenty minutes he drives while talking about it, and I sit in silence and hidden outrage. I look over at him, but realize I'm now looking beyond him, straight through him. How is this possible? I watch him speak, spouting nothing but lies. He knows it's all lies, but thinks I believe it. I'm no longer listening. I'm now in my own world, silently screaming. I truly just want to stop it all, make him pull over and call him out. I don't know if I have the strength to do this. If he can lie to me like this, so comfortably and convincingly, then how many times has he done this before?

He pulls up to the Delta departures gate and jumps out to help me with my luggage. I'm struggling not to say anything. My husband, my best friend, the one person in life that I thought I could depend on the most just spent twenty minutes lying straight to my face.

"I'm proud of you for staying back for the business," I say as my gut wrenches.

We kiss, hug, and then I turn to walk away.

"But just don't go to the casino," I say, turning around, looking him in the eye and rolling away with my suitcase. Stabbing him with these final parting words is such a low blow, but I can't help myself. I have to say SOMETHING.

"What?" he says loudly and in an annoyed tone.

I quickly continue on, making the distance too far between us to be able to say or hear anything more.

He has no clue at all that I know. I can only imagine the turmoil that is going on inside him right now as I'm walking away and no longer looking back. And then I wonder, what if it actually doesn't bother him? What if this has no effect on him beyond the inconvenience of what he has to do patch things up?

Well, if I get to have a moment, I'm taking this one now. Normally, he wins. Not today though. I have proof. I know the answers he can no longer deny.

Chapter 33

When I hear the wheels of the plane crank out below me, I recognize my emotions too are being pushed far beneath me in preparation for landing back home. This is my vacation and my girl time. I will not let Charlie's lies ruin this for me.

At arrival, no one is at the ticket counter to get my rental car, so I throw the heavy bags at my feet. Whew, I packed a lot. I guarantee I will only wear half of it. Options, I remind myself. A girl has to have options.

"I'll be right with you," says a girl with striking blue eyes and long, golden locks as she whips around a corner and then disappears again into another office door.

"Okay, thanks!" I reply as my phone starts to ding.

I open the lock screen and find a handful of new messages from the girls. One-liners matched with emojis are flying back and forth among the group.

The missing counter attendant finally emerges and finds my reservation in the system before handing over the keys to the rental. I text Mom and the rest of the family on my way to Cara's to let them know I've landed and am officially back in town. I then switch over to phone mode and call Marie and we talk on the forty-minute drive ahead of me. I let her know everything that happened. I proudly share that I didn't crack, and then embarrassingly admit that I did sneak in a stabbing line at the end.

We both exchange our frustrations and questions, and then she talks about plans for how to handle everything once we are all back home. Reality hits me for the first time. I anticipate with fear what the future holds in front of me. Beep, beep.... Her words fade and my phone drops the call. I'm pretty far north in the country now and hit a dead spot. Saved by the country! I wipe my tears and prepare for fun again.

"Woooooo hooooooo!" I swing open the car door and Cara comes running out from the garage. We throw our arms around one another.

A few tears sneak out, mixed with excitement, sadness, and just an overwhelming flood of emotions that take a hold of me as soon as our arms wrap. Even though I haven't seen her since Christmas, Cara and I talk all the time, so she knows a lot about my situation already. The rest of the girls pull in a few minutes later and I quickly pull it together and pretend all the rottenness doesn't exist right now.

We get all gussied up and head out to a local dive bar for a bite and drinks. Before we leave, I reach into one of my bags and pull out an old Polaroid camera and box of film I had ordered online. I had found the camera at a garage sale. Best $1.50 I ever spent. Luckily, the cameras are coming back into style, so the film was easy to find. It's a bit pricey at $30 a cartridge, and you only get 8 prints, but it's a fun way to capture our memories tonight in a special way.

After the bar and back at the pool house, we are slinging back shots and drinking beer, staying up into the wee hours of the night under the stars with our feet dipped in the water. We talk about everything and anything good, dumb, and trivial in life. For the night, I let go and just enjoy us.

The next few days spent with Cara end up being a mixed bag of fun and determination to get some "business" done. We go for rides on the golf cart and get high, lie at the pool listening to tunes, head into the city to see more friends, and monitor Charlie's email.

This morning, over coffee, Cara suggests we make a calendar to visually track and see every time Charlie has gone to the casino. Every time he goes, because he is a *players* member, it sends a confirmation to his email with the points he earned on the visit. I wish it said how much money he spent, lost, or won, but at least it's proof of how often he's going. She sets her cup on the dining table and walks over to the home office. I open up his email on my phone and she opens a desk drawer, grabs a stack of paper and two pens.

Week after week, month after month, we're able to see now that he goes on average three days every week, and sometimes more. What shocks me most are the days of the week that he's going. There are week days like Mondays and Wednesdays, and more often than not are Sundays. After we would get home from the cottage, he would always say he needs to go to the shop to catch up on work. Now I know that was also a lie. It's clear that instead of going to the shop or onsite to do work, he's going to the casino to gamble. I flashback to the countless number of times I've had to answer the business phone at my work because he wasn't picking up. Our business account is through a phone service that allows us to connect to our cell phones; if he doesn't answer, then my phone is next in line to ring. I wonder, how many times didn't he answer because of the obvious rings and dings of the casino?

For our last girl day, Cara and I spend it at the pool in the sun, paddling around on the paddle board and boasting about the indisputable evidence we've pulled together to make a case with Charlie. There's no way he can deny this proof, nor can he wiggle his way out of this one with his clever wit and charming stories that are good enough to bend anyone's ear. This time, he has to admit and answer to his lies and there is no smooth-talking his way out of it. I can only hope that he will admit to everything, and do it humbly. I want everything … I want us … to get better. The crazy thing is though, that I can't shake something else I'm feeling—this really terrible feeling I have.

"There's no way!" Marie shouts in dismay as we're chatting on my drive from Cara's house back to the city to Charlie's new family home. I'm staying there tonight and helping with their move into the new house. They started moving earlier this morning and Charlie arrives in town tomorrow.

"I know," I sigh in response. "But I checked our bank account and he went out again last night. His tab was $130 dollars. I know drinks are expensive in D.C., but why is he all of a sudden drinking?"

"Michelle, he loves you so … " she starts to say, but I interrupt.

"And then I also saw he went to lunch at a restaurant yesterday and the bill was clearly for two," I continue to gab away, not intentionally trying to interrupt her. "He never goes to lunch at a sit-down restaurant unless it's with a client, but he used our personal account to pay. If it was business, he'd use the business credit card—right?"

I'm working myself up again just venting to her. Marie is really the only one who knows and is in the thick of things with Charlie and me. We've been living with her now for some time. She knows *most* everything. She knows the struggles, the many questions I have had, and vague answers I always get. She knows of the many late nights I've cooked dinner and waited for him to get home but always end up sticking it in the microwave with a note. She knows how many times I've answered his work phone, responded to emails, and dealt with unhappy customers who are annoyed by his lack of communication. She knows about the money that should be coming in from the business but continues to get delayed or is unpaid for one reason or another. There has been a lot that has continued to happen and more so, more often.

Marie sighs, "I don't know what is going on. But, Michelle, I do know, without question, he's not cheating on you. He loves you very much. He is lying, and about a lot of things, but his love for you is never at question."

"Okay?" she asks, making sure I'm listening.

"I know," I hesitantly agree.

I pull in the drive and hit my foot on the brake at the top of the hill in disbelief and awe of what I see.

"Marie, this place is insane."

The pictures online do not do it any justice. The home is absolutely beautiful, huge and breathtaking. The driveway itself is nearly a quarter mile long. There's a creek, a little bridge, three buildings, a double wooden door entrance, circle drive, gorgeous landscaping, and all surrounded by an untouched, private forest.

Marie and I exchange goodbyes, good lucks, and hang up. The long, winding drive leads down a slow sloped hill to the charming home framed and shadowed by rolling hills filled with deep wooded forest. A large moving truck is still in the drive. There are stacks of boxes strewn all around the ground outside and a handful of boys dressed in similar shirts going in and out of the house.

The walkway, steps, and stoop are made of brick pavers and lined with flowering pottery. I can hear the sounds of a river that runs nearby. To the left is a four-stall garage. I can't believe Charlie isn't here to see this.

I squeal, squeezing everyone so tight. Coming home and seeing them is honestly just as exciting as seeing the girls. They all take a break and we enjoy a beverage together, but are continuously interrupted by the movers who need direction where to put things. After a toast and unloading of my own personal bags, we all get to work and have the entire truck unloaded before dark.

"I just can't get over it," I push out through a yawn, grabbing my neck and then throwing myself on the couch. "This place is amazing."

My eyes scan the room. There's an enormous stone fireplace that serves as the only wall in the main, central living area.

"We are just so happy to have you here," Katie leans over on the couch and gives me a big hug.

"I wouldn't miss this for the world," I squeeze her back. This is such an important time for the family."

"Remember when you laid all the stones for the fireplace at the old house?" Katie reminisces, looking at the fireplace in front of us and then over to Big Pops.

"We're going to have some great fires in this place," he assures her and then looks over to me.

"Especially on Christmas morning!" I exclaim.

They had built the addition on their last house and Big Pops had hand-selected and carefully laid every stone in the fireplace by hand. They would joke that it was a nightmare, but you always knew they were so proud of all the hard work that went into it.

We spend the next few hours sharing stories and tirelessly yawning over slowly sipped cocktails. Now lying in the cloak of dark by myself, I can't keep my mind off Charlie. I still can't shake this feeling, nor can I keep my fingers off my phone. I feel determined again. There's more to this, I just know it, and I'm going to figure it out. As much as I loved tonight and everything about this vacation, my anger and hurt now sit with me in this darkness. I wonder what he has been doing while I have been here helping his family move into their new home.

I check his Facebook out of desperation, but as I knew it would be, it doesn't offer up anything new, but on his LinkedIn I find a new connection that I don't know. Who is she? She's a pretty girl. She's from Baltimore. I click the side button with my thumb to turn the screen off and set my phone down to my side. What am I doing? I ask myself. Am I going crazy?

I toss and turn all night. I'm sleeping on a couch placed in the middle of a large living space with windows all around me to the woods outside, beautiful in the daylight but creeping me out in the dark. The sun finally starts to peek at the horizon and my phone is no longer the only light in the room. I honestly can't help myself. I check my bank account again. He went out again last night. The transaction is at another bar between the house and the shop.

We didn't do it right away after we got married, but once we moved to D.C. and started the company, we finally decided to combine our bank accounts. The only money that goes into our shared account, though, is not from the business. It's only what I earn every week. And what goes out are both of our expenses, plus whatever the business needs. I took a screen snapshot and send him the pic of the over $100 bar charge made to our personal account again last night.

· ◆ ·

You have fun last night?

CHARLIE

> What's this? I'd hope you think I'd do better than
> that.

· ◆ ·

A few hours later Charlie sends a pic of him and Bernie in the truck. They're both smiling (well, Bernie with his tongue out) and he says they're on their way. I'm back at the airport returning the car and am sitting in the median waiting for Katie and Charlie's sister, Anne, to pick me up. I close out his text, and all the rest of my open apps, when a Facebook notification pops up on my home screen. It's an alert that we have two new followers on the company Facebook page I built and manage for the shop. I click it open and see two small profile bubbles—they are both young, cute girls.

My stomach drops. This is strange, and the feeling I have hits my gut like a checkmark. We own an electrostatic paint company. Why are two young girls liking our business page?

I click on each girl's profile to learn more. I see that they're both connected and are friends and live in the same city as the shop. Enough is enough, I decide. It's time to know the truth.

My body is trembling again.

I already know.

I already knew.

Chapter 34

I'm still sitting in the median at the airport waiting to get picked up and I send both girls who had like our Facebook page a private message. I thank them for liking our company page and ask how they heard of us. I explain that we're new to the area and would be grateful for an honest response—humbly and mostly because my husband and I have recently had troubles. One of the girls messages back right away with her number to call, just as Katie pulls up. I am silent in the backseat the entire ride back to the house, letting them chatter while trying to keep my emotions at bay.

Neither of them notice me duck out and go downstairs when we get back to the house. I go outside through the basement door to the backyard but only to find out that I have no phone service. I walk around the house and down the long narrow driveway.

I look again at her message before calling. She says she knows Charlie and that I should call her. I realize it really must be true; you only see what you want to see. All the doubts and questions I've ever had—it's always easier to just let it go and not think about it. This time, once again, I wouldn't. I dial the number with shaking hands.

"Oh, sweetheart," she answers.

"Thank you so much for letting me call you," I say.

I am pacing back and forth now. I can barely breathe. I had no idea what she would say next. All I know is that it's likely going to be enough to open a hole beneath me.

I see Katie open the front door and now she's watching me.

"He did tell me about you," she continues (her voice sounds young). "He just told me about you last night."

Any words have escaped me.

"I went to his house and I saw a picture of you," she says. "He told me you were engaged to get married, but he wasn't sure if it was right."

"We've been married for five years," I manage to interrupt, insisting she know the facts. "And we've been together for more than ten."

"We had sex last night," she interrupts back.

I drop.

I hit the pavement and my phone goes flying across the driveway. I could only have hoped that I could break like glass, so it could just all end.

I can't understand; I can't comprehend this new reality.

Katie runs over as soon as she sees me drop and picks my phone up from the ground.

"Who is this and what is going on?" she demands.

Without hesitation, I rip the ring from my finger and throw it. The rest of any conversation and my thoughts are spotty. It's as if my brain shuts everything off. I have entered a fighting ring I'm not prepared to enter and am taking heavy blows that would surely reach my K.O.

Anne runs out as soon as she sees what's happening. I'm still on the pavement, hurled over holding my stomach.

"Where's Charlie?" Katie asks with her hand covering the phone.

"He just sent … me a picture … him and Bernie … they are … on the road," I stumble to let her know.

I think about the picture. And then back to the thought of him having this girl over to the house and having sex with her last night. I am going to get sick....

Anne finds my ring in the bushes and calls my girlfriends. They all arrive to the house within the next hour. I am a hot mess, even more so now than when it all went down. The more time I have to let it all sink in, the more devastation I feel. My world is collapsing, flipping upside down.

Where do I go from here?

My phone dings and Anne grabs it from the bedside table. She looks to me in question.

"It's her," she says, wondering if she should read it.

"What does it say?" I ask.

"It's a Facebook message … " she says.

"What?"

Lo jumps up and grabs the phone from Anne and looks at me.

"Let me see!" I yell and reach my hand out.

The girl tagged me. She posted a screen cap of my profile pic with Charlie and me together, and then tagged me in the post: "I just found out this ******* I've been dating is married! What he doesn't know is that now I have become friends with his wife."

This girl actually feels entitled to broadcast it to the public for all my family and friends to see! Oh, woe to her? Does she not realize this is my actual life? Does she have no empathy nor understand how embarrassing and devastating this is?

I message her and plead to take the post down. Within minutes, the post comments raise to the *hundreds*! When she finally untags me, she still leaves the post up on her page.

"I'm taking my Facebook down," I tell the girls, frantically navigating to my settings.

"Do it!" the girls all say in unison.

And with a click, my entire profile is down. I'm gone. With the flip of a switch, it's lights out and I fade to black.

I'm still curled up on the floor when my phone dings again. Anne goes to check it. I keep trying to stop crying and be somewhat normal, but I can't. I'm an absolute mess.

"Thank you so much for being here," I look up at Lo wiping my snot. "I'm so sorry."

"Michelle, you have NOTHING to be sorry about," she scolds me and wraps her arms around me.

I hear a distant cry from Anne and then she and Cara come running in the room. They only look at Lo, intentionally avoiding me.

"You HAVE to see this," they tell her holding out my phone.

"Stop it," I say in disbelief and feeling queasy again.

"What's going on?" I demand. "Who is it?"

"It's her," Cara says finally acknowledging me with disconcerting eyes.

"Lo, go ahead," I say confidently looking over to her. "If you know I can't see it, then delete it. I'll believe you...."

Lo leaves the room with them and I feel the weight of emptiness in the silence. I'm questioning how much more I can handle. What did she send? Is it a picture or screen cap of his messages to her?

After a few minutes, she walks back into the room alone.

"How are you doing?" Lo asks.

I look at her knowing exactly what that means.

"Seriously?" I lower my head, understanding what she's not saying.

"Yeah," her words linger quietly. "I'm so sorry."

I cover my face and take a deep breath. I don't know what she just saw, but I know it's bad.

"Did you delete it?" I ask with my face still in my hands.

"Yes," she affirms.

I'm done. I can't handle any more of this. I have to get out of here. I jump up and start getting all my bags together. Without saying a word, Lo starts helping me.

I catch Katie at the top of the stairs.

"I'm so sorry," I wrap her in hugs and slobber.

This should've been their time, their moment. It was their big move, after all these years of hard work with their business. Lo packs me in the car and Cara and I drive back north into the country.

Charlie never calls. All I get is a text from him.

CHARLIE

> It's just so hard trying to be good all the time.
> Sometimes it's just easier being bad.

What is that supposed to mean?

· ◆ ·

JOURNAL ENTRY

August 14, 2015

When the morning sun rises here, it shines a warm copper glow on everything it touches. When you look out the window, there is an endless field of corn and blue sky lightly peppered with white marshmallow-like clouds. Everything in this room is deafening silence, but through the window I can hear the morning risers. The songs of the morning birds, alarms of the roosters, and distant howling from the neighboring farm dogs.

I'm home.

And while my heart should be so happy and warm like the rays of the sun shining on this page right now, I lie here broken and empty.

Charlie, my husband, has been lying to me. He's been gambling and cheating.

It's hard even writing these words ... admitting that my life, everything that I thought was real, is all a lie.

It's been three days since all of his lies were exposed. And today it is yet again a blank canvas.

I am broken.

I'm so ashamed. I'm disgusted. I'm humiliated.

I'm scared and I'm tired. I'm hungry, but I can't eat.

And the one person that I always go to for my shelter, love, comfort, and hope ... is gone. And now I'm left questioning if he ever was really even there.

I'm home, back in Michigan. Where I know I need to be, but it feels backwards. I just don't know where else to go. And to make it on my own and pick up all my broken pieces, I had to come home.

The waves of emotion I feel are unreal. Sometimes I'm so angry. I want to just pick everything up and throw it so hard and just break everything around me. I want to get out of my own skin. I feel like a prisoner.

I can't think of or ever possibly imagine that anything could ever get worse, but I also know that there are some hard times ahead.

Chapter 35

"Sometimes when things are falling apart, they may actually be falling into place."

That was a text from Lo today. This is my last day being home before flying out tomorrow. I'm absolutely terrified to face the truth and go back to D.C. The next few weeks will be the true testament of my strength.

Today is a beautiful summer day in Michigan. I drove into Grand Rapids to have breakfast with Katie and Anne. As soon as we sit in the booth, it's obvious that we all immediately try to snuff out the elephant in the room with aimless conversation. Katie is mid-conversation about the couches she ordered from Art Van for the new house when I drop my head into my hands. I thought I could do it. I tried so hard to keep it together but couldn't last any longer than fifteen minutes.

We order our food to go. I feel terrible but seeing them just brings all the feelings flooding in and it hurts. I love them so much. They are my family. But how does this work now?

I never called Dad. I just keep putting it off. Sitting back at the pool at Cara's, I muster up some strength.

"I just need a few," I tell Cara and she winks as I walk away.

The courage swept over me out of nowhere. I don't know how long it would last or if or when it would come back. I need to take advantage of it now. I walk to the backside of the garage where there's a door and a tree swing. I open the back door to the garage and grab a towel to dry off my bathing suit. I sit on the swing and open my phone to call Dad.

I get his voicemail. I hang up and call Alice.

I get her voicemail.

I hang up again and send Alice a text.

> Hi! I have something kind of important to tell dad, but he's not answering the phone and

I'm wondering if he's not feeling well? I hope everything is okay. Please give me a call whenever you are free. XOXO

⋅ ♦ ⋅

Around 1:30 a.m. my phone rings, but I don't hear it. Instead, I notice the voicemail when I wake early this morning and grab my phone to use its flashlight to go to the bathroom. I close the bathroom door, flip the light switch, and hit play.

"Hi, Michelle. It's Alice—your daddy's not doing well."

I take a seat and keep listening....

"I'm on my way to the hospital. It's probably electrolytes or something. He was doing better this morning. Anyway, I'll keep you posted. He doesn't want me to let you know. He doesn't want anyone to know anything. But I'll send you a text as soon as I do."

⋅ ♦ ⋅

JOURNAL ENTRY

August 16, 2015

I finally slept past 6am. But I'm still waking up throughout the night. And even though I did get some rest, I want to crawl back under the covers and hide from today. My stomach is in knots about a message I got from Alice. And later today, I have to fly back to D.C. My dad IS sick. And now I have to deal with that as well as my own reality.

If he really is that sick right now, I could leave everything. I have nothing, and I could go take care of him.

⋅ ♦ ⋅

Battling Cara's new terrorist kitten, King Arthur, out of my hair, I un-hook his claws and toss him across the bed. I grab my phone from the bed cover and flip it over to read the screen as it rings. No caller ID. I know it's Alice. I run down the back stairs and out to the tree swing.

"Alice!" I answer without pausing. "How is he?"

Her voice is shaky. "He was just taken to ICU," she says and starts crying.

How can I continue to take these beatings? It's as though I am just taking a quiet stroll with Bernie when someone passing by randomly stops and hurls a clenched fist right in my face.

Alice starts to explain the most recent reports from the doctors, and for the first time, everything with Charlie all of a sudden feels irrelevant and unimportant.

"So, tell me," she finishes while clearing her throat. "What did you need me to tell your dad?"

"Nothing," I say. "It's not important right now."

Cara shows up on the golf cart and finds me cowering by the corner of the garage. I could've done a better job hiding, I'll admit. I look over to the two large bushes just a few feet away I could've stepped behind. I cough out a laugh, but it muffles past my lips and gets soaked in snot. The pain I'm enduring right now physically hurts. I can handle losing Charlie, but now I have to realize I may lose Dad, too.

I jump on and then quickly back off the golf cart just before Cara hits the gas. She looks at me perplexed.

"I'm going to say a prayer," I tell her and say nothing more.

I grab the tree swing and pull up to sit, wrapping my arms around each rope and lifting my feet from the ground. My eyes close as I clasp my hands together in prayer and I whisper quietly, "Dear God, if you must take my father and it is his time to go, I will understand."

I sit in silence for a few moments, slowly swaying back and forth. Cara doesn't interrupt me as she usually would. I grab my phone from my pocket and slide my finger to type a message.

> I just said a prayer. I'm so sorry. My heart is hurting so bad. I wish I could be there with you. I never even got to tell him I love him. Will you tell him that for me?

ALICE

> Yes, of course I will.

"My life is a joke," I mutter to Cara, getting back on the golf cart.

"Michelle," she says in a motherly tone. "Your life is more real now, than it ever was."

My phone dings again.

ALICE

> Your Dad:
> If you had been a prolific gambler and cheater, then there would be cause for embarrassment, but you are not and therefore have no cause for feeling embarrassed. I regret to hear the circumstances because the doorway out of compulsive gambling is very low. XOXOXO, Nate

Chapter 36

I take a sip from the glass of wine freshly poured by the bartender and read the text from Alice again. I'm on layover in Detroit and am squeezing in a glass before my next flight. And I won't be surprised if I get another one, too.

I keep reading Dad's message. He shared some really good thoughts and words of wisdom I needed to hear. While he didn't return an "I love you," that's OK and also (clearly) not in his character.

A new patron takes a seat next to me and the bartender lets him know that he'll be right with him. I send Alice another message to check in and it dings back right away.

ALICE

> I found a good intensive care doc who put him on Albumin, agreed with me that he is dehydrated. Started taking Albumin and blood pressure is looking better. Keep the prayers coming. Today I could see how much he truly loves you.

A drop falls and splashes on the screen. I try to stifle the emotion and gulp it down with the rest of the wine.

"Have time for another?" the bartender asks as he walks by.

"I don't," I say with a small crack of a smile, "but I'll take another one."

The bartender walks away and grabs a fresh glass off the rack and I open my wallet for my debit card. I hurriedly drink the second glass and make my way to the next gate. The last few stragglers board after me, and once the wheels are up, I say another prayer. I'm so nervous to go home and confront everything.

When we land in D.C., I take my phone off airplane mode. There's a message from Marie.

MARIE

> Call me when you land. I'm going to come pick you up. Charlie is not staying at the house and has promised he will stay at the shop.

. ◆ .

Despite my argument that I can take a cab (I mean, honestly, the house is only a few miles from the airport), Marie picks me up. The ride home is awkward and we're both distraught.

"I'm going to head to bed," I say stepping out of the car and closing the door behind me. She reaches up and clicks the garage door button above the review mirror.

"I understand," she says stepping out of the car and turning her head towards me in the light, revealing her now red puffy eyes.

"How is your dad?" she asks shutting her door.

"I don't know," I shake my head. "I don't think it's good."

"Well," she says, now behind the car slamming the trunk shut after pulling out my luggage. "Let me know if you need anything."

"I will," I hug her and head upstairs.

. ◆ .

My phone dings again. It's been a while. I had already unpacked, showered, and brushed my teeth when I hear it. I run to the foot of the bed and flip over my phone. It's Alice.

ALICE

> We need big prayers, not doing well. His blood pressure is unstable and he's in and out of consciousness.

> Oh, Alice. I wish I could be there with you and I can't believe you are alone. Please tell me what I can do. Do you want me to call you? Do

> you want someone to talk to tonight? Just let me know. I love you so very much.

ALICE

> I'm okay. I will keep you posted on text. Get some rest.

I manage to pass out on top of the covers holding the phone in one hand and his red clown nose in the other. The short text updates continue to come in throughout the night and wake me up. I look over at the clock. It's 1:25 a.m. I feel numb, and I'm so tired. This all feels to be too much for one girl to carry. Maybe I should be the one in the hospital slipping in and out of consciousness.

3:17 AM
ALICE

> I just went to hold his hand and kiss him. He did not respond. My heart is breaking.

> My heart is breaking with you.

4:27 AM
ALICE

> What does this mean? Oh no! Please tell me he's not gone. Please, how is he?

ALICE

No. But it won't be long now. I am so very sad.

5:24 AM
ALICE

Just went over to give him a hug and a kiss. He is unresponsive. This is so very sad. This month is 29 years together.

Don't lose hope. He's a strong spirit and soul. I'm with you. I love you.

· ◆ ·

I lie here feeling like a zombie. I need sleep, but now is not the time. After all the hours tossing and turning, I finally roll myself off the bed and head to the shower.

I stand mindlessly under the shower head hoping to wash away everything that has happened. When there's a knock on the bathroom door, it startles me. With the water still running, I step out and wrap my body in a towel and crack open the door.

"Morning," I say to Marie who is fully dressed with heels and lipstick on.

"Morning," she says sweetly. "Is everything okay?"

"Yeah," I say without conviction. "He's not doing well at all."

"Are you still going to work?" she asks with concern on her face.

"I am," I remind myself aloud. "I have to take care of things."

After a few moments of silence, she eventually responds, "Okay, well I'm leaving now, but just let me know if you need anything."

"Yes, I will. Thank you."

· ◆ ·

7:48 AM
ALICE

Just lost him now. Poor baby.

▪ ◆ ▪

When the text comes through, I crumble and fall once again, but this time on the bed. I realize I have no one here to help or comfort me. I have to pull myself together. I get up and like a trained soldier, or mindless zombie, I walk over to the bedroom closet and pull out a black, button-up dress. I pull it over my head and tie it at my waist. I pull my hair up into a ponytail and look at myself in the mirror. The girl I see looking back is tired, pale, and has puffy, tear-soaked eyes, but she is also determined. I grab my thick black-framed glasses off the dresser and throw them on to hide my face.

"I can do this," I say out loud to myself in the mirror. Just as easily as the words flowed from my mouth, so flows their continuous repetition in my mind.

I finish getting ready, grab my purse, and am closing the door when the phone dings again. This time it's Cara.

CARA

You got this!

Incredible, I think, questioning the universe. I continue to repeat the words over and over and walk out the door.

▪ ◆ ▪

JOURNAL ENTRY

August 18, 2015

Does it get worse before it gets better? I honestly don't know how I'm going to come out on the other side of this. My dad died yesterday, and I've been set on auto-pilot ever since. The only thing I can be thankful for is that my father gave me a real reason to have something to be sad about. I'm thankful that I don't have to give Charlie my tears anymore. I just keep telling myself to stay calm and focused on what I have to do to get out of here.

When Charlie found out I put in my two weeks, he started with verbal threats. I know I shouldn't have answered the phone, but I really didn't expect he would act like this during such a heartbreaking time.

I withdrew half of the cash from savings today and walked it into a new bank to set up my own separate bank account. I just can't trust that his threats to drain our accounts are empty words. I also couldn't decide what would be most fair to not upset him, so I left everything in checking. Even though it is all my pay.

· ♦ ·

Charlie's at the house when I get home from work. He had come home to take a shower and timed it so that we would run into each other. I was hopeful that when we finally did see each other for the first time in person we could have a civil conversation, but that hope is met with deep regrets. His words can be so cruel and they cut so deep. The finger is pointed at me now, because I am the one leaving. But what he seems to not understand is that he is the one who gambled. He gambeled with our relationship and our business. And he is the one that lost.

I know now that I was just a pawn in his grander game, and now I'm looking to protect my queen, my most powerful player ... me.

Chapter 37

Marie knocked at the bathroom door again this morning and put an idea in my head. I'm not sure if it's the best approach, but it is the next thing I need to figure out. Sitting at the kitchen table, I reach for my glass of coffee and take a big gulp before running my index finger down the thin yellow page.

I stop at The Myerson Law Group and read that they are located on Sunrise Valley Drive, just down the road from where we live. I google the office to learn more. Their team seems diverse and it's a woman-owned firm that specializes in family law and divorce. I would want female representation. Women work hard, we get into details, and we have compassion. I call to set up an appointment and find out they can fit me in this afternoon at four o'clock.

Okay, wow, this is happening. I hang up the phone, flip the Yellow Pages shut, and straighten my skirt. I got this, I remind myself again and may actually be starting to believe it.

Work goes fast and the boss tells me to wrap it up and get out of town this weekend, if I can, and by that she means go home to Michigan. At first thought, it had seemed to be impossible, but after thinking about it, I realize she's right and I should jump on the opportunity. I can take my computer with me and work remotely for a week or so, as needed. I text Cara from the office to see if she can fly in sooner and she sends an immediate thumbs up.

After work, Martin and I drive to the cottage to collect my belongings. I share most everything with him on the long drive. I appreciate Martin. He's cool. Always rock solid and one of the most interesting people I've quite possibly ever met. Despite answering all of his questions honestly, it pains me to not share something Marie asked to keep between us— Charlie's gambling. I'm not aware of her reasoning but do respect her wishes. I do know that Charlie is in debt to them. How much now, I have absolutely no clue. Only Marie has this knowledge. I don't think it's a lot, but then again, I also didn't know he was gambling. I also don't know what invoices have been paid and which ones have not. Marie is a CPA and our company accountant, so I've been trusting her with all of our company finances.

Just before we hit the road, I had visited the lawyer's office. No one knows yet. I signed and paid to file for a divorce. To sit in that office and make such a huge decision all by myself and to sign those papers was one of the hardest decisions I've ever had to face alone. The only thing I know and have to hold on to is this opportunity to rise up and recognize that I deserve better.

"I cannot guarantee any of this will seem fair," the lawyer had assured me, "but the most amicable way to dissolve a marriage would be to do what you are doing."

I just want to be fair. I don't want anything. I just want out. That's it. I don't want to hear the lies anymore. I don't want to be drawn in by this ridiculous love I feel only to end up trying to have faith in something that never exists. And I don't want to be scared anymore. I'm good. I put myself in this mess and now it's up to me to get myself out. All I want out of this is myself.

"How are you doing?" Martin asks as we approach the last exit before home.

"I'm good," I say peering down at the unmarked blue folder resting near my feet; inside are the signed papers from the lawyer's office.

- ◆ -

JOURNAL ENTRY

August 20, 2015

I sat in an unfamiliar office today with legal documents staring me in the face. I kind of understood what the papers meant, but for the first time in a long time, I didn't have anyone to ask.... Such a major, life-changing decision, and the only one there to make it was me. I am getting a divorce.

How am I doing this? I'm running on fumes, barely any sleep, and only scraps of food that I force down to make sure I don't faint. I'm making checkmarks on my list faster than I can turn my head. I just keep telling myself, don't look back—you're not going that way.

- ◆ -

There are days when it's 6:00 a.m. and you wake suddenly for no reason, go searching for the clock, still tired and hoping it's the middle of the night, but it never is. It's so irritating, usually, but not today. Today is different.

I roll over and get myself out of bed. Pure determination is now at play as I pull to my feet and head all the way downstairs. I touch every wall on the way down as if it were my last, thanking them for all the joy and memories this home has given me. I stop in front of my work closet, grab a tote from the stack I brought home from the cottage yesterday, tear off the lid, and slide open the door.

I stand looking at the open closet door for longer than necessary, mindlessly staring into the abyss of work jackets, blouses, pants, and suits. As the reality slowly soaks in, I reach in and start slipping off each suit jacket from its hanger, folding it and laying it in the open tote. It's still barely early morning light and I hear the rumble of a faucet upstairs.

Someone's up. I nervously take a seat on the edge of the couch behind me. Down walks Marie with a look of concern on her face. In the last three years living together, I have never woken before her. She usually leaves the house before I am even out of the shower. But this morning, I've been up for at least thirty minutes already.

I move off the backside of the couch to meet her as she approaches. The tension is thick. I can feel it as she takes the last step. She walks past me, taking a seat on a chair in the living room. I can tell she's upset. She starts with small talk and a bunch of Q & A's about tomorrow's plans for unpacking the storage unit, but it quickly turns weird when I start talking about Cara flying in later today. I stop mid-sentence as soon as I see her squirm. She doesn't know, but I've changed my plans and want everything of mine packed so that Cara and I can hit the road tomorrow.

I remind her that her assistance in anything we do is always so much appreciated but is not necessary—especially if she is going to feel uncomfortable. I get it; it's her son. I also don't want Charlie knowing that I'm leaving town tomorrow. I don't want him to know until I'm on the road—and we both know the many reasons for that.

"I can't do it," she says. "If he starts to ask me questions, I can't lie."

Fair. I assure her it's okay. Cara and I can pack everything ourselves. She doesn't need to help. She apologizes, and the tears break through as she makes her way back upstairs.

Alone again in the dark, hanger after hanger, I reach in and pull off a blouse, a jacket, a skirt, pants, and fill up the totes. Just as I finish and snap the final lid shut, I hear more steps coming down from above. It's Martin. He stops halfway down the stairs.

"Michelle, I'll help you tomorrow," he says in an upset tone.

"No, it's okay Martin," I say with an exasperated sigh. "I can do it myself."

"You can't do it yourself and I'm going to help you," he insists. "And I'm the only level-headed person around here to deal with this mess."

A smile cracks on my face. Martin makes his way down the rest of the stairs and we talk about my plans. Marie makes her way down again and apologizes. She tries to explain to us both that Charlie may be rude and scary to me, but when he closes the door and talks to her, he opens up and everything is okay.

So what exactly is that implying? I wonder. Because he's nice to you it makes it okay to be mean to me? The dialogue in my mind begins whirling into a storm. I frantically and without thinking start grabbing the four totes I just filled and carry them out to the garage while they continue arguing.

I rewind back to the other night when I got home from work and Charlie's truck was in the drive. When I opened the door, my nerves and anxiety were met by the sound of the running water in the shower downstairs. There on a side table next to the bathroom was a freshly made cheeseburger on a plate, waiting there for Charlie when he gets out. I can't blame her. He's her son. And I know how good he is. I probably would have cooked him a damn cheeseburger, too. And made some French fries and left it all with a sweet love note.

Making my way back inside, the incredibly uncomfortable conversation finally starts to come to an end. We start discussing the plans for picking up the U-Haul tomorrow morning and then the two of them start fighting again. Martin is on the couch and Marie is now sitting on the stairs. They're cussing. I've never heard them fight like this or speak such cruel words to one another. They're feuding about who should pick it up. I'm telling myself, "Well, it's definitely not the both of you!"

My girlfriends had all fought at one point, too. They argued about who will make the flight to D.C. to help with the move. Emotions are high. I feel at fault for all of it, even though I know it's not true, but it's all because of my messed up life. What if I could've resolved, predicated, or called the right shots sooner? I've already admitted, I saw all the stupid flags and still volunteered for this life with Charlie. I actually believed love would win. Now I'm wishing I could shove myself inside of one of those totes!

I leave Marie and Martin to their growingly uncomfortable conversation and make my way back upstairs to get ready for work. I pause at my reflection in the mirror. I realize that, without intention, I had dressed myself in black again. It's another knee-length, buttoned up, collared dress with a waist tie. I look like I'm going to a funeral. It's actually perfect, I think to myself, grabbing at its spaghetti thin strings to tighten the framing around my waist. Today, I am attending a funeral— it's the death of Charlie and me.

I grab my purse and work bag. This is my *last* day in D.C. living and working. The floodgates to reality are inching open more and more quickly now. Audibly quiet but with nerves ready to explode, I start repeating to myself, "I am not alone … there is a plan … I can do this." Over and over, I whisper the words and then fill up my coffee mug and head out the door.

Chapter 38

ALICE

ALICE

> Book it.

Alice's text confirms my proposed flight to head back west for Dad's funeral in San Diego. He is to be cremated and requested no special attention, no surprise. So, Alice has planned a get together at her sister's house.

Dad's brother, Uncle Frank, will be flying in on Thursday, September 3rd. Great Aunt Maura and Dad's other brother, Uncle Ed, are planning to fly in for the "celebration of life" on Friday. Dad's best friend from high school, Ted, is also heading into town for the gathering. I've only heard things about him in passing, most recently about a purchase of an Airstream and then some commentary on a film script. There was also something about him living in the desert and being a director. He has known Dad since grade school and they grew up together. It's my understanding that he also knew nothing about me—my dad had a "secret" daughter. Oh, that mysterious Nate. Not shocking, I'm sure.

At the break of morning light, I find Cara already awake as well. We agree to get up and get to it. We're both dressed in less than fifteen minutes. We grab only what we need and head out the door. On the road, we realize we're so early that we can't pick up the truck yet and stop at Starbucks to eat up some time.

Cara's flight got into D.C. around four o'clock yesterday. Charlie showed up at the house again later that night while she was there and we hid her upstairs just in case. He knew I was going home, but he had no idea when or that Cara was coming into town to help. Unbeknownst to him, we're leaving town tomorrow. His character was so far off and deranged you'd swear he knew. He stood behind the kitchen counter interrogating me for nearly thirty minutes. His hands planted on the countertop, he kept flexing his muscles and stiffening his neck to intimidate me. After he left, a mixture of fear, anxiety, and stress kept both Cara and me up for most of the night.

Arriving at the U-Haul pickup location, we pull into a dirt parking lot and walk up to the only building on the lot. It's a parked trailer with a make-shift sign that reads "OFFICE." The trailer, or office, is smaller in size than some of the U-Haul trucks on the lot, and assuredly smaller than the truck I reserved. We walk into an uncomfortable conversation between another customer and an unkempt lady sitting behind a desk filled with stacks of papers and dust. Nearly twenty minutes later, Cara and I joke that we woke up, got dressed, and stopped for coffee faster than they are completing their transaction. The lady puts up her hand to pause their conversation and answers the phone.

"That's correct, sir," she says into the phone, staring at her monitor. "We don't have that size right now but I can call to see if there's one at an office nearby. Hold on."

The customer she was dealing with is now upset and walks out, clearly signaling to the woman behind the desk that he's had enough. I'm so annoyed that I nearly high-five him as he walks past. The salesperson doesn't realize he had gone until she hangs up the phone and sees only me.

"I'm so sorry," she says with a perplexed look on her face and stands up to peer out the window looking for the customer who just walked out. "Can I help you?"

I tell her I have a reservation and pray she'll be capable enough to find me in the system.

"Follow me," she stands up and waves her hand to bring me outside.

Cara's been outside smoking since the customer walked out, so I wave her over when she sees us. We're led to a huge truck parked at the end of the lot. It's indeed the BIGGEST one there and I look over to Cara to confirm; we're both in total shock. The lady starts walking us through all the procedures and details. And then, as if the ten-by-fifteen-foot truck was not intimidating enough, she reminds us that we have a car trailer to hitch up behind it.

Cara and I are suffering uncontrollable laughter as we pull the monster rig out of the parking lot with my car towed on the trailer behind. Turning the wheel requires both hands. I'm nervously looking in all the mirrors. It's a first-ever that twenty miles per hour feels oddly comfortable to my speedster heart, and the shocks on this bad boy are terrible. The road feels like a bumpy bike path! Ah ha, we laugh hysterically as our seats bounce up and down.

Martin is waiting for us when we pull into the entrance of the storage unit facility. Thankfully, he helps direct me in backing up, turning around and getting the truck to the unit through the narrow drive. I put it in park and we step out at the same time the doors to a rusty, white pickup truck parked a few units ahead open. I hired a few extra hands to help out.

"Ohhhh," Cara mischievously comments.

"Michelle," she taps her little finger strongly on my shoulder as we stand waiting at the back of the truck. "Did you smell them?"

"No!" I laugh. "Smell them?"

They are kinda' cute, I admit. I open up the storage unit door and we get to work. I divide out what I can as evenly and fairly as possible. Rule is: electronics, equipment, machines, tools, and other "man things" stay in storage so he can have them. All décor is mine. The kitchen, we can split box for box. Everything else, besides what is obviously mine (girl things), is up for debate. In most cases, it will likely end up with me saying, "I don't want it," because I could not care less.

Every time Cara crosses paths with the movers, I see her little sniffer go in the air and her cheeks rise in a cute, mischievous smile. With the help of Martin and the hired, good-smelling help, we pack the entire truck full in just two hours.

I reach up and pull the storage unit door down for the last time. As the door falls to close, I catch sight of a banker's box and pause the door. The box is marked now with fading black marker in my handwriting, "WEDDING PHOTOS." I release the door and let it slam closed.

We stop back at the house to load up the rest of my stuff and Marie greets us with tacos.

"Did you get everything you wanted?" she asks.

"I did," I assure her. "Thank you so much for thinking to get us food. I'm so hungry!"

Cara agrees and immediately grabs a taco out of the bag. With a mouthful, she starts telling Marie about how crazy it is riding in the U-Haul with the trailer and car towing behind when my phone starts ringing. It's Charlie. I hit the button to silence and ignore the call. I can't talk to him yet. I'll call him once we've hit the road and I'm a few hours out of town. I am not allowing any chances of detour at this point. I am determined to get on the road and continue as planned. The only mode my brain is on at this point is "GO." I'm doing this. My phone ring is silent for mere seconds before Marie's starts ringing.

"It's Charlie," she says. "Do you want me to answer it?"

Of course answer it, it's your son, I think to myself. But why do I have to tell her? How does she not know what the right thing is to do and how to handle the situation? Does she *really* want me to tell her? She must be so torn and trying to be respectful and loving to both sides. I do appreciate her.

"It's your son, Marie," I reassure her.

She answers, and it's obvious how uncomfortable she feels. She's paced at least twenty-four circuits back and forth between the family dining room and the kitchen within the first five minutes. When she hangs up, she surprisingly approaches me with a direct and stern voice.

"You need to call him and tell him you are leaving," she demands.

"Yes, absolutely, but I just want to get on the road first," I remind her, feeling small and intimidated.

"It's not fair to him," comes the heart-defying, sound-deafening, soul-defeating words from her lips.

I roll my eyes and feel my heart turn to anger over her words now exploding in my head. Fair to him? He did this. My life is turned upside down. I don't have a home or know what I am going to do for a job. Where will I live? How will I support myself? I went from knowing everything to not a single thing in my life. This is all a result of his decisions and actions, not mine. Again, I silently ask myself, fair to him? I storm past her, not answering, and find Cara in the kitchen mid-bite into her taco.

"You ready?" I ask her with a look so transparent that she knows what I mean is we have to go now.

She disappointedly returns the look and then looks at her taco and shrugs. She knows it's not an option; we are going. She scores a few more bites before wrapping it up and returning it to the bag with the rest of the food on the counter. I walk over to Martin sitting on the sofa in the far corner of the living room.

"I'm so sorry," I whisper leaning in and reaching for his shoulders to hug him.

I turn back to see Marie and nearly choke on my pride. I should do the same, hug it out and let it all go, but it's incredibly awkward and feels disingenuous. I walk past her again, looking down this time in shame, and leave the room to walk downstairs and outside to the truck. I grab the few last bags sitting in the garage and start stuffing them in the back seat of my car still hooked up on the trailer. I see Cara walk out with the bag of tacos. I shut the car door and then see Martin walking out hurriedly. He's headed straight towards me. He's either determined or mad. I'm not sure how to read his face, but he continues to walk closer and then jumps up on the trailer with me.

"You okay?" he asks.

I shake my head no and he grabs me, giving me a tough hug. I needed it and it breaks me. I break down in his arms. I almost left here in the worst possible way. I don't want this. I don't want any of this. I love them both so incredibly much. This is my family, my home, and I have to say bye…. I shouldn't do this in a spiteful way. I lighten my grip and pull my head up from his shoulder. When I wipe my eyes, I see Marie. Now she's walking out. I tap his back and pull away. I can see her intentions and quickly jump off the trailer to meet her halfway.

"I'm so sorry," I incoherently choke out reaching to hug her.

And just as suddenly, my phone rings and startles me. I'm so caught up in the moment that the ring pierces through time. Oh no, it's Charlie again, I think, reaching into my pocket. My heart stops. I flip it over to see the caller ID but it says it's Dad. What the…. The confusion sweeps over my face and Cara notices.

"Who is it?" she asks.

"My dad?" I question, uncertain how to respond.

"Um, that's impossible, Michelle," Cara says.

I turn the phone screen towards all of them so they can see, and in disbelief we all stand in silence, staring, listening to the rings….

Chapter 39

My hands are death-gripped to the wheel and I'm sitting so straight you'd think I had on a back brace. Cara is in the passenger seat exchanging squeals with rambunctious, nervous laughter. We're driving the big rig through the narrow, rollercoaster cluster of streets and hills of downtown Pittsburgh. What seemed to be a fun detour has quickly turned into a frightening joy ride. The Liberty Tunnel and crazy amount of bridges are disorienting.

On a positive note, we're making some good memories. I successfully jack-knifed the trailer a few hours earlier at a gas station. Taking too quick of a turn coming out from the gas pump, I jammed up the trailer with my car on a guard rail. The more I tried to correct the trailer, the worse it got. We had to un-hitch it. Thankfully, two cowboys driving by saw us unhitching and turning around to ask if we needed help. Within fifteen minutes, the gallon-hat boys had us unhitched, straightened out, re-hitched, and back on the road. Feeling nothing but pride with our dirty, greasy hands, we clasped them together and thanked the cowboys for their help as they tipped their hats and wished us well on our way.

After a few hours driving through downtown Pittsburgh, we find a way out of the maze and decide to head straight back out of town. We find and stop at a Walmart on the way and buy a lock for the truck gate, a case of beer, and two Steelers t-shirts to always remember the crazy ride.

We arrive to the first quiet little town outside of the city and check into the first hotel we find. It's nearly twelve o'clock and we're *exhausted*. We throw on our new Pittsburgh Steelers tees and walk to the only restaurant nearby.

"We'll have a glass of Pinot Noir, a Bud Light, and two shots of tequila, please," I say to the bartender, pulling up my stool to the bar.

. ◆ .

JOURNAL ENTRY

August 24, 2015

I awoke early this morning in a place that shouldn't feel foreign but does. I'm home. We drove back into Michigan late last night. I showered and got ready, still living out of a suitcase, but I'm no longer on vacation. The life I knew today is gone.

I feel like I did in Africa. I'm in a whole new world filled with nothing I've ever known before. I have only the clothes and provisions I can carry on my back. I'm stepping out, preparing to explore and embark on a journey far from my comforts and known reality, yet more real than anything I've known.

·◆·

Cara's kitten, Arthur, is always hiding under furniture waiting for me whenever I walk into a room. I had just run over to the pool house to grab a hoodie from the mess of boxes and totes we moved in there last night. Like an animal and little monster he is, he lunges out from below a chair when I walk in the room. He jumps with full force and wraps his paws around my ankle, sinking his tiny little teeth into my skin.

"YOWCH!" I yell out and try to shake him off.

I unhook his teeth and claws from my skin and toss him to the floor. He's quick; he shows right back at my feet in less than seconds. He's a tiny terrorist.

The guys I hired to help are meeting us at the storage unit in fifteen minutes. When we pulled in last night, we unloaded most of what I knew I would need to stay here, living in the pool house, and kept the rest on the truck to put in storage until I can find an apartment.

When we crossed the state border and entered Michigan yesterday, I noticed our landscape for the first time. Cattail fills the ditches along the highway and beach grass covers the rolling hills everywhere. It's somewhat of an island surrounded by fresh water. And the sunset last night, oohhh wee! I almost forgot how undeniably gorgeous Michigan sunsets are, and each one like it's never been seen before. A brilliant gold ring outlined the clouds by the horizon, while a colorful array of bright oranges, pinks, and purples painted the sky.

Two guys pull up in a van at the same time we arrive. I pull a few units ahead of my new storage unit so I can open the back truck gate and pull out the walking ramp. Cara is in her car and starts to unload a few boxes. The boys mean business. They have the set face to get things done. Jason and Dan are their names, stitched in white lettering on dark navy blue t-shirts along with their business, "Just Us Moving Company."

"So," Jason stops, moving a stack of three boxes and watching me. "What brings you to Michigan? That's a California number, right?"

"It's D.C., actually," I tell him, grabbing and carrying the stack off the truck. "Northern Virginia. I'm from here. I'm moving home. I'm getting a divorce."

As soon as the words come out, I want to choke on them. Why did I just say that!? Is this what I am going to do now, just obnoxiously call out my new sad status to every stranger I meet or who asks anything about me? Is this how I get comfortable with it? I can feel the blood rushing to my face.

"Good for you," he says and grabs an oversized living room chair.

The sincerity of his quick affirmation is unexpected and nice to hear.

"This is an exciting time in your life," he says, turning around and looking over his shoulder. "It's an opportunity for a fresh start."

"Thank you," I say, moving another stack of boxes near the door gate. "I needed to hear that."

Jason and Dan unload the truck at an amazing pace. They organize and stack up boxes in the unit and leave walking paths to get around everything, so I have easy access to everything.

"You always smile that much?" he asks walking past again.

"Aw," I pause and blush. "I'm really thankful for your help. You guys are doing a great job!"

We exchange handshakes and payment for their services. I watch as their van drives away and haul down the large rolling unit door, sliding the latch and locking it in place. I pull myself back up into the U-Haul truck cab and close the driver's door. A huge sigh releases from my lips and I throw myself back in the seat. This is a moment to release tension and emotion, and I sit in the silence alone to reflect.

I awake the next day before my alarm goes off. The birds are chirping. When you no longer have an obligation that you have to wake up to, you realize that you love waking up. I roll out of bed with serious ambition. I throw on some running clothes and grab my ear buds. The sun is just above the tree line and there's still dew on the grass. There's no traffic out here and I can run right down the middle of the dirt roads. After a mile, I stop to take a break. It's been a long time since I ran. I've always loved to run—it comes easily and is a great release—but many times throughout life I lose the passion and time to commit.

On the side of the road, I jump through the brush at the tree-line and hike to a clearing where the land meets sky—it's the beautiful rolling hills of Northern Michigan. I pull out my ear buds still playing Frank Sinatra and let them dangle around my neck. I find an old stump and take a seat to breathe, enjoying the peaceful, untouched land that surrounds me.

Back at the pool house, I place fresh flowers picked from alongside the road in a vase for Cara's mother. I take a shower, plug in, and begin my first week of working remotely to start tying up loose ends after leaving D.C. so suddenly. I end up working straight through, from 7:00 a.m. to 7:30 p.m., and continue nearly every day, followed by unpacking and trying to get settled in my new little living quarters in the pool house.

Every morning, I find myself a bit more exhausted but not enough to stop or change. I'm on a mission and am going strong like the Energizer Bunny. After only a week, I'm able to wrap up work and ship my laptop back to D.C. I also start working on passing off my company management details to Charlie and Marie. Checklists, logins, passwords, and instructions are all organized. I'm applying for jobs, transferring company intellectual data, updating billing addresses, crossing off personal checklists, and hanging out with Cara doing arts and crafts in the garage until midnight. Sleep is not a priority right now. I need to get stuff done and I also need to unwind.

Last night around 10:30, I checked the final task off my list. I emailed both Charlie and his mom an updated spreadsheet accompanied with a full instruction manual for all office procedures, including our company website, phone account, internet access, utilities, the sign guy, business cards, ordering sites, etc., etc.

· ♦ ·

JOURNAL ENTRY

September 3, 2015

I don't know how I did it, but I did. I wrapped up work and crossed off everything on my list that I wanted to get done before taking the first step to getting back to me and finding where and how I can get back on my feet.

I checked the last thing off my list last night, packed my bags, and awoke to my alarm this morning at 4 a.m.

And now I am on a plane again. I'm going back to California for Dad's funeral. It feels kind of strange to be going back out there alone. Also crazy to put it in perspective: I'm going to visit my father who is now gone and without my husband who is no longer a part of my life. This should be an Alanis Morissette song, "A little too ironic ... yeah, I really do think."

What could possibly be the meaning to all of this? They say everything happens for a reason. I can only hope that this weekend with my dad's friends and family will hold some answers and give some healing. I'm eager to discover any meaning to all of this.

Maybe I did put Charlie's dreams and our ambitions together over anything of my own. And maybe it's time to feel confident and strong on my own, and not need to rely on the love of anyone but my own....

Chapter 40

"Welcome to San Diego," the flight attendant says over the intercom.

I see Alice and Great Aunt Maura in Dad's van when I walk outside from baggage claim. They are both looking fabulous with their beautiful skin and sophisticated, California style. Each has on a pair of large, fashionable sunglasses; their clothing is dark and tight on the bottom, loose on top. Alice's wispy brown hair and Great Aunt Maura's stark white locks blow in the wind as they wait to greet me.

"Shall we grab lunch?" asks Alice. "We still have a few hours before Ed and Bettie arrive."

We all agree without hesitation. We jump in the van and find a lovely harbor-side restaurant down the road.

At our table, we order wine with our meal and when it arrives, pick up our glasses to toast. The smiles, love, and cheer are echoed in the clinking of our glasses, as we sip and set them down. As we do, we look up to find Alice with her head down in quiet tears.

I'm speechless and heartbroken. I don't know what to do or what to say, and I also want to break down with her, but I cannot. I need to be strong for her. Once she manages to stop the tears, she apologizes and starts telling us a story about how Dad recently bought an audio tape that is supposed to lead them on a journey to find their power animal. Not knowing what she is talking about, I listen intensely. She tells us how she ended up listening to the tape with him, and without even realizing it, she was the one who became entranced and met her "white wolf," but it did nothing for Dad. We all laugh, but then I have to ask, "What is a power animal?"

Great Aunt Maura does her best to explain and then, with her soothing, entrancing words, tells me to close my eyes and relax as she begins trying to lead me down an entranced path to find my own. At first, it wasn't working at all. Then, with my eyes closed listening with content, I see a bunny. Too obvious, I tell myself and open my eyes to thank her for trying.

After lunch, we head home. Not long after we arrive and unload, I realize how tired I am and feel like I could take a nap. Sitting on the same couch where Dad and I had the revealing talk about his cancer, Great Aunt Maura walks over and sits down next to me on the couch. She places a hand on an un-socked bare foot and assures me everything is going to be okay.

"You're tired," she says looking me in the eye. I assure her I'm fine, but she continues, "Why don't you go lie down and rest your head."

And like a young girl who listens to her wise mother, I agree and give her a hug before walking quietly to my room. I close the door and fling my body on the bed. On the California King, a white, down comforter poofs and then deflates under me. I lay my head on a pillow and exhale all the anxiety built up the last few weeks. And then, determined once again to resist sleep. I turn myself around to the foot of the bed and throw my hands up under my head. Leaning on my elbows, I look around the room. I keep thinking about the idea of a power animal that they spoke of at lunch when my gaze halts on a machine in the corner on the room. During lunch, Alice talked about Dad's "dying days" and how he had grown so weak that he couldn't make it up the stairs to their bedroom. She had purchased an expensive machine for $4,000 that she was confident would have helped him, but it was too late. And there the machine sits. And here I lie.

A soft tap on my shoulder awakens me. It's Alice.

"Aunt Maura said I should come wake you or you'll sleep the night away," she says with a big, sweet smile.

She points to my eyes and I immediately lick my fingers and wipe what I know must be mascara pooled underneath.

"Ed and Bettie are here now too and we'll be going to dinner shortly," she continues.

I look at the clock on the nightstand and can't believe it's been a few hours. I assure her I'm getting up and apologize. She lets me know that they're glad I got some rest and closes the door. I peel myself from the comforter and make my way to the bathroom. I turn the faucet on and soapy my fingers. Drying them on the hand towel I see it. Stitched on the towel is a mountain cat with spots.... It's a leopard.

Hmmm.... Maybe? I question.

Nah.

I'm still not a believer, I decide. That's silly.

I nervously get ready and then walk out to the main living room where everyone is gathered. I meet the rest of the family and we all exchange what feels like an uncomfortable "it's-nice-to-meet-you." Uncle Ed makes his way across the room to sit next to me on the couch. Alice grabs her phone and snaps a pic of the two of us sitting side by side.

After dinner in downtown Escondido, Alice, Great Aunt Maura, and I return to the house alone. It will be just us girls this time, under Dad's roof for the weekend. Alice helps me bring my suitcase and bags upstairs to the office. This time, I will be sleeping on the couch so that Great Aunt Maura can have the bed in the spare bedroom. Alice says she wants me to use Dad's bathroom and closet, accessible only through the office, as my space this weekend.

"Oh," she whispers and pauses just before we walk out. "I have something for you."

Her smile was as devious as I was curious. She walks back through the bathroom to Dad's closet, opens the door, and disappears for a moment before coming back out with an old black file box. She sets it on the ground and removes the lid with one hand and starts pulling out wrapped items with the other. As she lifts out a soft, Tiffany-colored turquoise cloth, she looks at me again with that smile. She continues to pull out items and soon a collection is set to her side, including a martini glass, broken watch, and gold pen.

"What is it?" I ask as she reaches over to place the Tiffany blue cloth in my open palm. The cloth is soft to the touch. It's evidently old, but fully intact and made of fine quality. I flip it over and unfold the sides. It opens out in the palm of my hand. There are two tiny pockets and inside each are two pieces of tarnished but beautiful sterling silver baby flatware. Then she hands me a second cloth, of equal quality but gray in color that opens to more tarnished sterling silver pieces. Inside this cloth is a baby whistle and a more evidently used baby rattle with scratches and a dent. The rattle is engraved H.E.B. in a fancy swirling scroll script.

"I think this is all your dad's," she says as I gaze in admiration at the tiny treasures in my hands. "Nobody knows about these, and I think you should have them."

"I wonder if any of this was Grandpa's?" I ask Alice, examining the rattle again with the initials H.E.B.

"I'm pretty sure that is Nate's, too," she says.

I am speechless. I am holding in my hands some of the most precious antiques that one may come across in a collection of family heirlooms and they're my dad's—this is seriously so cool. In utter admiration, I keep intently looking closely at every piece, until she distracts me with another treasure that she puts right under my nose. I set the silver trinkets down and grab the new treasure from her hands. It's a martini glass, and it's made of really thick glass, filled with all kinds of colors and streams of gold.

We tuck the items safely into my suitcase and I hug her tight. I'm beyond thankful to not only see and touch these treasures, but that they can come home with me. Back downstairs, the three of us, now in PJs, all squeeze together on the couch (also my bed for the night) and watch a movie.

▪ ◆ ▪

JOURNAL ENTRY

September 5, 2015

We went to a pool party today, but no one actually went in the pool. Lame. I wore my bathing suit underneath my dress and was ready to soak in some California sun. Instead, we enjoyed wine and hors d'oeuvres sitting under a covered porch and admired the sun and pool from afar. Clear difference between Michiganders and Californians.

▪ ◆ ▪

When we return from Alice's sister's house, I sneak back upstairs to Dad's bathroom and do a little snooping. I feel terrible, but I can't help myself. This is his most intimate space and I want to explore it. I close the door behind me and open his closet to look around. It's a decent walk-in, so there are lots of options to look through. I pull down a weathered, brown, leather briefcase with large tarnished gold clasps. The clasp springs nearly hit me in the chin, I have my face so close trying to open it. Startled, and nervous, I return it without looking through its contents. I decide I'll take that as a sign. Ugh, I so badly want to snoop, but now I am nervously holding myself back.

Backing out of the closet, I notice a wall hanging near the door. It's large, and even from the back I can see that it was professionally framed. I try to pull it up from the floor and flip it around with one hand, but it's so large and heavy that I nearly drop it and tumble over a stack of boxes. I reposition my footing and attempt again. Balancing my arm now on my knee and using the other to hold my grounding, I reach again to flip it and see its face.

It's his diploma. And it's massively large. It's from National University in recognition of a Doctorate of Jurisprudence. But his name.... I've never seen it this way: Nathaniel Henry Edward Brunhoff III. "Nathaniel?" I question. So typical Dad. I can't help but think he's ridiculous. He probably did that on purpose.

Now satisfied in my secret hunt for hidden discoveries, I pause and stand there peering in again at the closet and all its contents. His dress shirts are on hangers and in the middle of those that are pushed aside by Alice, hang my blouses, one bright orange and another soft pink. It feels kind of symbolic and I hope to never forget the sight. There I am, "hanging" with him—father and daughter.

· ◆ ·

JOURNAL ENTRY

September 6, 2015

I took a shower in Dad's bathroom this morning. I stood there thinking, today is the day. It's my final day here and also the day of Dad's celebration of life. I want to soak in every moment. I want to remember every feeling and sight. Including how the sun so perfectly shed a stream of light on the small, stuffed terrier dog that Alice brought home from the Netherlands years ago to comfort him for the loss of his dearest dog "Wookie."

There are so many pieces of lost time in Dad's life. I wonder what else I don't know about him. If there is any day, today may be the only good day left to inquire.

Chapter 41

A few hours before the celebration, the immediate family meets and gathers in Dad's living room. Uncles and aunts are all seated in extra chairs pulled in the room earlier in anticipation of their arrival. Uncle Ed has his computer connected to the extra-large flatscreen on the wall and is playing the video tribute I made for Dad. It's a mix of old family photographs with Shakespeare quotes that slowly flash on and off screen. I quietly take a seat. After it finishes, it starts on repeat, and everyone naturally starts individual quiet conversations amongst themselves. Normally, I would join in or even just participate as an observer, but tonight I'm speaking up and asking more loudly than normal to try to get some answers. All the pictures the family sent me include many with their mother, but there was not a single picture of their father.

"Does anyone have pictures of your dad?" I ask.

"Yours, not mine," I remind everyone after silence swept the room.

"I think I have a few I could send you," says Bettie. "I'll look when I get home and email them to you."

"That would be great," I thank her and realize I want more than that. "Did you know him well?"

"I didn't," she admits, glancing over to Ed and then to Dad's other brother, Frank. "The only time I met him was at our wedding."

She shares her story aloud with the rest of the family in the room listening intently. She admits she had a preconceived opinion and poor outlook of him before they met. Her idea of what he would be was based on everything she had heard from the family, especially stories from the divorce. She explains that the boys' father had tried to make the divorce as hard as possible. He fought with their mom, Grandma Marti, with disdain and the determination that she would not get a penny—not even for child support. It was after her move back home to Sterling, Colorado, that she started developing agoraphobia and confining herself to her own home.

I sit back and listen but can't help but remain headstrong in disagreeing with the diagnosis. Did she really just develop this "full of fright" disease or did she develop it out of loss or from *fear* of her ex-husband? Her life, too, was turned upside down, just as mine, when she learned he was cheating. Everything she knew was ripped suddenly from her and revealed nothing more than a life of lies. And back then, I imagine the embarrassment would have been far greater than today. The man would have been right, and the battle was not one she could win. She would have been shunned and looked down upon. Nor would she have any means to support herself and her children. Oh, how my heart breaks for her; I cannot even imagine.

What if he was threatening her (even her very life) on top of it all? She must have lost sight of how to live healthily. Whom could she trust? What was her husband capable of? She was now a girl on the run, trying to protect her family from the one she once loved and believed in, and believed loved her, but is now her enemy. How do you make sense of that? You can't. And you shouldn't because it shouldn't happen.

Aunt Bettie continues her story. At the wedding, she recalls being annoyed because he brought the "other girl" with him—the one he had cheated on Grandma Marti.

"She was mean.... There's not a single sliver of warm blood running through those veins," Great Aunt Maura confirms. "But beauty.... That girl, she did have great beauty."

I'm on the edge of my seat now. In June, 1979, not long after the wedding, a few days later, after the murder, Bettie had to run home from a family gathering to grab a party plate she had forgotten when the phone rang.

"My stomach dropped when I heard his voice," she says. "He had never called us."

We are all listening intently now.

"It was him," she says again and pauses.

"I had already suspected it was him, you know, that he had hired a hit man," she admits. "So when I heard his voice, I was petrified, and he was so coy. He said he was calling to see how things are going and pretended to have no knowledge of the recent shooting."

Bettie tells us that just as soon as she hung up the phone, she called the police and wrote a full deposition following the phone call. Yet, the case still remains open today.

Uncle Ed tries to break the tension and reminds us that we need to make our way to the celebration of Dad's life. In a car full of ladies now gossiping, I find myself stuck in my thoughts of this story and everything I'm learning about my family.

"Michelle!" Alice shouts back from the driver seat. "Why are you so quiet?"

"I'm okay," I say, embarrassed. "I'm just thinking."

I think back to my first visit, riding in this van, staring out this same window nervous and timid. I remember Dad interrupted everyone's conversation at one point and said the same thing, "Michelle! You've been really quiet."

We arrive at Alice's sister Lisa's home, which is really a mansion. Detailed wrought-iron gates open to outdoor marble floors and enormous columns so wide that no less than three people can wrap their arms around one and they reach high to the sky. A koi pond is built into the stonework with a fountain in the center of the grand entrance that then stretches the length of the entire center courtyard.

We're welcomed at the main doors to the home by an older, dignified gentleman dressed in elegant comfort with striking white locks and two very large, well-behaved poodles. Just behind him are a group of servers dressed in tuxedos passing trays of champagne and wine. We're escorted to the north section of the center courtyard and to an area of the home that opens with a large, open-concept kitchen. A chef is running around busily giving orders to his staff preparing tonight's meal. We're told that it will be made with all ingredients from Dad's favorite store, Jimbo's.

Dad loved that store. Uncle Ed said every time he'd walk in they would call him by name. Alice also said the staff swore they saw him walking the aisles of the store the day he died.

A lovely woman, slightly underdressed, suddenly interrupts my conversation. She has soft brown eyes and blonde hair highlighted with bright strands of silver.

"You must be Michelle," she says confidently and reaches out her hand.

I feel a bit overdressed compared to her casual appearance. I'm in nude heels, a navy skirt, and a peach blouse with gold buttons. She is in khakis, sandals, and a collared blouse.

"Yes, I am," I say incredulously and reach out my hand.

"I'm Lynn," she says, almost reassuringly, as though I should know her. "Ted is so excited to meet you!"

Ah, this must be my dad's best friend's wife, I realize.

She looks to her right, "He's on his way over now."

We clasp hands, and she places her other hand on top of mine as I follow her gaze to a man approaching, short and older, with graying hair. He's a bit quirky but cute. He appears to be of interesting character and is stylish. But when his bright and totally contagious smile fills his face it outshines the distraction of both their cargo pants.

"Michelle, you have no idea how excited I am to meet you," he says as soon as he's within earshot and continues once closer, "Wow, this is just so neat."

"Likewise," I say with a half sincere smile and overwhelming perplexity about the situation.

"Your father was a very intelligent and funny man," he says. "And he was never afraid to play a prank."

He re-introduces his wife, Lynn. She stands sweetly next to him, smiling and nodding her affirmation. This is really neat. I am meeting my dad's best friend, and one he's had since grade school. This is his best friend and questionably the only constant Dad has had throughout the entirety of his life. Just as I think to ask for stories, he starts sharing them....

"Growing up," he says, "I was known as 'Shoes'—because you would never find me in anything but my tennis shoes."

"For graduation," he continues, "I was told that if I tried to wear my tennis shoes at commencement they wouldn't give me my diploma. So, your father had the idea to sneak me a pair of his dad's size thirteen dress shoes, so that I could wear them with my tennis shoes inside them."

He lets out a good chuckle. His eyes light up and so does my heart.

"Once I got past the screening at the front entrance," he boasts, "I took them off and left them at my seat to accept my diploma in my tennis shoes."

Frank walks up and hears the story. He starts to share another story about when Dad was sent to private school and was not happy about it ... at all. He had always worked on Volkswagens and knew everything about them inside and out. So, it turns out that Dad noticed the headmaster also had a VW. One night, while everyone was sleeping, Dad disassembled the headmaster's VW enough to roll it in through the cafeteria doors and put it back together inside. Set on display for breakfast in the morning was the headmaster's VW for everyone to see, both students and faculty. Needless to say, he was expelled.

Ted had left briefly during the story and returns holding a manila envelope with words written in all caps in black, felt-tip marker: HANKABILIA (78-83). He pulls out a large photocopied image and hands it to me. It's a black and white news article with a photo of a pole barn and some strange, poorly decorated trailer on the roof. He says the clipping is from when they were seniors in high school working on homecoming floats. Dad wanted to put the junior class's float on top of the barn. Ted thought Dad would just give it up after a few days, but he didn't. It took him about a week to figure it out, he says, but one night, under Dad's direction, they hauled the float on top of the pole barn using two-by-fours, some rigging, and Grandpa's Land Rover. Ted hands me the newspaper article.

"It will be better in your hands anyway," he says.

Like an undercover agent who's been given the goods, I swiftly carry the Hankabilia to my purse tucked away in a closet and sneak away to the bathroom.

"Oh," I say, surprising myself as I walk into the room with a large wall of mirrors and greet myself. "Why, hello there."

Wow, this place is intense. I turn, grasping the brass handle behind me and quickly pull the door shut to lock it.

I sit down and look up to see behind me, opposite the mirrored wall, stretched from floor to ceiling is the most beautiful, intricately designed and elaborate piece of tiled art. Rich in colors of black, tan, and gold, with piercing yellow eyes, long white fangs, and a bright pink tongue that appears in the mirror as though it's licking me on the top of my head, with both paws stretched out at each side of my shoulders. The enormous animal mural behind me, and that I see in the mirror in front of me, is a leopard.

Is *this* my power animal?

On the flight home, my heart hurts and the sadness comes in waves so large that they knock me down, but I have to remember that there is an answer to all this. Even though I didn't get the answers I sought from Dad's celebration, I remember that I set out on this journey to discover more and I'm still determined to do so.

My story doesn't end here.

· ◆ ·

JOURNAL ENTRY

September 30, 2015

I wasn't sure when I would write again or what would be my last entry in this journal. These last few weeks I've wondered if or how I'd complete this story and if I should share it?

But today, something happened.

I opened my laptop and on a clean Word document, I typed a title to something that now feels like a book, "Saving Scout."

In a determined desire to be as factually correct as possible, I pulled out my "dad" file and started thumbing through to the find the first printed page, the start of it all. And it's with no coincidence that I find it and scan to see the printed date in the footer ... 09/30/2014.

No way.

I pull out my phone and double-check today's date. It's September 30, 2015 ... 09/30/2015.

It's been exactly one year ago, to this day, when I received that first notification and message on the family Brunhoff Facebook page.

And so the story continues....

. ♦ .

There is a greater plan to this life.
    On this journey, I thought all I wanted was to find him.
    But really, what I was looking for was me.

IF YOU ENJOYED THIS BOOK, WILL YOU HELP ME SPREAD THE WORD?

There are several ways you can help me get the word out about the message of this book...

- Post a 5-Star review on Amazon.
- Write about the book on your Facebook, Twitter, Instagram, LinkedIn, – any social media you regularly use!
- If you blog, consider referencing the book, or publishing an excerpt from the book with a link back to my website. You have my permission to do this if you provide proper credit and backlinks.
- Recommend the book to friends – word-of-mouth is still the most effective form of advertising.
- Purchase additional copies to give away as gifts on my website at www.AuthorMichelleChristina.com.

The best way to connect is by visiting
www.AuthorMichelleChristina.com